WINDING THE CLOCK

O'Rahilly and the 1916 Rising

TO MY MOTHER

WINDING
THE CLOCK
O'Rahilly and the 1916 Rising

Aodogán O'Rahilly

THE LILLIPUT PRESS
1991

First published in 1991 by
THE LILLIPUT PRESS LTD
4 Rosemount Terrace, Arbour Hill,
Dublin 7, Ireland

A CIP record for this
book is available from
the British Library

ISBN 0 946640 65 3

Jacket design by The Graphiconies
Set in 10 on 12 Baskerville by
Phototype-Set of Drumcondra
and printed in Dublin by
Colour Books of Baldoyle

Sing of the O'Rahilly,
Do not deny his right;
Sing a 'the' before his name;
Allow that he, despite
All those learned historians,
Established it for good;
He wrote out that word himself,
He christened himself with blood.
                    How goes the weather?

Sing of the O'Rahilly
That had such little sense
He told Pearse and Connolly
He'd gone to great expense
Keeping all the Kerry men
Out of that crazy fight;
That he might be there himself
Had travelled half the night.
                    How goes the weather?

'Am I such a craven that
I should not get the word
But for what some travelling man
Had heard I had not heard?'
Then on Pearse and Connolly
He fixed a bitter look:
'Because I helped to wind the clock
I come to hear it strike.'
                    How goes the weather?

What remains to sing about
But of the death he met
Stretched under a doorway
Somewhere off Henry Street;
They that found him found upon
The door above his head
'Here died the O'Rahilly.
R.I.P.' writ in blood.
                    How goes the weather?

(W.B. Yeats, 'The O'Rahilly')

Contents

List of Illustrations

O'Rahilly with his wife, Nannie, and three children, Mac (seated), Niall (below left) and Egan (author).

The author (centre), his brother Mac (left) and cousin Emmett Humphreys in their Fianna uniforms at 54 Northumberland Road, *c.* 1915.

between pages 174 and 175

The O'Rahilly, in his Volunteer uniform, *c.* 1915, photographed by his sister Anna in the garden of 54 Northumberland Road.

The O'Rahilly family home, 40 Herbert Park, where they lived from 1910; The O'Rahilly left it for the GPO on Easter Monday 1916.

Four pencilled notes (part-overwritten in ink) sent by The O'Rahilly to his three sons and wife from the GPO during Easter week.

between pages 206 and 207

Barricade at end of Moore Street which The O'Rahilly was trying to storm when shot. It is identified by the name of the butcher's shop, 'Simpson and Wallace'.

The burnt-out shell of The O'Rahilly's De Dion Bouton in Prince's Street after the Rising, now buried under 'Hill 16' in Croke Park.

A letter from the author to his father written during Easter week and sent to the GPO. On its reverse The O'Rahilly pencilled a farewell to his wife, after being hit by a bullet, which passed through his tunic, puncturing the paper.

Preface

This is the story of a young Irishman who believed that the British would not release their grip on Ireland until they were compelled to do so by being defeated in an armed struggle. It tells how he came to this conclusion and of the steps he then took to make the armed struggle possible. It may be of interest to historians of the period from 1910 to 1916 and to Irish people who are curious about the pressures that finally led to the withdrawal of the British army of occupation from twenty-six of the Irish counties.

The armed struggle to compel the British to release their grip on Ireland is not now a popular doctrine. Nor was it when it was first proposed to the Irish people almost eighty years ago. In 1912, Michael O'Rahilly urged the men of Ireland to arm themselves if they wished to free themselves from British domination. What he had in mind was that the Home Rule Bill had been passed by the House of Commons and could be delayed by the House of Lords for only two years. This meant that there would then be a Home Rule Parliament in Dublin.

This Irish Parliament would have no army, but if a body of Irish Volunteers was under its control, there was nothing the British government could do to disband it. It would have to be a 'volunteer' army because the Irish government would have no power to raise revenue to pay a regular army, and the British government was not likely to provide funds for this purpose. Such an armed force, under the control of the Home Rule Parliament in Dublin, would be as effective as a regular army. It was just such a force of Volunteers, in 1782, which enabled that Irish Parliament to obtain substantial concessions from the British government.

O'Rahilly's call to the manhood of Ireland in 1912 went

unheeded. But less than twelve months later the Ulster Volunteers were organized to resist, if necessary by force of arms, the passionate desire of 80 per cent of the Irish people for a Home Rule government, to look after Irish interests. This Irish Home Rule Bill had been enacted by a majority of the Westminster House of Commons, but, despite this, Carson, with the support of senior members of the British Conservative Party, was recruiting a volunteer army to resist its enactment.

Those people who now issue routine denunciations of the 'men of violence' should spare a passing malediction for Carson and Bonar Law and the leading members of the British Conservative establishment, who, in 1913, financed, organized and gave their full support to a minority, whose doctrine was that if they could not achieve what they wanted by normal political activity, they were entitled to take to the gun and obtain their objectives by the bomb and the bullet.

The existence of Carson's Ulster Volunteers made it easy for O'Rahilly to convene, at the end of 1913, the meeting that led to the formation of the Irish Volunteers. These Volunteers made the rebellion of Easter 1916 possible. This biography spells out how O'Rahilly set about calling this meeting and forming the Irish Volunteers.

For many years following 1916, there was a general belief that the Rising was an event of which Irish people could be proud, but in recent times a 'revisionist' school of historians has been promulgating its conviction that, on the contrary, the Irish should be ashamed of it and should try to dissociate themselves from any approval or pride in it. Whether we approve or disapprove, there is general acceptance that the Rising of 1916 was the most important event in the history of Ireland since the Act of Union of 1800, and for this reason the events leading up to it and the actions of those who played leading roles in it are of historical interest.

Eóin MacNeill was president and chief of staff of the Irish Volunteers, the organization that provided the main body of the rebels, although the role of James Connolly and the 200 men of his Citizen Army was of critical importance. MacNeill himself did not take part in the Rising and there has been much controversy about his actions in the events leading up to it.

It is now seventy-five years since the Rising of 1916, which led directly to the Black and Tan War. No one will ever know whether

we might have loosened the British grip on Ireland by constitutional agitation, but we should bear in mind that the men of 1916,
who invoked the ultimate appeal to arms, accepted that their efforts
were likely to cost them their lives, and many of them did die. No
man can do more for his country.

If there is an implied criticism in this biography of the 250,000
Irishmen who served with the Allies during World War I, it is not
intended. These men, 50,000 of whom never returned, were as dedicated as were the Volunteers who fought and died in 1916 to what
they believed to be their duty to Ireland, and they deserve to be
equally honoured.

O'Rahilly's life would have had nothing of sufficient interest to
justify a biography if it had not been for his part in the formation of
the Irish Volunteers, and his death in Moore Street, leading a
charge against a British barricade. There was an earlier biography
by Marcus Bourke in 1967. The justification for a new one twenty-
five years later is that many family papers have since come to light
which fill in details of O'Rahilly's early life. Other important
documents have also become available, especially the notes that he
wrote from the GPO during Easter Week.

It would be impossible for me to write an objective biography of
my father. I was eleven years old at the time of the Rising, and my
father was to me then, and still is, the fountain of all knowledge,
wisdom, courage, virtue and honour. If this is a biased view, it is
relevant to mention that a French reporter who came to Dublin in
1917 to write about the Rising acclaimed O'Rahilly as 'Le Bayard de
1916, sans peur et sans reproche'. (Bayard was a famous French
knight, 'without fear and without blemish.')

The book is dedicated to my mother, who had to endure many
years of lonely widowhood after her husband's death. It would never
have been written without the encouragement of my wife, who urged
me to persist in completing it when I had lost heart in the effort. I
also wish to express my thanks to the publisher, Antony Farrell, and
to his editor, Jonathan Williams, for their corrections and sugges-
tions in an effort to make this biography readable.

Finally I want to acknowledge the help I received from Miss Emer
O'Riordan, who did much valuable research for the book.

Clondalkin, County Dublin   *Aodogán O'Rahilly*
March 1991

1

The Background of the Clan

Ballylongford is a small town in County Kerry, on the south-west coast of Ireland. It is near the mouth of the river Shannon and has a harbour on the river which was formerly used by small sailing vessels to discharge their cargoes for distribution in north Kerry and south Limerick. This harbour was an important commercial advantage for the town, before the railways were built linking Kerry to the ports of Cork and Limerick.

In such towns, in addition to the many small shops catering for the needs of the local people, there are often one or two larger ones which dominate the economic activity of the area, supplying hardware, building materials, fuel and drapery, as well as food and drink. Rahilly's in Ballylongford was such a shop towards the end of the last century.

Richard Rahilly was the owner of this shop in 1875. He had inherited it from his mother about ten years earlier and had built it up into one of the largest of its kind in north Kerry; it did more trade than any similar shop in Listowel or Tralee.

Richard's wife, whose maiden name was Ellen Mangan, had come from Gourbane in County Limerick. In 1875 they already had two daughters and Ellen was again pregnant. On 21 April in that year a son was born, and was christened Michael Joseph after his paternal grandfather. It would have been a normal expectation that when this son grew up, he would inherit his family's profitable business and further increase the substantial fortune that his father had amassed, ending his days as a well-respected and affluent member of the newly emerging Catholic bourgeoisie.

Any such expectations were not realized. Michael Rahilly, who became known as 'The O'Rahilly', was the prime mover in the formation of the Irish Volunteers in 1913, and was one of the leaders of the 1916 Rebellion. He was killed in the fighting near the General Post Office as he was leading his men against a British barricade.

There is today a plaque in Ballylongford commemorating its connection with the 1916 Rising, but the town had an earlier claim to fame. In 1900 it was prominently marked on a school atlas, published for Irish children by the British Ministry of Education. A footnote on this map explained that Ballylongford was the birthplace of Kitchener of Khartoum, the famous British military commander. He had achieved this fame when re-establishing Britain's authority in the Sudan during the last decades of the century.

These two Ballylongford men died within weeks of each other. One was the supreme commander, in World War I, of the vast assembly of Britain's armed forces, while the other was in effective command of the handful of Irish Volunteers in the GPO who were rebelling against the British occupation of their country.

Kitchener and O'Rahilly (the 'O' had been dropped during Penal times, but Michael restored it some years before 1916) were at opposite ends of the political spectrum. Kitchener's family were Anglo-Irish and had come to Ireland where land was cheap after the Famine. Kitchener, like so many of the young men of Anglo-Irish families, had made a career for himself in the British armed forces.

The Rahillys were an Irish Catholic family, who had known hard times when the Penal Laws were enforced in the sixteenth and seventeenth centuries. These laws debarred Irish Catholics from owning property or entering the professions. If an Irish Catholic owned a horse, any Protestant could take it from him by paying him £5, even though the horse might be worth many times this amount. The loss of a horse, when horses were the only means of transport or of cultivating the land, could be a crippling blow. However, in 1875, when Michael was born, the Rahillys were prosperous shop-keepers.

If it was usual for members of Anglo-Irish families to enlist in the British armed forces, it was by no means common for members of the emerging Catholic bourgeoisie to end up as revolutionary Irish nationalists. Most Irish Catholics were mild, constitutional nationalists, as were many Irish Protestants, but a sizeable minority of them had carved out comfortable niches for themselves in an

Ireland governed by Britain. Such was the case with Michael Rahilly's family. There was no trace in his upbringing of the convictions that were to lead to his death on the barricades. These may have begun when, as a young boy he began to take an interest in his family background. Michael's father came home one day and told the family that he had met an old woman in Tralee who told him that he was related to the Kerry poet Aodhagán Ó Rathaille. Michael set about investigating the connection. He discovered that there were many Rahilly and O'Rahilly families in Kerry. The name had acquired some distinction among *Gaelgeoirí* – enthusiasts for the revival of the Irish language – following the establishment of the Gaelic League in 1893. Michael then learned that Aodhagán Ó Rathaille, who was writing in Irish at the beginning of the eighteenth century (the same time as Dean Swift was writing in English), was one of Ireland's greatest Gaelic poets.

The descent from one of the poet's nephews to the family who settled in Ballylongford early in the nineteenth century is easily followed. An O'Rahilly, who was one of the poet's nephews, had been evicted from land near where the poet had lived, and had spent some years in Killarney before moving to Ballylongford where he had opened a shop. In the next generation, a son, also a Michael Joseph and the grandfather of the 1916 Michael Joseph, had married a Margaret McEllistrim about 1837. He died in 1847, the same year as the birth of his youngest son. His wife had borne him five children, three boys and two girls.

At the time of his death the Famine was devastating Ireland. It was a cruel time to be left a widow with five young children to support. People were dying of starvation and famine fever all over Ireland. Hundreds of thousands were leaving the country. Many of them had to sell everything they possessed to get the fare to board the 'coffin ships' out of Ireland, and many died on the voyage from starvation and disease. Within ten years, the country's population was reduced from 8.2 million to 6.6 million, whereas up to the Famine it had been expanding rapidly. There is no record of the cause of Michael Rahilly's death, but he may have caught the famine fever like countless other victims.

Not only did Margaret Rahilly manage to bring her five children to maturity in good health, she succeeded in getting them well educated, thus giving them a good start in life. Her success in running the shop and educating her children suggests that she was a woman of strong character, but she could not have had any influence on her grandson, because she died in 1860 before he was born. Only two letters of hers have survived. In one, she is expressing her concern about a member of the family who is gravely ill. The other is written to Michael, her eldest son, who was then studying medicine. One of the subjects he required for his medical studies could not be provided in Cork and he had to attend lectures at the medical school in Dublin. She had not heard from him for a week when she wrote the following letter on 20 June 1868:

If nothing has happened to you why did you not write to me for the past week, knowing my anxiety?

Oh, for God's sake write, or if anything prevents you get someone else to write and tell me all.

The most frightful things are occurring to me, may God of Heaven preserve me from trouble, for he knows that I have had my share of it already. If I don't hear from you by some chance to-morrow, if I have sufficient strength of body or mind, I will be on my way to Dublin.

Or if there is more trouble in reserve for me, I hope, without harm to my soul, that the Almighty will take me before I live to see it.

Did you get the five pounds which Richard enclosed yesterday week?

From your tortured mother

The five children were prolific letter-writers, and kept in touch with their mother wherever they were. Many of these letters have been preserved and throw some light on the family into which Michael Joseph was born in 1875.

Margaret Rahilly knew the importance of a good education for her children. Even though Catholic Emancipation had been achieved in 1829 and Catholics could own property and enter the professions, secondary and third-level education was still at an elementary stage of development. She needed energy and determination to provide the education she wanted her children to have and was able to run the shop so well that it could generate the funds to enable her to pay for this education. Her children would have been taught what were then called the 'Three Rs' (Reading, Writing and Arithmetic) in the local primary school. The eldest boy, Michael, was then sent to boarding school, first in Ennis and then in Killarney. In his first letter home from Killarney, in the early 1850s, he told his mother about the school routine and the sort of food they were given:

I now remember how anxious you are to hear all particulars so that I will

4

now give you an account of how we are situated. Rising at 6 when prayers and a lecture from Challoney Mod read by Father Gaughton. Breakfast bread and milk 9 o'clock. School 9 till 1 at which hour dining. School resumes at 2 till past 4. Walking and exercise till 7, at which hour we have bread and milk for supper.

Prayers 8 and bed 9 o'clock.

Father Sullivan on last Sunday took us to the Chapple and showed us a certain seat formerly belonging to my family, which was at present un-occupied and desired me to go there on Sunday with whatever boys I wanted. It is in a rather dilapidated condition, but yet not very bad.

I had just finished the last sentence when the bell rang for breakfast, and I was surprised to get instead of milk TAY. The reason for it is I am sure that one of the boys got sick yesterday and I got a headache from taking milk. This one of the masters told us at dinner yesterday, so that I am sure that we will get tea for the future.

From this school Michael went to Queen's College in Cork to study medicine.

There is no record of where the second boy, Richard, went to school. He was the father of the 1916 leader. A letter written in his late teens indicates that he was then helping his mother in the shop. Tom, the youngest boy, went to a seminary in Limerick to study for the priesthood, but he soon found that he had no vocation and left that institution. He next comes to light in a letter to his brother Richard from Harrisburg, Pennsylvania, in August 1866. He was then seventeen years old, but there is nothing in the letter to indicate what he was doing in the United States or who was paying for his upkeep.

My dear old Dick,

I wrote you a kind of letter about 4 or 5 weeks ago, which I hope you got alright. I am just after getting up after last night's fun. I had a jolly good night at the ball, lots of the handsomest girls I ever saw, but the worst of it was I am not able to dance, but they put it down to Ireland being such a wild place. Many's the time I wished I had you with me here, and many's the time I think over the great smokes we had together.

We will be going to the 'Falls of Niagara' soon and when we come back I intend to settle down. This is a great place for fun; every night I can go to a ball or boating or woodcock shooting, or, in fact, anything that I like to do. I'm entirely my own master NOW. Marlo tried to keep me down but he saw it was not good, so he gives me plenty of pocket money now. I am as happy as a king. . . .

I must go and take a glass of iced champagne to settle my stomach . . .

very cheap every kind of drink is. . . . I see Jack Haid sailing down the river in his boat. . . . I wish he stayed away as I'm too 'top heavy' just now.

I'm just after dismissing him and I'll give you a description of him. There he goes with the 'helm' in his hand, in his shirt and trousers, smoking a big cigar, with a jar at his feet and a negro fanning him, a regular fast fellow.

My dear fellow I am bothering you with this rigmarole of a letter. Goodbye. Excuse this shaky hand of mine. Ever your afft. and dearly attached
>   Tom

Tom never got over his addiction to alcohol, and on his death-bed confessed that there was never a day in his life that he did not have an irresistible craving for drink. It seems likely that Marlo was a friend or relation of the Rahilly family and that Tom had been sent out to him to learn a trade or business. If this was the purpose of his time in the US, nothing came of it. Eventually Tom returned to Ireland where he spent the rest of his life. He had a family of fourteen children, a number of whom became brilliant scholars.

The two girls of the family, Margaret and Marianna, when they had obtained whatever education was available in Ballylongford, were sent about 1850 to a convent school in France. The perfect French in which they wrote home indicates that they were several years there. Margaret wrote that she found it easier to write in French than in English, and signed her name as the French would write it phonetically 'Margaret Raleigh'. It is unlikely to have been common at that time, or indeed since, for girls of an Irish family, living in a small town, to be sent to school in France, although it is possible that the tradition of having to go to the Continent for education in Catholic schools was continued even after Catholic Emancipation.

Michael Rahilly was the first student of Queen's College, Cork to be conferred with a medical degree. He was interested in languages and, while studying for his medical examinations, was becoming proficient in German and Italian. After he had qualified as a doctor, he became a medical officer on board a British battleship. While he was waiting to board his vessel at Queenstown (now again called Cobh, its original name), he wrote home to his brother Richard asking to be sent 'my favourite book, the History of the Rebellion of 1798'. The author was W.H. Maxwell and the copy he carried on the battleship was found among his grandnephew's books. It did not seem incongruous to him that the book he brought with him on the battleship conjured up visions of an Ireland free from British domination.

These foreign travels by Michael Joseph's uncles and aunts meant that he grew up amongst close relatives who had lived abroad. His Uncle Michael had many tales of adventure in foreign lands on board the battleship. His Uncle Tom no doubt had tales to tell of how he had enjoyed himself in the United States. Both his aunts had lived for a number of years in France and spoke French fluently.

Thus, even if Michael Joseph grew up in a small town in Kerry, almost two hundred miles from Dublin, he heard stories of many other lands. However, when we look for evidence of radical Irish nationalism in his upbringing, the only trace of it was that request by one of his uncles to be sent his copy of Maxwell's *History of the Irish Rebellion of 1798*.

Richard was the son who gradually took over the running of the shop, which he did successfully. As a young man, he wrote to his elder brother in Cork on 7 April 1858 about a new suit:

As I am at present divided whether I will get a new suit, I warn you to keep all old articles of yours for me in that line, as you can have the new and yours will do me beautifully.

The youth of eighteen who was willing to wear his brother's cast-off clothing to save expense was not likely to dissipate the family fortune in extravagant living; nor did he. It would not be possible to amass a fortune just by being careful about spending money, but it helps. Catholics who were in a position to make money had one great advantage in building up a fortune. Since they were not received in the 'county' set of 'hunting, shooting and fishing people', with the expensive entertaining that this socializing involved, they did not have to waste their money trying 'to keep up with the Jones's'.

There is no record of what arrangements were made among the members of the family to enable Richard to end up owning and running the business, but it seems to have been an amicable one, and the Rahillys remained a closely united family. The family business that Richard Rahilly took over from his mother in 1866 was to expand greatly over the next thirty years. When it was advertised for sale, some years after Richard died in 1896, it was handling, in addition to the usual food and drink business, a large trade in coal, timber, steel and other building materials. An indication of the nature of the trade emerges from a letter that Nell, Richard's eldest daughter, sent to her brother Michael while he was at boarding school at Clongowes. She told him that they had just discharged the largest vessel that had ever come into the port of Ballylongford, a sailing vessel carrying 200 tons of coal.

Before the railways were built, about the middle of the nineteenth century, small ports like Ballylongford were used for the discharge of cargoes of imported commodities, which then were moved by horse and cart to inland towns and villages. All this changed when railways were built to link the main ports to the inland towns. Large ships then discharged their cargoes into the railhead ports and these were sent by rail across the country. This put an end to the small ports which did not have railheads and could discharge only small ships; but since there was no railway line to Ballylongford, the port continued to be used for the unloading of various commodities which were then distributed to the surrounding area. The Rahilly shop also had the agency for the Ballantine flour mills of Limerick, and small steamers laden with this flour were discharged in Ballylongford for distribution from the Rahilly business.

Richard Rahilly had ideas for the development of his business. He realized how useful it would be for a shop if a machine were available for recording all cash sales. There were then no cash registers on the market, so he set about inventing one. A family story tells how a salesman from an English firm was shown the half-made cash register and was told how it was going to work. He went back to his company and told them what he had seen in this remote Irish town. The firm were in the engineering business and, realizing that there was a vast market for a such a machine, proceeded to design and manufacture one of their own. Richard spent £100 getting legal advice on the possibility of winning a legal action against the firm, but he was advised not to proceed with the case.

There was another development that Richard investigated thoroughly. The river Shannon at that time was one of the largest and most prolific salmon-fishing rivers in Europe. Shipping these salmon to the towns and cities of the British Isles would not have been possible before the completion of the railway network. But, with the railways in operation, it would have been possible to send salmon on the midday train from Listowel and they would arrive in London early the following morning. However, if the weather was hot, the fish would not arrive in good condition unless they were packed in ice.

The manufacture of artificial ice was then known to be technically feasible, although probably no plant was making it in Ireland. The process began with a boiler in which there was a roaring fire to generate steam. The steam was then used to operate a steam engine which drove a compressor. A suitable gas, such as ammonia, was compressed and became hot. The hot compressed gas was then cooled by passing it through pipes cooled by water. When this compressed gas, now at atmospheric temperature, was allowed to expand, it became very cold and could be used to freeze water into ice.

Richard Rahilly saw an opportunity to ship salmon all over Ireland and Britain if he installed an artificial ice-making plant in Ballylongford. His wife, Ellen Mangan, was unhappy about the risks involved in making an investment of £20,000 and dissuaded him from going ahead. It was a substantial sum of money and would have been a serious loss to the family if the project had failed. Many years later, when the venture was being discussed at home, Michael Joseph said that he regretted that his father had not carried out the plan. He added wistfully that if the ice-making plant had been installed, he might never have left Ballylongford.

In addition to making money running his business, Richard Rahilly also discovered how money could be made on the stock exchange. During the years when he was building up his fortune, London was the financial capital of the world. People who had capital and the talent for anticipating commercial developments could find opportunities for making money by trading in stocks and shares and Richard Rahilly became competent at such trading.

One family tale recounts how Ellen and her daughters, Nell and Anna, came home from a shopping expedition to Limerick. Richard noticed that, instead of buying thread in hanks and then having to wind it on a piece of timber or paper to enable it to be used, they had been able to buy it ready-wound on little wooden spools. He realized that the firm who made these spools, J. & P. Coats, would prosper, and so he bought shares in this company. Over the years these increased in value many times.

As Richard's children, Nell, Anna and Michael, were growing up, they became aware that, in addition to the successful operation and expansion of his own business, their father was increasing his fortune with stock exchange investments. They also learnt about buying stocks and shares, but found out that there could be losses as well as profits from financial transactions. Anna told of the family's dismay when they got word that the Munster Bank had failed in 1885. She did not say whether her father had held shares in the bank or if it was money on deposit, but the family knew it would be a serious loss for them. Richard was out sailing on the Shannon when the news reached Ballylongford. They could see his yacht becalmed on the river and dreaded the advent of a wind that would enable him to sail home because then they would have to break the news to him.

2

Family and School Influences

If Michael's father, Richard Rahilly, had not been able to leave his son sufficiently well-off to live comfortably without working, Michael could not have devoted the last years of his life to his efforts to get the British occupation forces out of Ireland. Yet, although business interests were important in the Rahilly household, family members were by no means exclusively preoccupied with their business and financial investments. Richard Rahilly was actively involved in other matters. When he wanted a larger house, either in anticipation of his marriage, or shortly after it, he designed and built it himself. It was a three-storey house and is still one of the largest houses in Ballylongford. He enjoyed sailing and, when he wanted a small yacht for this hobby, he built one for himself. Michael Joseph grew up in a family in which there was a tradition of making the things you wanted, and this competence became one of his most notable characteristics.

Richard was also a member of Listowel Urban District Council; he attended meetings regularly, riding his bicycle the ten miles from Ballylongford to Listowel. In a letter to Michael while he was at school in Clongowes, his sister Nell said that her father had gone into Listowel to make arrangements for starting a co-operative creamery there. This creamery became the Kerry Co-op, now one of the largest business organizations in Ireland.

Another feature of the family atmosphere in which Michael Joseph grew up was his father's interest in poetry. Anna told us how when he came on a poem that appealed to him, he would read it aloud to his family.

Michael's family were deeply devoted to the Catholic religion. Every dogma was accepted without question, and every discipline

11

imposed by the Church was faithfully observed. There was a family rosary every night and grace was said before and after meals. There was no possibility of Mass being missed on Sundays or on Church Holy-days, or that meat would be eaten on Fridays or on fast days. Michael's sisters and his wife went to Mass and Holy Communion every morning all their lives, a practice they had acquired in their youth. The Rahilly family were in no way unusual in this commitment to the Catholic faith.

A love of music was an abiding interest among the members of the Rahilly family. In those days, if you wanted music and you lived in a small, remote town on the west coast of Ireland, you had to make it for yourself. Professor Alfred O'Rahilly recalled a visit he paid to Ballylongford in 1895, when his cousin Michael was away at medical school in Dublin. Michael's father was obviously proud to be able to show Alfred a musical box that Michael had made. The father's interest in music, and the educational importance he attached to it, emerges in the first letter he wrote to his son on 23 September 1890, when the boy had arrived at Clongowes Wood College in County Kildare in 1890: 'About extras, you can say that I wish you to be taught piano and vocal singing for the present. If the banjo was taught I would not mind your going in for it.'

In the Rahilly house there was a piano, an organ and a violin, and all the children were interested in music. When one of Michael's sisters wrote to him at school, after she had been to London, she said: 'We bought a lovely bust of Beethoven yesterday which we will put on the piano.'

Michael never lost this love of music and singing. One of his companions in the political movement was Seán T. O'Kelly, who later became President of Ireland. When asked what he could remember about Michael O'Rahilly, he replied that if there was a piano in the room at any party, Michael would sit down at it and sing songs to his own accompaniment. The song that Seán T. remembered best was a music-hall song about a horse race in the Southern United States, 'The Camptown Races', which he heard Michael sing several times.

A cousin of Michael's, a nun, was asked when she was over ninety what she could remember about him. She said that when she and her sister were at school in Eccles Street, Dublin, Michael had paid them a visit. There was a piano in the visitor's room and he had sat at it and sung Mangan's poem 'My dark Rosaleen'. She said that, even after seventy years, she could still vividly recall how moved she had been, both by the words and the music, and the great feeling with which her cousin sang.

In an account that Michael's sister Anna gave to the Military History Society, she said that shortly before Easter 1916 Michael paid his customary Sunday visit to their house in Northumberland Road. He had sat down at the piano and had sung 'Aghadoe'. When she recalled this after the Rising, she realized that it was in the nature of a swan song which he was singing for them. She said that he had a lovely tenor voice.

This musical association also emerges in the poem that W.B. Yeats wrote about Michael O'Rahilly. Yeats wrote several poems about 1916 within a few months of the Rising, but twenty years later wrote one about Michael entitled 'The O'Rahilly'. Three of the verses begin with a reference to singing. The first two verses begin with the line 'Sing of the O'Rahilly', while the last verse begins 'What remains to sing about'.

Yeats may have associated Michael with singing as a result of a memory of a party they had both attended at which Michael had entertained them with his singing, but it could also have been from inquiries Yeats made of some notable characteristics of O'Rahilly. Michael hoped his children would also have this interest and talent for singing and he spent many hours giving us singing lessons, mostly Irish songs, while he played the tunes on the piano.

Another interest that Michael shared with his father, and never tired of, was handicrafts. As a boy, he had become familiar with woodworking from helping the local carpenter who was employed in the family business, and from this beginning he taught himself cabinet-making. There is a bookcase that he made in our house in Herbert Park which would be a credit to any cabinet-maker's skill.

The first mechanically propelled motor car was made in the early 1890s and Michael got his first car in 1902. He never lost his interest in driving, overhauling and tuning cars and devising new gadgets in the hope of improving their performance.

As far as is known, the Rahilly family were nationalists, but they were certainly not radical nor revolutionary. The only evidence of political interest during the nineteenth century is a collection book for the Repeal Movement, dated 1840. The Repeal Movement had been more or less active since Daniel O'Connell had won Catholic

Emancipation in 1829. Many people believe that if O'Connell had campaigned for Repeal of the Union, instead of for Catholic Emancipation, he might have got the British out. He was in failing health when he won his first objective, and he died without making any progress in his efforts to get Repeal.

Irish political life was moribund for the next fifty years until Parnell infused new life into it about 1880. Then in 1890 Parnell's liaison with a married woman, Mrs Katharine O'Shea, was used to destroy him politically. The tension and worry of the scandal led to his death the following year and created a bitter split in the Irish Party. When Michael was in his early twenties he was a committed Parnellite, but there is no evidence as to which side the family supported at the time of the split. In one letter from his father to Michael in Clongowes, he said that one of the girls would have gone to a meeting at which Parnell was expected to speak, but some domestic problem had prevented her. In another letter, the father wrote: 'They expected to meet Patt Fitzgerald there to-day, as Patt, of course, with his usual aberration of intellect is a rabid Parnellite and must attend the meeting in Shanagolden.'

Regardless of whether the Rahilly family were pro- or anti-Parnell, there is no doubt that, in the eyes of Dublin Castle, the headquarters of the British administration in Ireland, they were typical of the emerging sensible, respectable, middle-class Catholic bourgeosie whom the Castle were anxious to cultivate in their aim of achieving the anglicization of Ireland. It was in pursuit of such a policy that Richard Rahilly was made a Justice of the Peace about 1880.

The conferring of what was generally considered to be the 'honour' of being made a JP was an expression of confidence by Dublin Castle that the office-holder was someone who had no subversive feelings about the British occupation of Ireland. On the occasion of this honorary legal appointment, a number of local people gave Richard Rahilly a flattering testimonial.

The signatories of this testimonial included both Catholic and Protestant clergymen and four local JPs. During the last quarter of the nineteenth century the Rahilly family were truly part of the British establishment in Ireland. One brother was a JP, another an officer in the British navy, and a third, who had been in the Royal Irish Constabulary, was now a clerk of the Petty Sessions – another Dublin Castle appointment. The RIC was screened to ensure that no radical nationalist was allowed to join, but Tom Rahilly would

Michael Joseph Rahilly with his parents and two sisters.

The main street of Ballylongford, County Kerry. The Rahilly birthplace and family home is the three-storey building on the right.

Michael Rahilly as a young man.

Nannie Rahilly, née *Nancy Brown of Philadelphia.*

Slieve Luchra, Philadelphia, USA, the Rahillys' first home, 1905-09.

have had no trouble in enlisting because, in the files of the Castle, the Rahilly family was clear of any taint of subversion.

Family letters show that there was an active interest in French among three generations of this Rahilly family. One of Richard's sisters, Margaret Rahilly, who was sent to school in France in the mid-1850s, wrote home to her eldest brother: 'Knowing how much you love the French language, I have decided to write to you in French.' In the next generation, Nell, Michael's sister, wrote a letter home in French from Mount Anville convent in Dublin. In another letter, in English, to her young brother, she said that she hoped that he was studying hard at his French, so they could have conversations in that language when she came home on holidays. Sighle O'Donoghue, daughter of Nell Rahilly, has recalled how pleased she was when her American cousins came to live in Dublin, but said she could not speak to the youngest boy because he spoke only French. The result of this interest in French was that Michael Joseph grew up in a family, many of whom spoke French and several of whom had lived in France and knew that there were other worlds beyond that of the English language and culture.

Having taken over the management of the family business in the mid-1860s Richard Rahilly worked hard, spent carefully and invested any surplus in quoted companies that seemed likely to develop. This enabled him to build up a fortune of at least a hundred thousand pounds, equal to millions of pounds in today's money.

There is no evidence that the Rahilly family was actively involved in politics, or even interested in them. In all the letters that have been preserved, the only allusion to the Irish language (even though most of the people in the area where they lived were Irish speakers in the middle of the nineteenth century) is a jocose reference in a letter home about 1860 from the eldest son Michael, who went to study medicine in Cork. Michael said that he had lately met a boy called Sigerson (this was George Sigerson, who later became famous as a Gaelic scholar) who had urged him to study the Irish language because he was certain to do well at it. Michael commented that he would surely be at the head of the class since probably he would be the only one studying Irish! At that time the Rahilly children would have known Irish, but any idea that an Irish person had a Gaelic heritage worth preserving does not seem to have occurred to the boy who met Sigerson at Queen's College, Cork.

These uncles and aunts of the young Michael Joseph, with their tales of foreign travel, may well have stimulated a desire in him to travel abroad, although his parents were probably the most important influence in forming his character. Much is known about his father, Richard Rahilly, who was a successful small-town business-man, but there is nothing to suggest that Michael's radical nationalism, which became a consuming passion, was influenced by his father.

Little is known about Michael's mother, Ellen Mangan. Only a few of her letters have survived. I cannot recall my father or either of my aunts speaking about their mother. The only member of the family whom I questioned about her was Alfred, one of the sons of Tom Rahilly, her brother-in-law. Alfred was an old man, who had retired as President of University College, Cork, when I asked him about my grandmother. He replied to my question by saying that he could sum her up in one word. I thought he was going to say that she was a saint. Instead he said: 'She was a bitch.'

Alfred Rahilly's description cannot be accepted as unbiased. His own father was a failed businessman and an alcoholic. He also knew how his Uncle Richard gave financial and other help to his family. My Aunt Anna told me that it was a regular chore for her father to get word that Uncle Tom was on the booze again; her father would have to drop everything and go off to Listowel to take Tom to a 'drying out' clinic in Roscrea or Mount Melleray. If Alfred knew or suspected that my grandmother disapproved of the help his father was getting from his brother, and possibly tried to stymie it, this would have been responsible for the poor opinion he had of her. She may not have been as unworthy as Alfred's description of her suggested.

When he was about five years old, Michael was sent to the local national school, just as his sisters – Nell (six years older) and Anna (four years older) – had been before him. This school was a coeducational institution. According to Marcus Bourke's biography of Michael O'Rahilly, the boys were supposed to be sent to the boys' school at six years of age, but Mary Carmody, the headmistress, insisted on keeping them in the girls' school until they were seven-and-a-half. The headmaster of the boys' school, Patrick O'Connor from Dingle, was a native speaker of Irish and an enthusiast for the language; so much so that, according to Bourke, he gave lessons after class to some of the boys, and one of these was young Michael Rahilly. If Michael did get these Irish lessons, he does not mention them in a letter he wrote later to his cousin Frank, when he began the study of Irish in Philadelphia, but Patrick O'Connor may have planted seeds of interest in the Irish language and Irish nationalism.

When Michael was fifteen, he was sent to Clongowes, regarded as one of the best of the Irish Catholic boarding schools. The fathers of these Clongowes boys would have been professional men, senior civil servants, substantial shopkeepers, and the occasional large farmer or cattle dealer. The training and the curriculum would have enabled these boys, if they had the ability, to pass the university entrance examination and themselves become professional men, or enter the British civil service. (James Joyce went to Clongowes two years before and gives an account of the school in *A Portrait of the Artist as a Young Man.*) When they left Clongowes, the boys who did not take up a professional career might return home to take over the shop or the farm.

The raison d'être of this Jesuit school was to implant firmly into the minds of the future leaders of the Irish community an un-questioning belief in Catholicism, and a faithful adherence to the disciplines of the Catholic Church. The Jesuits hoped, as a bonus, to recruit some of the boys into their order.

There may have been priests in Clongowes with radical nationalist views, but there was no possibility of the school making a conscious effort to instil into the students any pride in their Irish heritage, or any belief that it would be a desirable objective to get the British out of Ireland. With the exception of Michael O'Rahilly and his nephew Dick Humphreys, twenty years his junior, there were no other ex-Clongowians in the 1916 Rising, nor many who played any major part subsequently in the efforts to expel the British from Ireland. But these ex-Clongowians, with their secondary and university education, were well placed to grasp the many opportunities that became available when the new Irish State was established. They were able, as Milton put it, 'To creep and crawl and climb into the fold.' Marcus Bourke, in his biography of O'Rahilly, lists many of those who did this most successfully. If Michael Rahilly got no radical, revolutionary Irish nationalism from his family background, or in the environment of Ballylongford, he certainly got none from the beliefs then prevailing in Clongowes Wood College.

In Clongowes, Michael was reasonably successful in his studies and in sport. Soon after his arrival, he was awarded first prize for an essay, and he was able to report home that he had done well in the Euclid examination (geometry was then called 'Euclid'). This evoked the comment from his father, written on the back of an envelope, 'I am more than pleased at your getting on so well in the Euclid exam. 450 out of 500 is A.1.' But the father was insatiable in his desire for his son to do well in his studies. There are exhortations in almost every letter. In his first letter, written on 20 September 1890, he writes:

Whatever you did in the past, I beg of you, my dear Michael, try hard to show a good record now. I know you are heavily weighted in the contest by want of Latin. But if you only determine and stick to your work, no matter what may tempt you away from it, believe me you will succeed. Now my dearest boy, I depend and calculate on your doing this and don't allow me to be disappointed.

This letter implies that the boy had not been a model youth up to then. The father's cause for complaint is not specified, but was obviously known to both of them. In another letter, Richard wrote: 'Now that you have commenced work in earnest, I beg of you to work at your studies in a way that we will be proud of you, and during study think of nothing whatever but what you are at. Concentrate yourself on it and you will succeed. Whatever you go to do, do it with all your might.'

In the school sports Michael won races, and at the end of the first year he won a prize of £10, but the letters do not tell us whether it was for sport or for studies. Ten pounds in those days would be equivalent to many times that amount in today's money. In all the letters his mother wrote to Michael and in many of his father's, they expressed anxiety about his health, which caused them much concern. He suffered from frequent colds as well as from tooth-aches and earaches. In other letters, the family were making arrangements for new suits, which he would get fitted as he was passing through Limerick on his way home. This was a far cry from the letter that Michael's father had written to his brother at Queen's College, Cork, in which he had 'warned' him to keep all his cast-off clothing, because they 'will do me beautifully'.

None of Michael's letters home have been preserved, but in the letters from his family there are numerous references to their being pleased that he was happy at school. He does not seem to have found any difficulty in complying with the strict disciplines of a Jesuit boarding school. Despite his assuring his family at the time that he was happy at school, I can recall him telling Mother that none of his children would be sent to Clongowes. He did not elaborate. It may have been his recollection of the West British atmosphere in the school. When he said this, he was a revolutionary nationalist and he wanted his children educated in a school where such ideas were understood.

Among the letters that have been preserved is one from his father of 22 June 1886. Michael may have been on a retreat at which he made his first communion. It is a strange letter, part of which reads:

My Own dearest Michael,

I cannot tell you, my darling child, how pleased and happy the receipt of your first and truly welcome letter made . . . above all your approaching the Holy Sacrament with such good disposition, which I trust, with God's help and assistance, may always remain with you. From my heart, my dear child, I freely forgive you for any pain or annoyance you have ever given me, and in return I have to ask your forgiveness for the far greater crime which I have committed against Almighty God and against you, when I gave you so frequently, I regret to say, bad example in many ways, especially do I allude to my having [word cut off the letter] than I ought on our trip to Queenstown, but which I trust that you will never again see from your father.

The key word is missing; it was on the bottom corner of the page, and it seems certain that it was cut off by Michael. What can the father have done on that trip to Queenstown? It must have been something of which Michael was ashamed. Most likely Richard got drunk, which seems to have been a weakness with all three brothers.

The father wrote in another letter during November 1890 something that tends to confirm this speculation:

I send you enclosed one of the nicest copies of the Sacred Heart Messenger I saw for some time, and one remarkable also in another way. Your uncle Thos F. was so struck by the article on Temperance by Dr Norman Kerr that when by mere accident, I said to him that he ought to try the 'other side', and if he did I would again join the Total Abstinence cause with him, that he at once agreed, so that we are all joined in the League of the Cross now, but the beauty of it was that it was the little article that first induced him to think of it and my fortunate suggestion finished it.

As far as his studies were concerned, Michael did all that his father could have expected of him. In a letter of December 1891, his father wrote: 'I looked over the list of examinations you sent us and must say you made a most creditable record and I am more than pleased.' In another letter he had this to say: 'I cannot tell you how pleased I was at your getting 3rd prize in English. This is what I like to see.'

The father's obsessive concern that his only son should have a successful academic career seems strange considering that there was a thriving business waiting for the boy to manage. The explanation may be that those who have not themselves had a university training often feel a sense of inferiority arising from the lack of it. Another consideration in the father's mind may well have been the social stigma that attached to the retail trade in those days.

W.B. Yeats spelled out his low regard for shopkeepers in his poem 'September 1913'. It is a lament for John O'Leary, the Fenian idolized by Yeats:

> What need you, being come to sense,
> But fumble in a greasy till
> And add the halfpence to the pence
> And prayer to shivering prayer, until
> You have dried the marrow from the bone?

Whatever the reason for the father's desire that his son should enter the professional classes, Michael's parents had no reason to be ashamed of the cultural atmosphere in the family home. All the family loved music and this was an interest Michael absorbed in his youth. Gardening was an activity in which the parents and the two daughters took pleasure, although Michael never pursued this hobby. Literature, especially poetry, was an abiding interest of the father's and if Michael had only a minimal love of literature, it was not his father's fault. Manual craftsmanship was a hobby of the father's which Michael shared and he never lost his taste for it.

Michael remained at Clongowes until 1893 when, to his father's great delight, he was accepted as a candidate for the matriculation to the new Royal University in Dublin and there was enrolled in the medical faculty. His father wrote to him on 15 October 1893:

I am more than pleased at finding your name to-day on the list of successful candidates for the Matriculation and most earnestly congratulate you, my dear boy, as it proves that you are not neglecting your opportunities, and I hope in God that he will give you grace always to continue to do so, for believe me, dear Michael, that it is only those who do, and are determined to do, all they can, in whatever position in life they are placed, that will succeed in that position or rise out of the bulk.

3

Courtship and Marriage

Having passed his matriculation examination, Michael had to decide which subject to study at university. In those days there were no restrictions on the number of students admitted into any faculty. If the student could pay the fees, he or she could decide the discipline into which to enrol. No explanation is known for the decision to enrol Michael in the medical faculty. It is most unlikely to have been his own choice because his interests were always in practical matters like engineering. But the social status of a doctor was then higher than that of any other profession, and it was probably his mother who wanted this prestige for her only son.

During the summer holidays of 1893 while Michael was waiting to go up to university, he was invited to a party given by a north Kerry farmer. This farmer had a brother who was a parish priest in Philadelphia; one of his parishioners was a widow named Brown who had five daughter. That summer Mrs Brown and her daughters were on holiday in Ireland, and the American priest had asked his brother to entertain them when they visited that part of the country.

The Browns spent some weeks in Kilkee, County Clare. The north Kerry farmer lived near Tarbert and there was a ferry across the Shannon from Clare to Tarbert. The farmer organized a party for the Browns to which he invited several eligible young men from the locality, including young Michael Rahilly from Ballylongford.

Nannie was one of the Brown girls. That evening at the farmer's party it was love at first sight between Nannie Brown and Michael Rahilly.

Emigration from Ireland to the United States has been going on for centuries. At the time of the Famine, there were the floods of starving emigrants who fled from Ireland in the 'coffin ships', but for a hundred years previously there was a steady flow of Irish people hoping for a better life in North America than they could get in Ireland. Most of these were the Irish Catholics who had been made second-class citizens by the Penal Laws, but a recent survey has shown that there was also considerable emigration from the northern ports, which would have included many Protestants.

No records of the Brown family have been found, but a William Brown settled in Philadelphia during the first quarter of the nineteenth century. He was such a staunch Orangeman that he was nick-named 'Orange Billy' in Philadelphia. He had a knowledge of the woollen trade, which he probably acquired in England because English law had prohibited the export of woollens from Ireland. The manufacture and export of woollen goods was considered to be of such basic importance to England that it was known simply as the 'trade'. Wool was regarded as 'the flower and strength and revenue and blood of England'. The English had no intention of allowing the Irish to compete in this trade and the easiest way to avoid such competition was to make Ireland's export trade illegal.

William Brown realized that in a developing country, in which there was heavy protection for native manufacturers, there would be a good opportunity for the manufacture of this basic commodity. He probably had some capital to enable him to get started, but as a white, Anglo-Saxon Protestant he was able to obtain an entrée to bankers and other people of influence in Philadelphia, a very Protestant city. Whatever way he achieved it, by the middle of the century he was the owner of a large woollen industry in the centre of Philadelphia. He had two sons, Robert and James. When he died about 1850, Robert took over the management of the woollen mills.

Robert Brown had married a Catholic girl, Mary Hickey, whose family had come from Emly, a small town on the borders of Limerick and Tipperary. All we know of this family is that Nannie's mother, speaking of her father, had said 'my father, my dear, was a scholar and a gentleman'. For a Catholic, at that time, to be so described suggests that he may have been a schoolmaster.

When Robert died about 1880, his wife had borne him five daughters, the youngest of whom was only two years of age when he died. Robert's brother, 'Uncle James', as Nannie called him, took over the running of the mills. James did not relish the day-to-day drudgery of this work. He was convinced that there were easier ways of making money and he never stopped trying to find some new idea in which he could invest in the hope of making a fortune. A family story tells how a man named Bell came to James and said that he had invented a means whereby two people could speak to each other even when they were miles apart. James decided not to back him. This became the Bell telephone system. A small initial backing would have ended up worth millions.

Nannie told us that James left the running of the mills to a foreman named Kelly, and Uncle James's lack of attention was a major factor in the failure of the mills.

When Robert died, his widow was in receipt of an income of $20,000 a year from the mills. In those days, this made her a wealthy woman. She continued to live in Philadelphia for some time and the children began their schooling in the Sacred Heart school of Eden Hall. Mary Brown then moved to a house on fashionable 5th Avenue in New York. This was a step up the social scale and would help in getting suitable husbands for her five daughters.

In those days an education in Paris was considered desirable for girls whose parents could afford it. Mrs Brown could afford it and her children were entered in a boarding school in that city, while she stayed in a hotel. The family usually spent the summer holidays in Long Branch, New Jersey, where they had a summer home, but in the year that Nannie and Michael Rahilly met they had decided to spend their holidays in Ireland.

That evening, after the party in the farmer's house, Mrs Brown and her daughters took the ferry back to Clare and it seemed likely that the flirtation between Nannie and Michael had run its course. But Michael had been hooked. During the weeks that the Browns were still in Clare, Michael used to ride his bicycle to Tarbert, catch the ferry to Killimer, and then ride to Kilkee where they were staying. When he was asked at home where he had spent the day, he told them that he had been to Tarbert to visit his cousins; this was the truth, but not the whole truth.

At the end of the holidays, the Browns went back to Paris, and the liaison between Michael and Nancy would probably have been forgotten by both of them were it not for a lucky bet that Michael had on the horses. Backing horses was one of his foibles at this time, and one day he had an important win. During his first term at university he put £1 on a double event and when both horses won he collected £20, equivalent to many hundreds of pounds today. With this sum added to his allowance from home, he headed for

Paris, travelling third class on the train and steerage on the boat. Before he left Dublin, he wrote a series of letters to his family, each one post-dated a week from the previous one. He gave these letters to his room-mate, a student named Arthur Conway, with instructions to post them in a certain order. Conway, who later became Professor of Mathematical Physics at University College, Dublin, failed to post the letters in the correct order.

If the letters had reached Ballylongford in the correct order, his family would have been happy in the belief that Michael was working away at his medical studies. They would not have been pleased if they knew that he was gallivanting over in Paris chasing a schoolgirl he had met in Kerry.

When the letters were posted in the wrong order and some of them arrived in Ballylongford 'before' they were written, the family had some questions to ask Michael when he arrived home for the Christmas holidays. It is not known if he was able to concoct a plausible story then or if the truth emerged only much later.

It is possible that Michael proposed marriage to Nannie during that secret visit to Paris, but there could not have been any question of a formal engagement between Nannie, a schoolgirl of sixteen, and Michael, a schoolboy about to enter medical school. Their letters during the remainder of the year have not been preserved, although there was a Christmas card from Paris, dated 1893, and on it the simple message, 'With best love, Nannie'. This was probably a daring avowal in those reticent days, and Michael preserved it carefully by pasting it to a sheet of paper.

Michael passed his first-year examination the following summer. Mrs Brown and her daughters remained in Paris until the summer holidays, but there were no further doubles on the horseraces and Michael did not pay them another visit.

Within eighteen months of Michael and Nannie meeting at the party given by the north Kerry farmer, there were fundamental changes in both the Brown and Rahilly families. In the early summer of 1895, Mrs Brown and her five daughters embarked from France, homeward bound. Mrs Brown became seriously ill on the journey home and, when the vessel docked in New York, had to be taken on a stretcher to her home on 5th Avenue, where she died shortly afterwards.

Some time later the eldest of the girls married a young New York businessman, to whom she had been engaged. The other girls continued to live in their New York home. Their aunt, Miss Hickey, their mother's sister, looked after them and finance was provided by Uncle James.

Soon after Michael returned to college in September 1894, he was stricken with tuberculosis, which was widespread in Ireland at that time. Michael went home and was nursed back to health by his mother and sister, Anna. The eldest sister, Nell, had married a doctor, David Humphreys, some time previously, and was now living in Limerick. This doctor was himself stricken with tuberculosis some years later, but failed to make a recovery.

Michael was still convalescing at home when his father got caught in a heavy shower riding his bicycle home from Listowel. He was wet and cold when he reached home and was in bed the next day with a severe cold, which within a few days developed into pneumonia. Some days later his heart failed and he died on 24 March 1896, in his mid-fifties.

Everything had now changed for the Rahillys of Ballylongford. Michael, as the only son, had to take over the management of the business. This ruled out the possibility of his going back to Dublin to continue his medical studies. I recall him in later life regretting that he had no formal training which would have enabled him to pursue a professional career, but this lack may only have impinged on him when he was older.

Ellen Rahilly inherited her husband's considerable estate and had to make fundamental decisions about her own future. If Michael had settled down in Ballylongford, as everyone assumed he would, it was a normal expectation that he would, before long, find himself a wife. His mother may have considered building a new house for him, but decided instead to move out herself. An attractive house came on the market, and was bought by the widow. It stood outside Limerick, on eighty acres of land, not far from Ardnacrusha, where the power station to harness the Shannon was built in the mid-1920s. When she moved to Quinsborough House with her younger daughter Anna, Ellen Rahilly was quite close to her elder daughter, Nell, in Limerick city; and Michael could visit them by a train journey of less than two hours from Listowel.

The Rahillys were now 'county'. Anna, who was keen on riding, could keep a horse and go hunting with the Anglo-Irish landowners.

If the move for Mrs Brown, from beside the woollen mills in

Philadelphia to fashionable 5th Avenue in New York, was a step up the social scale, the move from over the shop in Ballylongford to a country mansion outside Limerick was an even greater advance socially for the Rahillys. They could now join the golf and tennis clubs, which were reserved for army officers, professional men, senior civil servants and large landowners. No shopkeeper, however wealthy, could hope to be accepted in the 'county' set.

Following Michael's visit to Paris, in the autumn of 1893, to see Nannie, who was a boarder in a Catholic convent school, they did not meet again until he went to New York in 1898. During those three years the courtship was carried on by correspondence. Michael was a prolific letterwriter, but none of those letters to Nannie have been preserved. The most likely explanation of the absence of any letters from this period is that she kept all Michael's letters until she received and accepted (or was about to accept) a marriage proposal from another suitor, and then she destroyed them. Michael would certainly have kept her letters, because he made a life-long practice of keeping letters, even those he had received from home when he was at Clongowes. But Nannie was determined that none of her girlish love letters would be available for public scrutiny. She even took this reticence to the point of making me promise, when she gave me the letters that Michael had written to her from the GPO (these were documents of considerable historical interest), that these would not be published while she was alive.

In the years following the death of Michael's father and Nannie's mother, whatever romantic dreams the young lovers may have had, the omens for their realization were not propitious. When Michael's father died, he had little choice but to remain in Ballylongford and look after the business. Even if he had wanted to return to the university, he was too late to pick up what he had missed in the lectures given during his illness, but all the evidence suggests that he had no relish for medicine and was probably glad of an excuse not to continue his medical studies.

However much in love the young couple believed themselves to be, the reality was that they scarcely knew each other. They had chatted and maybe danced together at the farmer's house on the night they met, and he had paid those visits to the hotel in Clare where the Browns were staying. Then there were the few weeks

Michael had spent in Paris. In those days fifteen-year-old girls would not have been allowed visits from their boyfriends and Michael could see Nannie only at weekends and then probably in the presence of a chaperone.

Any thoughts of marriage involved difficult decisions for them both. Michael was now the proprietor of a business in a small Kerry town, far from Dublin. How could Nannie contemplate settling down, so far from home, in a place she had never even visited, and in which she did not know a single soul except Michael?

If she had sought advice from anyone – and we can be sure she was given it whether or not she asked for it – it would be difficult to imagine any advice other than that it would be wise for her to wait, and to look for a young man with a similar background to her own, so she could keep in touch with her family and friends. Nannie was young, good-looking and attractive. The change from the lifestyle of an affluent New York young woman to the remote wilderness of north Kerry must inevitably lead to difficulties; and what did she really know of this young medical student, who had abandoned his studies and who, since his father's death, was looking after the family business. How could Nannie be sure that he was not looking for an American heiress so that he could live on her money?

These conflicting thoughts, desires, fears and forebodings, and no doubt advice from her friends, were going through Nannie's mind when a young New Yorker, whom she found congenial company, began paying attention to her, and then proposed marriage. If he was an eligible young man, anyone would have advised her to accept him, which she did. We know nothing about this young man except that his name was Marx. All I can tell is that one day in Kerry, probably in the late 1940s, Mother and I were alone in the bungalow when she volunteered the information that, before she had married my father, she had been engaged to a man named Marx.

Foolishly I did not question her about him. What was his background? Where had she met him? How long had she known him? What did he do for a living? Had he given her an engagement ring? How long had she worn it? How did she come to break with him? Did she write to break off the engagement or tell him face to face?

Michael's decisions in the love affair were just as difficult. His heart was set on this young American girl. She was quite small,

28

about 5½ feet tall, with a touch of ginger in her hair. He knew she was fond of him, but he also knew she would not cut her roots in New York and Philadelphia to come and live in Ballylongford.

The business Michael was now managing had been in the family for almost a hundred years; it had expanded greatly under his father's ownership, and was running at a useful profit. All the indications were that in Ballylongford he could look forward to a secure income for the rest of his life, without unduly exerting himself. The Browns were a well-off family, but there were five girls and he knew nothing about their finances, even if he could contemplate being dependent on whatever allowance Nannie might receive from her family. Giving up his own business was not a choice based on considerations of the main chance.

Michael's father, by any standards in rural Ireland, had been a wealthy man. He had worked hard to build up his fortune, but he had left everything to his wife, and Michael had nothing in his own right. He was financially dependent on whatever his mother gave him.

When his mother went to Limerick, Michael was left alone in Ballylongford. He had plenty to occupy him looking after the business, and there was no lack of recreational activities. He could enjoy sailing on the Shannon during the summer; in the winter there were ample opportunities for shooting. Michael was interested in horse-riding and bought and trained a racehorse, winning a large silver cup when he rode the mare in the Ballylongford races.

There were plenty of invitations to parties from families with unmarried daughters. Michael was a gregarious young man and was the life of any party with his singing and joking. It would have been a pleasant, carefree existence if he had not been haunted by his yearnings for his sweetheart in New York.

He was still undecided when he got word from Nannie about Marx. Maybe when Mother said she had become 'engaged' to Marx, she intended to convey that she had received a proposal of marriage, and without giving a firm commitment to Marx, had written to Michael to say that, since there did not appear to be any prospect of anything further between them, she was going to accept Marx's proposal. This news convinced Michael that it was now or never. He had to persuade his mother to sell the business and settle sufficient capital on him to enable him to get married. If he could do this, he could cable Nannie to say that he was on his way over.

His mother held the purse strings, so he had to begin by settling matters with her. It is easy to understand her reaction of incomprehensible disappointment at the suggestion that her only son, whom she had just nursed back to health from a bad infection of tuberculosis, was proposing to walk away from the family business, which her husband had spent thirty years of hard work developing. The business had become a fundamental part of her life, and she assumed her son would one day take it over. Instead of which, he now intended to reject it all in pursuit of his infatuation for this American schoolgirl, whom she had never even met.

No records exist of what arguments and rows took place between Michael and his mother about his proposal to leave Ballylongford, but it seems certain there were disputes. It was reasonable to ask why Nannie would not come to live in Ballylongford and share her future husband's lifestyle in the small Kerry town.

If Michael remained in Ballylongford, he could make a reasonable forecast of his future career. There would be managing the business, making money, investing some of it, local sporting activities and possibly, like his father, an entry into local politics. He was also keenly aware of the danger of becoming addicted to alcohol. The evidence of this addition was widespread in small country towns. I recall him saying to us on one occasion that if he had remained in Ballylongford, he was likely to have taken to drink.

The alternative of getting away from it all and embarking on an unknown and unchartered career appealed to his adventurous spirit. Matters were brought to a head when Michael received word that Nannie was about to accept Marx's marriage proposal. Whatever characteristics Michael had inherited from his parents, caution and prudence were not amongst them and he now had to make a decision he knew would shape his life. It was true that his mother could refuse to co-operate, but it was also true that if he refused to remain in Ballylongford, she could not herself manage the business.

In the end she decided that further opposition was of no avail. She agreed to settle on her son a capital sum of £9,000. This settlement was made conditional on his getting married, which suggests that at that time it was not certain if Nannie would accept him. This capital sum invested in the 'Funds' would provide a modest but assured income of £450 a year for the young couple.

It would be strange indeed if Michael's mother did not have

serious misgivings, wondering if the capital which she and her husband had amassed over the years by hard work and careful husbandry was now going to be squandered by Michael and this American girl in a few months of extravagant living in New York. She need not have worried. Michael was not acquisitive, but was keenly aware of the independence that an assured income gave him and had no intention of losing this privileged position.

With the marriage settlement from his mother in his pocket, Michael Rahilly set sail for the United States in September 1898.

Michael did not go directly to New York. He knew that girls in Nannie's income bracket attached great importance to having a diamond engagement ring, and he was not going to disappoint her. Jewellery was expensive in New York because there was a heavy import duty on precious stones. Diamond-cutting was a major industry in Amsterdam, and it was possible to buy diamonds there at bargain prices. Michael went to Amsterdam on his way to New York and bought a solitaire diamond for £100. He had the stone mounted in New York and presented it to Nannie. She accepted his proposal and sent him to Philadelphia to see her Uncle James, the effective head of the family. When he had seen Michael, he wrote to his niece on 28 September:

Dear Nannie,

Yours of the 27th July duly recd. and contents noted. Mr. Rahily [*sic*] called and of course I told him I was pleased and all that – he is to my mind a very nice young fellow and I think you are perfectly safe in trusting your future to his keeping and as you mean to marry I think that you have made an excellent choice. I like him very much. I am not in favour of long engagements of course you are both very young and can take your time.

Your loving uncle,
James Brown

It is a curious letter, beginning formally and even stiltedly, and then continuing almost without a punctuation mark. There is no mention of how Michael was going to support a wife, but Uncle James must have asked this question and been shown the settlement that Michael's mother had made in his favour. Probably in those days young girls were not supposed to be concerned with prosaic matters of this kind.

Uncle James was able to tell Michael that Nannie would get an allowance from the woollen mills, and it was assumed that Michael would find work, so there was no reason to delay the marriage. Nannie agreed to marry him, and Michael went back to Ireland to arrange for the sale of the business. That autumn the following notice appeared in the *Kerry Legal Reporter*:

Very Desirable Investment

To be sold as a going concern, the old established and flourishing grocery, spirits, drapery and general warehouse, and the extensive Coal, Iron, and Timber yards and stores at Ballylongford, where business has hitherto been carried on by the late Richard Rahilly. For further particulars apply to:

Francis Creagh, Solicitor, Listowel,

or Michael Rahilly, Ballylongford.

The business was sold and Michael returned to New York in the spring. The wedding took place on 15 April 1899.

Uncle James told the young couple that they could have a large wedding, to which all their friends and relatives from Philadelphia and New York would be invited. If they preferred a small family wedding, he would give them the money that had been saved by not having a large wedding breakfast, to spend on their honeymoon. They opted for a small family wedding and, after the wedding breakfast in Nannie's 5th Avenue home, boarded the S.S. *Seale* bound for Genoa.

The young couple stayed near Lake Como in Italy and Mother often reminisced about the pleasant time they had in that beautiful place. From there they moved to various Italian cities, and in a letter home Michael said how inexpensively they could live on the Continent.

Even on the honeymoon, Michael took the first step down the political path that would end in Moore Street in 1916. The occasion was the fiftieth anniversary of the coronation of Queen Victoria. There were fulsome articles in the European edition of the *Herald Tribune* in praise of the Queen and of the many blessings that her reign had conferred on humanity. This was more than Michael could stomach and he wrote to the newspaper to point out the miseries and devastation that Victoria's reign had inflicted on Ireland. The editor deleted some of his more severe strictures.

In their travels around Italy they kept as mementoes programmes of operas they attended, pictures of famous buildings they saw, and reproductions of paintings that appealed to them. There was no pressure on them to return to the US and they continued their 'Grand Tour' for as long as the money lasted. They had Michael's income, Nannie's allowance from her uncle, and the money saved on the wedding breakfast. Nannie became pregnant a month or two after their marriage, and they realized that, as the pregnancy progressed, travelling would not be comfortable for her.

In July 1899 they were staying in the Hotel de Florence in Paris. They had gone to Dresden and Prague on leaving Italy and were now on their way to visit Michael's family in Limerick. While they were in Paris, Nannie received a letter from Uncle James dated 17 July. He began by apologizing for not having answered four of her letters and then went on:

I suppose that you know that I would not consent that Sadie should get married to Mr Steingranat at the time that they had it set for. It seems to me too hurried and for some object. He is a foreigner and a Protestant and I don't like either and I am afraid that he simply wants Sadie for what he expects to get.

Sadie was one of Nannie's older sisters; Malte Steingranat was a minor member of the Swedish nobility. It seems strange that Uncle James should say that he did not like Protestants, when his own father must have been a staunch Protestant to have been nick-named 'Orange Billy' in Philadelphia. Maybe Uncle James believed that Sadie, having been brought up in a strictly Catholic family, would not be happy in a 'mixed' marriage. He also probably knew that it would be impossible to find a Catholic church in Sweden outside Stockholm. But apart altogether from religious differences, Uncle James would have realized the strains to which Sadie would be subject when she found herself in a country house in remote Sweden, where nobody spoke a word of English, and where she would be thousands of miles from her family and friends.

Uncle James was correct in his fears about this Swedish suitor. There were two Steingranat brothers who had come to the United States to trade on their minor Swedish titles, with the brazen intention of marrying American heiresses. In his letter Uncle James asked Nannie and Michael to go to Sweden to investigate these Steingranats. This would help him decide whether or not to consent to Sadie accepting Steingranat's proposal. Uncle James undertook to pay all the expenses of the trip.

It was the sort of adventure that Michael relished, but Nannie decided to stay in Paris. She seems to have been quite sick from the pregnancy, and in his letters Michael urges her to take her medicine and to have her 'drive' every day, presumably in a horse carriage.

Michael's trip was their first separation since their marriage three months earlier. He wrote his first postcard from the Gare du Nord, while waiting for his train north. He was away a little over a week and in that time sent Nannie five long letters, five postcards and several telegrams. He was passionately in love with her and kept her informed of every detail of his journey.

Michael went to Hamburg via Cologne and then on to Kiel. There he saw six German warships, and photographed the Kaiser's yacht, the *Hohenzolleren*. He then took a boat to Copenhagen and from there crossed the sound to Malmö. One of his letters written in August ends:

I am writing this behind the station in a lovely grove of pines. By the way the finest weather I ever found is here. It is delicious. . . . I think that Sadie would die of loneliness here. Think of it, six hours to Stockholm or Copenhagen and 42 from Paris or Berlin or London.

Good-bye my own little love. I do hope that you are not lonely. Do try to nurse yourself every way to be well on Saturday and don't fail to drive every day. Go to the theatre if you can with the Tylers or somebody. . . . Fare thee well little dote. Be good and you won't have a good time.

       Yours M.J.R.

P.S. The most obliging people are in this country. They refuse tips.

Another that month concludes:

You ask do I miss you; are not the number of my letters sufficient answer. . . .

Will you ever read as far as this, I wonder. Farewell, I am going out to tea. Be good and cheer up little darling. It looks awfully cute for you to sign yourself 'wife'. I kissed the letter fifty times.

       I am darling your own husband
         Michael J. Rahilly

When he arrived in Stockholm, Michael engaged a banker, a lawyer, and finally a private detective agency, to discover what he needed to know about the Steingranats. Among his papers there is a family tree of this Swedish family that he was able to draw by consulting a book on the Swedish peerage.

The research and effort that Michael put into this investigation is remarkable, although it was not of much help to Uncle James.

Michael was able to report to him that the Steingranats were minor Swedish nobility. The brothers in America seemed to be now impoverished, although a rich uncle had just died, but because his will had not been published, it was not possible to discover if these two brothers were beneficiaries.

After the Swedish trip, Michael and Nannie were to meet in London and from there to set off for Ireland and visit Quinsborough House. Nannie had not yet met Michael's family and both parties were curious and nervous. Nannie knew what a united family they were and, if there had been any friction between Michael's wife and his sisters, it would have boded ill for the marriage.

Nannie's upbringing had been quite different to that of her sisters-in-law, Nell and Anna. The difference in their ages was also important. The eldest of the Rahilly sisters, Nell, was then thirty years old and Anna was only two years younger, whereas Nannie was just nineteen. Nannie had been brought up in an atmosphere of financial security in which money was plentiful, whereas in the Rahilly family every penny was carefully watched.

In Ireland the devastation of the Famine years was still a vivid folk memory. When the Rahilly girls were growing up in the mid-1870s, they would have known old people who had lived through those appalling times. If such a catastrophe had happened once, who could be sure that it would not happen again? The only way an individual could seek protection was, if possible, to build up a personal nest-egg. When frugality to achieve this became a habit, it remained a way of life.

The visit went well and the three women remained close friends all their lives. There was just one incident during the visit about which Nannie could sense their disapproval, although nothing was said. The sisters and their mother were walking in the garden with Michael and Nannie when she noticed that her shoelace was loose. She turned to her husband and said: 'Michael, my shoelace has opened.' In a flash he was down on his knees on the gravel attending to the shoelace. Nannie saw from their looks that these Irishwomen took a poor view of their beloved Michael tying the shoelace of his American wife, whom they regarded as a schoolgirl.

Ten years later when both families moved to Dublin, Nannie and his sisters-in-law lived near each other and remained in the closest intimacy. The two sisters were a great help and comfort to Nannie when she was left a widow in 1916.

Mother used to say that the honeymoon lasted for almost a year, but she must have been counting from the wedding day to the time when they had an apartment of their own in New York. Michael and Nannie arrived back in New York in the autumn of 1899, more than six months after their wedding. On 25 October Michael was writing to Nannie on the train en route to Galena, a town to the west of Chicago. He had been sent to investigate a lead mine there. The name was appropriate since the word 'galena' is the Latin for lead. In his letter, he tells Nannie about the trip so far:

Niagara we left last night and slept in the cars. We had three berths in a compartment and one outside. I had the outside, in the middle of the car, with everyone in a common room. I had an adventure too: my berth was lower 6 and when I drew the curtain to go in, I found a maiden there sleeping the sleep of the just. I withdrew.

To-day, when we were up she looked disappointed.

He then writes about Niagara, where they saw an experimental plant for the lead works, which Michael said seemed to be working alright. The trip was in connection with some new plant designed to extract lead from the ore, and Uncle James had either been asked to invest in it, or already had done so. Michael was sent out to check on the mine. Clearly Uncle James had already sufficient confidence in young Michael Rahilly, who had been married to one of his nieces for only six months, to send him on such a mission.

Michael compares the town of Niagara with Long Branch, a holiday resort in New Jersey, where the Brown family had a summer home. In another letter he says that he would have sent his wife a picture of Niagara, except that the 'scoundrelly hotel keeper' wanted to charge five cents for the card, which Michael said was worth only one cent. Michael watched every penny.

In telling Nannie about the visit to Galena, he says:

It is a nice little place, but considerably more remote than Kilkee, something like Ballylongford. It is quite a nice little city though and we were most interested in seeing the mines. They do everything as primitively as though the Indians were still here. They dig where they feel like it and keep on if they find anything. If not they stop. There isn't much lead coming out of these works anyhow. We did have an experience though in the matter of driving. A fellow, the man who sells the lead, took us in a wagon to see the place, and talk of up hill and down dale, over fences, mud heaps, trees or any old thing. We were all silently and secretly praying when we were a mile out.

There were four in the party, but there is no mention of whether or not Uncle James was with them.

The next we hear of Michael's activities is in a letter to his sister Anna on 23 January 1900. He tells her that his dividends have not arrived and adds: 'I am trying to buy a grocery stock for cash and cannot do this without the dividends. In the meantime I am paying £30 a month rent for the store which is idle for want of stock.'

The dividends duly arrived, and some months later he wrote to his sister Nell: 'I am getting on fine here now and have one store nearly ready and a good manager for it. I hope that I will be able to give you a present of a million or so before long.'

There was not another word about the grocery store in any of Michael's letters.

Nannie would not have been enthusiastic about a store. Retail trade, in those days, was not socially acceptable and she would not have been happy telling her friends that her husband was running a grocery store.

Although nothing further emerges in any of the letters about the grocery store, there is a clue that it may have been started and carried on for some time. Michael is reported to have remarked to a friend that one of the most satisfying experiences in his life was driving a horse-drawn ice-delivery wagon. He did not say where he had done this, but it might have taken place in connection with the grocery store.

On 14 March 1900, just eleven months after the wedding, a baby boy was born. He was christened Bobby after Nannie's father. She could scarcely remember her father, who had died when she was five years old. When the baby arrived, Michael sent a cable to his family, consisting of the one word 'Boy'. The reply from Quinsborough also consisted of one word, 'Joy'. The Rahilly family did not waste money on lengthy transatlantic cables.

The baby did not thrive at first, but then started putting on weight, and Michael was able to write home:

About the baby; he is getting on fine: he weighs fourteen pounds and is gaining every day since we went on ordinary milk. The milk he was getting at first was not manufacturers, but was supposed to be specially good milk, prepared with sugar and water, extra carefully. As a matter of fact it was water and chalk, I think. We have a splendid nurse. She was trained in a children's hospital, and keeps the nursery in apple pie order. She is ideal in every way, and is really cheap, although she gets $20 a month. We are going to Long Branch for the summer in about a fortnight.

Nannie did not recover her health after the birth, and her doctors said that she would have to have an operation as soon as she was fit.

They spent the summer of 1900 in the Brown's summer home in Long Branch. While they were there, Michael was sent on another mission for Mr Brown, this time to Cincinnati. In a letter home to his sister written in the early summer, he says:

I was very near going over last week. Mr Brown had taken two tickets for himself and Madeline and at the last moment he found that he could not go. He wired to us: Nan and I were in Washington at the time and he said that we could use the tickets, but we, of course, would not dream of going, so the tickets were lost and the vessel sailed without anyone. I was as far West as Cincinnati on business for Mr Brown, and Nannie came as far as Washington with me. It was quite a trip for a week and I saw some of the finest things in buildings and scenery in America.

Nannie is not as well as she might be. The doctors say that she will probably have to have an operation in the autumn when she is stronger. She was quite unwell, you know, and has not recovered the ill effects yet.

But Michael did go back to Ireland shortly after this. On 30 June 1900 he embarked on the R.M.S. *Lucania*, and wrote to Nannie just before he left New York:

My darling Nan,

Jim has just left me. We caught this all right after seeing the 'Waldersee' going out as we were on the ferry, but we were too far away to see Madeline or your Uncle, if they were up which is doubtful. Accept thousands of kisses and love for my own darling Nancy.

He wrote another letter as the ship was off Kinsale, just before landing at Queenstown, but there is no clue to indicate what brought him to Ireland. It seems to have been a sudden decision and he did not stay long: in September he was again writing to his sister from Long Branch.

In October Michael and Nannie moved into an apartment of their own on West 80th Street, just across Central Park from where the Browns lived on 5th Avenue. It was their first home since their marriage.

Nannie had the operation that month and was feeling very weak after it. During the winter she went down to St Augustine, Florida, with the baby and her two unmarried sisters. It was hoped the mild winter climate there would help her to recuperate. She wrote from Florida on 12 February 1901 to her mother-in-law in Limerick (whom she calls 'Mother') telling about her own and the baby's health:

Dear Mother,

It is a long time since I received your welcome letter. I have been intending to answer it, but I suppose you know from Michael that I have been feeling very ill this fall, and so put off from day to day answering you so I am sure that you will pardon my seeming neglect.

The operation I had performed in October has been entirely successful: since it I am daily growing stronger and, with the help of God, I will soon be as well as before the arrival of the baby. When I left New York I was feeling so ill that I thought that I would be an invalid for life, but after two weeks here I feel a different person.

The baby is a fine child and as healthy as possible: he is very large for his age: he weighs 23 lbs and has six teeth, and, of course, is in every way the most wonderful boy in the world.

How is Dr Humphreys? I hope the trip has benefited his health, and that he will return entirely well. You all have had your own troubles this year, but I sincerely hope that they will be over now. How are Nell, Anna, and the children? Give them my best love and wishes for a merry Christmas and a happy new year.

I suppose that you know that Michael is in Phila. He is working very hard. He is up at six so as to get to the mills at seven, where he stays till five. A very long day. Still I am glad that he is there, as I think that it is a very good opening for him. If I were only with him I am sure that we would all be very happy. However he wants me to remain here and get good and strong, and I suppose that it is the best to do so.

Your affectionate daughter,
Nannie

Christmas 1900 was the second Christmas of their marriage and they were separated. He was working in the mills in Philadelphia and she and their son were in Florida. Nannie sent him a pocket-book for Christmas and on 21 December he was effusive in his thanks:

My darling little Nancy,

Thanks a thousand times for your sweetly pretty pocket book. . . . It was so thoughtful and dear of you to send it. . . . I am delighted to find that you are quite well and that your touch of malaria was only to scare me; as you see, you succeeded admirably. . . .

I got a day of cheerful mail to-day, to make plain that the darkest hour is just before the dawn. I got a cheque from the M. and L. bank with Couts' dividend. Ballinrobe and the Income Tax was due on the year before last, altogether $830, so cheer up.

I shall buy, I think, Metropolitan for investment. I think that it has more future to it, as it will always have the short run traffic, while Manhattan will get longer runs as the surface system develops. If oil receded a little it would be good, although it has now very little room: few things ever paid more than 50%. Anyhow I have to wait till after the holidays and there may be a chance of getting in lower then. Manhattan is only the same price now as when I wrote you first.

I had a letter from Mamie [Nancy's sister] asking me to go over for Xmas. I shall see your uncle and may go.

I have some people in N.Y. to see that I could do then.

With all kinds of good wishes for a happy Xmas and fifty more. I am, my darling Nancy your grateful and devoted husband,
        Michael Rahilly

The pocket-book that Nannie sent him that Christmas was the one he was carrying when he was shot in the charge up Moore Street. It was taken from his body by the soldiers who went through his pockets after he had died. His sister Anna asked the British authorities to return it, but they said that they could not trace it.

Michael decided to accept the invitation to spend Christmas with his sister-in-law Mamie, and her husband, Jim Cremins. He wrote a long letter to Nell about the visit. Some interesting aspects of his maturing character emerge from this letter. It contains the first expression of his distaste for Britain and every aspect of Anglo-Saxonism,'which was beginning to colour all his thinking. His love of adventure comes out in his suggestion to his sister that the families should charter a 200-ton yacht and sail around the world, in search of the perfect climate which would lead to a cure for the tuberculosis that had stricken Nell's husband, David Humphreys. This letter also contains a clue about why he may have abandoned his proposal to start a grocery store. Michael wrote to Nell that 'Mr Brown will not hear of my going into any business over here.'

In a letter to Nannie, written on 21 January 1901, Michael reveals more about his work in the mills. He starts this letter with the words 'Mia piccola carissima', the Italian for 'My dearest little girl'. He had become fluent in French and was now studying Italian:

I just got your sweet letter after long silence of nearly a week. I thought you were mad with me and was miserable accordingly. My wrist is nearly better now except that I cannot open doors or pour out tea, but I am quite an adept with my left hand and feel no inconvenience.

About coming down. I think that we are sure to go but probably on Feb. 5th and to stay two weeks. There's an excursion then at a slightly reduced rate, $50 inclusive of sleeper and meals.

Do you really want me to go, dearie? I was afraid that you found spinster-hood so free and novel and possessing so many of the advantages set forth in that article on widows in the 'Philistine' that I sent you, that you might be sorry to have your paradise intruded by a 'mere man'!

I will get my hands into shape. However, it is hard as I have been weaving these days and the loom filthyfies them. Still I will get them nice as I am now taking more care than I was hitherto. You see I am working with all the pretty mill girls and they have to be captivated. By the way some are as pretty as pictures. It seems a pity to see them stitching and picking and driving looms. But the pity is wasted as they say they like working.

In another letter sometime later, Michael gives an account of his work in the mills. He did not assume that, as the husband of one of the women who owned the mills, he could start at the top. He began at the bottom, either of his own volition or at Uncle James's suggestion, and was learning how to weave the cloth by working at it himself.

There is nothing in the letters to indicate why this apprenticeship was abandoned. The managers of the different departments were not likely to have been happy to have this young man working as a labourer, perhaps seeing things that should not have been happening. One wonders how many other boys from Clongowes had taken off their coats and gone to work as labourers.

Michael and Uncle James went down to St Augustine, Florida, and on 5 March he wrote to his sister Anna:

Mr B. and I came down here a week ago and have had great times here since. It is a delightful place, the nicest in this country, I think. It is all Spanish and old, with narrow streets, old churches and a Fort, and magnificent hotels.

We have Sailing, Rowing, Golf, Horse-Riding, Driving and Walking. So we are well off. Outside of the town though the country is very unattractive. Low, flat and covered with short little trees. . . .

I think that this place is perfect, with my usual optimism, but the girls, except Nan, are already referring to it as a 'hole' and wanting to go. They will want to get out of heaven if they ever get there.

The next letter home is from Long Branch on 7 May. It seemed unlikely that Michael would ever go back to work in the mills. In a letter from his sister it emerges that there had been a disagreement between Michael and Mr Brown and, because of this, he had stopped working in the mills owned by Nannie's family.

On the way north, Michael and Nannie spent some time in Atlantic City:

Dearest Anna,

Many thanks for your letter and photographs which I duly received when at Atlantic City. Need I say how delighted we were that David is so well and that you are all together once more again!

Atlantic City you could not find on the map, because it is so new. 25 years ago it was nothing and now it has a summer population of 200,000. It is a hideous spot. Materialism run mad. Nothing in it but the material. Houses, Hotels, Board Walks, Piers. No cliffs, no scenery, no trees, nothing nice.

So Dick is spoiled by his Pappa. Well, they tell me so is Bob. He won't go out with anyone but me now, and is just getting interesting.

We are all splendid and have come down to Long Branch for the past few days. That will be my address for the present.

I have nothing to say except that I shouldn't wonder if we went to EUROPE this year. If we do we will go for good and settle down somewhere. Give my love to Mother, Nell, David and the children.

I didn't keep my promise long about weekly letters did I?

Your ever affectionate brother
Michael Ioseph Rathaile

His signature in Irish to this letter is the first evidence of any interest in that language.

In 1901 Michael Rahilly badly needed some congenial activity to absorb his superabundant energy. He was under no pressure to support his family since they could live comfortably on the dividends of his investments. He had decided not to spend his life as the proprietor of a profitable business in a small Irish town, and had given up the idea of running a retail grocery business in New York. We do not know why he left the Brown Mills. It may have been because he insisted on learning the technology of the business. The managers might have resented this, and Uncle James did not have the guts to stand up to them.

Michael had no serious interests or responsibilities to occupy his mind and probably he hoped to find something back in Ireland. He may have even begun to realize at this time that the British occupation was not for the benefit of Ireland and hoped that, back in his country, he could do something about it. If his thoughts were leading in this direction, he would have been no different from the vast majority of the Irish people who wanted Home Rule for Ireland.

In the letter written from Long Branch in the summer of 1901, Michael says that they may come back to Europe and 'settle down'. He had capitalized Europe because it was not Ireland that they had in mind.

The Rahilly family came back to Ireland sometime in early 1902 and, according to Marcus Bourke, Michael was soon attending informal gatherings and discussions with radical Irish nationalists in a shop called 'An Stad' in Dublin, and contributing articles to nationalist papers under the pen name of 'Raparee'. If Bourke is correct, these literary efforts are the first evidence of Michael's interests in Irish politics.

On 19 June Michael wrote to his mother from Marine Villa, Vico Road, Dalkey:

Dearest Mother,

Just a line to say that we have had the most awful weather that ever was known, and can do nothing but sit at the fire for two days. I suppose it is poor David who feels it worst. He went to an uncomfortable spot when he chose the Queen's Hotel. If he went to Sundays Well he would be far better off. But I suppose everywhere is equally bad now. They have snow in South Africa.

Tell Anna I got the atlas for which I am exceedingly obliged. We are expecting her up, but in this weather we would not have much to amuse her.

I am to get the automobile to-morrow, but in this weather it will be only ornamental.

It appears likely that Michael, Nannie and their young son had spent some time in the family home, Quinsborough, before moving to Dublin. The reason for the return to Ireland is not spelled out in any of the extant letters.

The Rahilly family moved from Marine Villa to Welford Cottage, outside Bray, about the end of 1902; the house was almost directly opposite the entrance to the present Woodbrook Golf Club. At that time Woodbrook was just a tennis club and Michael was a keen tennis player. As he and Nannie knew nobody in Dublin, the club enabled them to make social contacts.

Michael first appeared as a JP in the Dublin Castle lists of 1903. The right to sign your name with these initials behind it was a minor step up the establishment ladder in Ireland. The duties were similar to those performed today by a District Justice, but it was an honorary part-time job. To be appointed a Justice of the Peace indicated that you were, in the eyes of Dublin Castle, a subservient supporter of the occupation forces, or, at least, that you accepted the right of Britain to govern Ireland.

In the early months of his return, there was no evidence of any subversive leanings from this highly respectable young man, whose father had been a JP before him. Richard Rahilly of Ballylongford had performed his duties as a JP conscientiously and efficiently.

There were no formal rules governing the appointment of a Justice of the Peace. Anyone wishing to become one would make representations to those who had access to the 'corridors of power'. Irish MPs, especially if they were among the leaders of the Irish Party, would have influence in Dublin Castle, and a generous subscription to the party funds would not diminish your chances.

It is unlikely that Michael Rahilly exercised any initiative on his own behalf in this matter. He may not then have publicly committed himself to the detestation of the British occupation forces which later dominated his thinking, but neither can we believe that his anti-British convictions were a sudden 'road to Damascus' conversion.

Someone must have spoken on his behalf to the Dublin Castle authorities. It is unlikely that the Castle asked senior civil servants or police officials to seek out suitably reliable 'Castle Catholics' whose allegiance could be copperfastened by giving them such a minor title.

If representations were made on Michael's behalf, the suspicion falls on his mother. A cheque to the Irish MP for Limerick may have helped. She was then in declining health and, if she had told Michael of these representations, it would have been difficult for him to have written to her saying that he did not want and would not accept any such mark of approval from the occupation forces. For Michael to have written to his mother in such a vein would have implied a highly critical slur on his father.

Family letters written when the father was made a JP record how proud the Rahillys felt when their father was given this 'honour'. Richard's widow would have assumed that her son would be equally pleased to be able to sign himself JP. There was no formal accept-ance ceremony nor any swearing of an oath of allegiance to the monarch. The names of the conferees were announced in the Dublin Castle *Gazette* and were listed in *Thom's Directory*. Michael Joseph Rahilly's name appeared in the lists of JPs from 1903 to 1907. Once a man was given this mark of approval by Dublin Castle, he would continue as a JP until he died, unless he committed some misdemeanour, or asked for his name to be removed. It seems likely that Michael asked for his name to be removed.

Few young couples were so blessed with benefits as Nannie and Michael. They were deeply in love after three years of marriage and they saw eye to eye on all important matters. They were both in good health. Nannie had made a complete recovery from her illness and was pregnant again. The baby was due in midsummer. They both adored their little boy Bobby. They were not wealthy, but by careful spending they enjoyed a high standard of living. Michael had both a car and a motor-cycle and was always happy when tinkering about with these mechanical novelties.

He had already begun to spend much of his time in the National Library, reading Irish history and picking up details of Irish genealogy. He was also becoming familiar with important Irish manuscripts and the libraries in which they were to be found. The knowledge he was acquiring emerged some years later when an article he had written about genealogy was published. Michael's cousin, Frank Rahilly, read it and wrote to Michael about it. Michael said that he had been interested in the subject for about ten years. He was then twenty-eight, which meant that his interest in this subject had begun when he was still a teenager.

In June 1903 Bobby was developing well and seemed in the best of health when, for no reason, he became sick and ran a high fever. A doctor was called and prescribed some medicine. The fever got worse and the following morning Bobby died, just three years of age. The cause of his tragic death was never determined.

It was a devastating blow to his parents and was an enduring sorrow to Nannie for many years until even greater troubles put it in the background. Everything about Ireland that reminded her of Bobby was now distasteful to Nannie and she wanted to get it out of her mind.

The next baby, another boy, was born on 3 July 1903, the same day the Gordon Bennett motor race was held near Athy, County Kildare.

Michael went to Athy to see this race. When Mother was telling us about this, she was too loyal to her husband to express criticism of him, but it was easy to understand her resentment that he was enjoying himself watching the motor race while she was suffering the agony of childbirth. The baby was christened Richard McEllistrim, but because he had an Irish cousin who was also named Richard, he was always called 'Mac' to avoid confusion.

Mother's desire to leave Ireland, to get the memory of the Bray house and Bobby's death out of her mind, led to their decision to move to Paris.

Michael Rahilly (left) with his brother-in-law, David Humphreys.

Quinsborough, County Limerick, where Rahilly's mother, Ellen, lived after her husband's death in 1896.

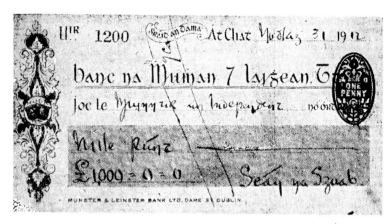

A cheque in Irish designed by O'Rahilly for Munster & Leinster Bank.

Plain:-

ABCDEFGHIJKLMNOPQRSTUVWXYZ
abcdefghijklmnopqrstuvwxyz

Italics:-

ABCDEFGHIJKLMNOPQRSTUVWXYZ
abcdefghijklmnopqrstuvwxyz

Seo an cló is ceart do beith agaib.

You can read English in this type.

C'est Parfaitement français aussi.

A new, simplified Celtic type designed by Michael O'Rahilly for printing in Irish in 1913 and used by An Claidheamh Soluis *and other papers until destroyed by fire during the civil war.*

4

Entry into Politics

It is not known how long the couple stayed in Paris, but some time in 1904 they moved to Brighton, where I was born on 22 September 1904.

In those days Irish politics consisted of what went on in the Parliament of Westminster. It was while we were living in Brighton in 1904 that Michael made his first tentative entry into Irish politics. He joined the London branch of the United Irish League. This was the name the Irish Party in Westminster had adopted in 1900 when the pro- and anti-Parnellite factions joined together under John Redmond.

If Michael was seriously thinking of becoming involved with the UIL, Brighton was a convenient place to live since it was only an hour from London by train. Brighton also attracted him, as Bray had, because it was on the sea. In London Michael could study the old Irish documents and manuscripts in the British Museum Library, where he appears to have spent much of his time.

James O'Mara, Michael's friend from Limerick (they had been in Clongowes together), was then working in London as the agent for the family bacon company. The two young men had much in common. James had been elected an MP and could introduce Michael to the leaders of the Irish Party. It was probably through him that Michael became acquainted with Joe Devlin, one of the top men in the party.

Among Michael's papers is a postcard from Joe Devlin declining an invitation to spend a weekend with the Rahilly's in Brighton. It seems possible that Michael was hoping to persuade Devlin that it was a futile waste of effort trying to obtain concessions from the British by parliamentary means. This constitutionalism had been going on for a hundred years and had produced no result. In Michael's opinion, a more effective policy would be for the Irish MPs to return to Ireland and to set up a mock parliament in Dublin. An account by Nancy Wyse Power of her recollections of Michael in the London branch of the UIL confirms that this is what he had in mind. She recalls how he had proposed a resolution to this effect. This became the basic policy of Sinn Féin, although that party had not then been formed. Even before Sinn Féin formally launched this policy two years later, there were radical Irish nationalists who believed that it was more likely to get results than any pressures the Irish MPs could apply in Westminster. The number of members of the London branch of the UIL who voted for Rahilly's motion is not known, but it was defeated, and soon after he left London his activities with the UIL ceased.

James O'Mara agreed with Michael that it was futile to hope to achieve Irish independence by making speeches in Westminster, and he resigned his seat in 1907.

Early in 1905 Michael, Nannie and their two children left Brighton and took a flat in London. Nannie had become reconciled to the idea of going back to live in Dublin, and Michael went there to find a suitable house. He stayed in Jury's Hotel in Dame Street and began to look at property. He was looking for a house with a mill attached to it, so that he could contribute to the development of the country in some tangible way. However, he found that any houses with mills that were operating profitably were not for sale.

As an alternative, he hoped to find a house adjacent to a turf bog which might enable him to begin the commercial exploitation of turf. At that time there was a general belief among Irish nationalists that Ireland's vast turf bogs were a potential source of fuel. However, Michael did not come across anything that seemed suitable. In one of his letters to his cousin Frank Rahilly, written about this time, he described himself as a 'licensed loafer'. He could live comfortably on the dividends of his investments, but he still wanted to find some useful activity to which he could commit himself. Early in 1904 Michael suffered another bereavement when his mother died at the age of sixty.

Michael and Nannie went to live for some time in Quinsborough, the family home outside Limerick. David Humphreys had also died and Michael's two sisters were living in Quinsborough with Nell's three children. During the summer of 1905 Michael and Nannie, with Nell and Anna, rented a house in Ballybunion and spent a month there with the five children. Michael loved this Kerry resort, where he could enjoy the swimming, the golf and the plentiful company. Nannie liked the golf, but she rarely went swimming.

That autumn, shortly after they returned to Quinsborough from the summer holiday in Ballybunion, Nannie left the two children with Michael and set off to New York to have a family council about the future of the mills. They were doing badly and had ceased paying dividends to the five girls. Three of the girls were now married, but Michael was the only husband who was free to take an active part in the management of the mills. The daughters hoped that, as a result of their meeting, there might be a reconciliation between their uncle and Michael, so that he could again work in the mills and perhaps make them profitable once more. The Brown girls, now in their twenties, realized that, while Uncle James had many agreeable qualities, he did not have the toughness and discipline necessary to run a large-scale business. He had never concentrated his energy on the woollen mills, because he was always hoping for a bonanza from some other source.

Nannie's mission succeeded in effecting the hoped-for reconciliation, and plans were made for the Rahilly family to return to Philadelphia and for Michael to take up a position in the mills with Uncle James's full co-operation. Soon after Nannie's return to Limerick, the Rahillys with their two children and an Irish nursemaid went back to Philadelphia. In a letter Anna wrote to Michael, she referred to the possibility of their going to live in Chicago.

Nannie was much happier moving to the city where she had spent her early youth and had many family friends than going to the mid-west. They settled in a suburb of Philadelphia called Lansdowne. The house they bought on Shadeland Avenue was the first they had owned since their marriage six years previously. When they moved into it, they both thought of this house as the permanent residence in which they would live out their lives. They named the house 'Slieve Luchra', the name of the district in Kerry where the poet Aodhagán Ó Rathaille had lived.

It was a substantial eight-bedroom house on seven acres, and Michael, who was never short of ideas for improvements, got to work making repairs and adding amenities. The central heating system needed major alterations, and the floorboards had to be caulked to make them draughtproof. Michael did this work himself. He was always happy when he could find something to do with his hands.

Nothing is known of the nature of the work Michael did in the mills. Our knowledge of his activities at this time usually comes from his letters home or to his cousin Frank Rahilly, but his work in the mills is not mentioned in these letters. When I asked Mother many years later what sort of work he did, she said that he was little more than a timekeeper. In those days, before there were time clocks for the workers to punch as they came on and off shift, a supervisor would have to keep a check on the timekeeping. It was common knowledge that the mills were on the point of collapse and needed much more than an improvement in the timekeeping if they were to survive.

Mother told us that two serious blunders had been made by management which led to the mills' closure. The first was that the company used all its resources to build a new mill when trade was booming, and when a slump came, the mills did not have the reserves to survive. A bad mistake was also made when all the woollen mills on the east coast of the US formed a cartel to regulate output and control prices. The Brown Mills, now called the Southwark Mills, thought that they were powerful enough to survive outside the cartel and they refused to join it. This was the rock on which they perished, because the cartel was able to squeeze them out of business.

Mother may not have liked to say it to us, but she knew that the fundamental cause of the failure was the lack of business capacity of her Uncle James.

In a letter to Frank Rahilly, written shortly after he settled in Philadelphia, Michael said that he had found an excellent library in that city from which he could borrow books for a few cents a week. It contained a good collection of books about Ireland and was another source of the extensive knowledge of Irish history which Michael displayed in articles he contributed to various papers and journals in later years. Frank had read one such article and was surprised at the range of information it contained. He wrote to say that he assumed that Michael had found an article on the subject and had cribbed the information, without citing the source. Frank found it difficult to understand how his cousin, who had led a pampered life travelling around the world, could have acquired so much knowledge as was contained in this article.

Defending himself against the accusation of plagiarism, Michael said that he had gathered the facts by means of what he called his 'envelope system'. He kept a series of envelopes, each one labelled with the heading of a subject in which he was particularly interested. He then obtained a supply of thin paper which he cut into a pieces so that they could fit inside the envelopes. Then, whenever he came across a fact relating to one of his subjects, he wrote an account of it on one of these slips and stored it in the appropriate envelope. When an envelope contained too many slips, he subdivided it. Michael told Frank that he found the system useful and he would recommend it to any journalist who made a living by writing articles. He said that he had used the system to collect information on the subject of his article over the past ten years.

During his years in Philadelphia, Michael had several inventive ideas. One of these was for a railway gate to reduce the accidents caused by trains travelling through towns and cities. We can assume that it was not feasible or cost-effective because the railways showed no interest. Another was for a folding camera, but this was also rejected.

While they were in Philadelphia, Michael and Nannie decided to speak French to each other and to their children. This served several purposes. It enabled Michael to improve his fluency, and was no trouble to Nannie, who was as fluent in French as she was in English. It also gave the children a basic knowledge that made it easier for them to acquire spoken French when they grew up. Finally, it enabled Michael to work off his phobia towards every aspect of Anglo-Saxonism.

But whatever other ideas occupied his mind, his thoughts kept coming back to what was happening in Ireland. His sister Anna regularly sent him the radical Irish weeklies, so he was well-informed of what was going on at home. This emerges in a letter he wrote to James O'Mara in 1908:

Only to-day I read in the papers the disheartening results of the Leitrim election. It is disappointing after Sinn Féiners have kept plugging away for nearly a decade, but nations move slowly and it seems hard to enlighten the men of places like Breffini ua Ruarc.

The Leitrim by-election to which he refers took place when C.J.

Dolan resigned his seat as a member of the Irish Party and fought the by-election on the Sinn Féin ticket. If Dolan had won, it would have been a serious blow to the Irish Party. Other MPs who were sympathetic to the Sinn Féin policy would have resigned and sought re-election as Sinn Féin candidates. When Dolan was defeated, this danger to the Irish Party was, for the moment, at an end.

If we know little about the work Michael did in the mills, we know quite a lot about his other pursuits and especially about his interest in the revival of Irish. This knowledge comes from letters he wrote to his sisters and to Frank Rahilly in Dublin.

It is clear that he was keeping closely in touch with events in Ireland, and was particularly interested in the efforts of the Gaelic League to revive the Irish language. Frank Rahilly was one of Ireland's leading Gaelic scholars and was later appointed Professor of Irish at Trinity College, Dublin. He kept Michael informed about the League's progress. Michael became so impressed by the Gaelic League campaign that he decided to learn Irish himself. He asked Frank to send him an Irish primer, one small enough to fit in his pocket, which he could study as he was travelling in the train to and from work. When he received this he wrote:

My dear Frank, Ten thousand thanks for the Irish Primer which duly arrived, and for which I daily thank you mentally. They [the exercises] are exactly what I need and truly well selected. My train journeys feel all too short when I have them with which to pass the time. I have not gone deeply into them as yet, but I can appreciate the delightful Gaelic of Father O'Cleary.

Michael also began teaching Irish to Nannie. The couple were such kindred spirits that learning Irish would have lost much of its pleasure for Michael if he could not have taught Nannie the words and phrases as he picked them up himself. She had a natural gift for languages and had no trouble acquiring a smattering of Irish.

Michael also decided to continue his study of Euclid, the subject in which he had obtained high marks in one of his first examinations at Clongowes. Besides studying the subject himself, he also tried to teach it to Nannie. She found it incomprehensible and laughed when she told us about his vain endeavours to interest her in geometry.

Michael and Nannie had a normal social life among the bourgeoisie of Philadelphia. The Brown family had been prosperous citizens there for many years and their woollen mills were an important commercial activity in the city. Uncle James was in a position to introduce his niece and her husband to both his business and personal friends. This led to invitations to their homes and, when Michael and Nannie reciprocated with invitations to 'Slieve Luchra', they soon had as much social life as they desired.

However, as early as 3 September 1905 Michael was already becoming disillusioned with his life there. He spelled this out in one of his first letters to Frank:

Your most interesting letter has reached me, and every line of it gave me pleasure, coming as an intellectual relief from the vortex of commercialism in which I am plunged here.

Two and a half years later, writing to James O'Mara on 23 February 1908, his opinions were unchanged:

There is, of course, no word of news from this stronghold of materialism. The Americans are just now in the crying stages of despondency over their want of business – the natural sequence to their recent debauch of prosperity. By prosperity they mean dollars, more dollars and yet more dollars.

When the Rahillys had been in Philadelphia about three years, it became clear to Michael that he could do nothing to stem the losses in the mills and that their closure was inevitable. He and Nannie realized that if this were to happen it would force them to make a fundamental decision about their own future. A third son, whom they christened Niall, had been born in Philadelphia in December 1906, and they knew that the decisions they made now would involve the future of their children. The eldest boy was six years of age and would soon be going to school. If they remained in the United States, their children would grow up as young Americans and this was not likely to have been what Michael wanted.

Nannie's perference was probably to remain in her native country, but she realized that there was an attraction, which he could neither explain nor resist, drawing Michael back to Ireland.

Mother told us that one of the possibilities that Michael considered at this time was the purchase of a seat as a stockbroker in New York. Stockbroking was not a profession like medicine or engineering and required no special training or qualification. Michael had learned about stock exchange transactions from listening to his father. Later, when his mother settled money on him, he had dabbled in a little trading himself. He had no doubt that he was capable of running the business of a stock-exchange/broker. The first requirement was integrity in looking after the client's interests and then one had to have the capacity to inspire confidence and to give sound advice. Mother did not tell us if he had actually negotiated for the purchase of such a seat. If he had, he might have found that he could not raise the necessary capital. It is more likely that the idea was superseded by his real desire to get back to Ireland. Michael's letters home confirm that he found utterly distasteful the preoccupation with the almighty dollar which was common among the people with whom they mixed in Philadelphia. He was not likely to have found the atmosphere in the New York Stock Exchange any more congenial.

Whatever options Michael and Nannie contemplated, they finally decided to return to Ireland. The first move was to sell 'Slieve Luchra'. While they were waiting for the agents to find a buyer for their house, Uncle James sent Michael on a final trip – right across the country and over the border into Mexico. We know nothing about the purpose of this mission, but it seems likely that Uncle James was chasing another will-o'-the-wisp.

Michael, as usual when he was away from Nannie, sent detailed accounts of the marvellous scenery, the perfect weather, and any particular adventures. Although the couple had been married for almost ten years, these letters were very like love letters. In his last letter, written on his way home, he said: 'it is dreadful to think of another week nearly before I see you.' Reading this letter it might appear that they had been separated for several months, whereas it can only have been a few weeks:

Bisbee, Arizona, Jan. 25 1909
My dearest little Sweetheart,
    I just received your long expected letter on my arrival here from Cananea, and you cannot conceive the relief it was to see your own dear handwriting after so long. You didn't date it but I suppose it was written Wednesday.
    It is dreadful to think of another week nearly before I see you.
    Thanks for all the news – I suppose the boys are well and yourself. We have had a fine time – such weather as you could not believe. If I had only had you with me I should have been perfectly happy.
    The joke of the trip occurred on the Mexican border to-day coming back. An inspector asked me where I was from. To which I replied 'United

States – American'. 'Where was I born?' In Ireland. 'Where were my papers?' I had none. Then I was an alien and must see the chief.

The chief maintained that I was a subject of Edward Wettin to which I replied indignantly that I was subject to no man, and if necessary would shoot Mr Wettin at sight – which saved me paying my $4.00 immigration tax.

Since then the fellows have christened me 'The Count', as it was my mustaches that caused all the attention. We hold our meeting to-night here. Have got everybody in line and hope to make a good arrangement. No word from your Uncle so I am going back direct to-morrow.

Your own (if not only) sweetheart, Ua Rathghaille

One of the documents found among Michael's papers were two pages of a daily newspaper published in Philadelphia. They are entirely taken up with a detailed description of the formation of a new Irish political party which had taken the name Sinn Féin. These words mean in English 'We ourselves'. There are three large pictures of the founders, John Sweetman and Edward Martyn, who were joint presidents, and Arthur Griffith, who was secretary. The policy of the new party was based on that adopted by the Hungarians in their efforts to secure some form of autonomy from their more powerful Austrian neighbour. The essence of this 'dual policy' was that the Hungarians refused to attend the joint Parliament in Vienna and insisted on setting up their own Parliament. According to the Sinn Féiners, it had succeeded in forcing the Austrians to relinquish some control over their neighbour.

Arthur Griffith wrote a book on the subject entitled *The Resurrection of Hungary.* John Sweetman financed its publication and it ran into several editions. As a result of the great emphasis that Sinn Féin placed on the analogy, they were frequently called the 'Hungarian Party'.

It is surprising that the editor of the Philadelphian newspaper was persuaded that there was sufficient interest among his readers to justify giving over two pages to a detailed description of this new political departure in Ireland. The fact that Michael had kept the pages carefully shows clearly his conviction that the Sinn Féin policy was the correct political strategy for the Irish to pursue in their endeavours to loosen the British grip on Ireland. When he returned to Ireland in 1909, he showed this belief by becoming an active member of Sinn Féin.

If the decision to return to Ireland in 1909 was of fundamental importance to the future lives of Michael and Nannie, it was equally important to the future of Ireland because from 1909 to 1916 Michael played a leading role in the developments which led to the withdrawal of the British forces from most of Ireland. If Michael O'Rahilly had not taken this leading role, someone else might have done so; but, as a matter of historical record, it was he who was responsible for the formation of the Irish Volunteers, which led to the 1916 Rising. He was convinced that the British would not leave Ireland unless they were compelled to do so by physical force.

It would have been impossible for anyone to have foreseen that this impeccably dressed young man who stepped ashore from the B&I boat on the North Wall in Dublin was going to set in motion a movement that would lead to the most powerful empire the world had ever known having to set free its first and most coveted colony.

An examination of the evidence does not indicate any logical or compelling reason for the couple's decision to return to Ireland. It appears to have been a case of 'There's a divinity that shapes our ends, Rough-hew them how we will.'

When the Rahillys and their three sons landed in Dublin that spring day in 1909, they went to the Imperial Hotel on O'Connell Street and remained there for some days until Michael rented a furnished house on Leeson Street. Some months earlier, his sisters, Nell and Anna, had left Quinsborough and had come to live in Dublin. Nell's husband had died five years previously and she also had three children, but there is no suggestion that the two families met in Dublin by prearrangement.

Sighle O'Donoghue, one of Nell's children, recalls how she was upstairs one morning in their house on Pembroke Road when the maid came up to her mother and said that there was a man downstairs, a Mr Brown, who wanted to see Mrs Humphreys. Nell said that she had no idea who this 'Mr Brown' could be, but she went down to meet him. Sighle watched over the banisters to see who was there. When her mother came to the bottom of the stairs, she turned to one side where the 'stranger' had been left, and as she did so Sighle heard her mother exclaim with delight 'Michael'! This was how the Rahilly family came together in Dublin.

Michael and his sisters remained very close for the next six years until Michael was killed in 1916. That summer of 1909 the two families again shared a house in Ballybunion for a month. They all loved this Kerry town and Nannie became quite keen on golf when she was there.

The Humphreys' children were older than their cousins, but there was not much difference in age between the eldest Rahilly boy and the youngest Humphreys boy and they too became fast friends.

The two families made arrangements for sharing a car. Michael and Anna each paid £200 for a small De Dion Bouton automobile. It was one of the leading French cars, the same make as the single cylinder car that Michael had bought in 1902, but this one was a four-cylinder model. The families had the use of the car on alternate days. Michael and Anna both became involved in the Gaelic League and drove to Feisheanna all over Ireland. At this time there were few cars on the roads and Michael also made a hobby of visiting places of historical and archaeological interest in many parts of the country, so the Rahilly car became quite well-known.

In the arrangements for sharing the car, which Michael spelt out in detail to avoid any possibility of misunderstanding, one of the clauses stipulated that he was to be paid one shilling and sixpence an hour for any mechanical work he did on the car. He loved tuning it and making new gadgets to improve its performance. In those days 'decarbonising' was a routine chore, as well as grinding in the valves and adjusting the valve tappets, and Michael always did this work himself.

A week or so before Easter 1916 Michael had just finished a major engine overhaul. He drove the car down to Liberty Hall on Easter Monday, laden with rifles for the Rising. The car was left outside the GPO at the corner of Princes Street, and was burnt out from the heat of the burning Post Office. When the Corporation was clearing up the rubble, they wrote a note to Nannie asking her for disposal instructions for the burnt-out car. At the time no one thought it would be an interesting souvenir of the Rising and Nannie told them to dump it. It is probably now buried under Hill 16 in Croke Park, with the rest of the rubble from the burnt-out buildings.

When this car was ordered, the chassis and engine were to be supplied by the French company, but the body was made in Ireland; Michael believed in supporting Irish industry. Bodies then were largely made of wood and were somewhat similar to those of horse-drawn carriages. The body was made by a Dublin firm of coach-builders and may have been the first to be made in Ireland.

The close ties between the two families continued when they both set up in more permanent homes, the Rahillys in Herbert Park, Ballsbridge and the Humphreys in Northumberland Road; again they were just ten minutes walk from each other. For some years they also continued to share a house for the summer holidays.

When Michael and Nannie settled down in Dublin in 1909, it is unlikely that he had any clear plans about how he was going to occupy himself. Ireland was undergoing radical changes, and in a number of fields of cultural activity a renaissance was taking place. Hundreds of thousands of young people had joined the Gaelic Athletic Association which had been formed to encourage the playing of Irish games. Before the GAA, the only games played in Ireland had been the English games played in the secondary schools, despite the fact that the Irish game of hurley was one of the best team games in the world.

In education, largely as a result of the Christian Brothers, a whole new generation of Irish boys was emerging with a good second-level schooling. The education given by these Brothers frequently included a firm belief in radical Irish nationalism. Indeed, they played a leading role in the forces then building up, to achieve for Irish people the right to manage their own country.

In literature, Irish writers, headed by such titans as Shaw, Yeats and Wilde, played a leading, and indeed a dominant, role in English letters.

The Gaelic League, formed for the revival of the Irish language, had thirty full-time teachers giving lessons, and it seemed possible that most Irish people could become bilingual, with Irish as the normal language in the home. The Feis Ceoil was stimulating an interest in music and helped develop such world singers as John McCormack and Margaret Burke Sheridan. The Abbey Theatre, with its peasant plays, was attracting interest in many parts of the English-speaking world.

The Co-operative Movement, formed by Sir Horace Plunkett, was teaching farmers to understand that by combining together in a non-profit organization, they could cut out the middle-men. They would pay less for their raw materials, as well as receiving the best market price for what they had to sell. The Co-operative Movement was also educating farmers in modern farming technologies.

Another important crusade that was making good progress early in the twentieth century was the Total Abstinence Association. Alcohol consumption and excesses arising from it had always been one of Ireland's most serious social problems. The Total Abstinence Association was spreading a general awareness that the only safe and certain practice to combat this addiction was to be a tee-totaller. Hundreds of thousands of young people joined this organization and took the 'pledge' to abstain from alcohol. The members wore a 'pioneer' pin which ensured that no one urged them to take a drink.

The Ireland to which Michael returned was alive with these activities and he was involved in many of them. Normal Irish political life consisted of the activities of the Irish Party in Westminster. Michael Rahilly would have had no trouble in getting nominated for an Irish Party seat in the House of Commons – the party wanted MPs who could support themselves in London without funding from Dublin – but he had no interest in such a role.

The Rahilly and Humphreys families returned from their 1909 summer holiday in Ballybunion about the same time as the *Sinn Féin Daily* published its first issue. Michael had not been involved in helping to launch the paper; this would have involved collecting the money, and then purchasing and installing the printing presses and recruiting staff. However, as soon as he returned from Kerry, he threw himself wholeheartedly into the newspaper project. He met Arthur Griffith, the prime mover in the launching of the *Daily*, and they became firm friends. Griffith had been preparing for this event for a number of years; he was convinced that until there was a daily newspaper to expound the Sinn Féin doctrine, they would make no progress in their efforts to convince the Irish people that the agitation of the Irish Party at Westminster would never achieve Home Rule.

Some months after the launch of the *Daily*, it became clear that there was no hope of its survival unless there was a substantial injection of finance to cover its initial losses.

The only hope of these Sinn Féiners, and it was a slender one, was that they might find business people in the US to invest in the paper in the hope of making a profit. They were not looking for people with any ideological commitment to the newspaper's policy, but simply investors hoping for a good return on their money if the paper became a success.

One of those involved in the launching of the paper was William Bulfin from Derrinlough, County Offaly. As a young man he had emigrated to the Argentine and had worked as a gaucho on the pampas. Later he developed literary talents and ended up owning and editing *The Southern Cross,* an Irish-Argentinian newspaper. He made frequent visits back to Ireland and got to know the Irish Irelanders who met at 'An Stad', the shop owned by Cathal Garvey. About 1905 he returned permanently to Ireland and made a cycling tour which he described in a popular book called *Rambles in Eirinn.*

Michael O'Rahilly and William Bulfin volunteered to travel to New York to look for American investors. They did not even approach John Devoy, the head of Clan na Gael, the leading radical Irish-American organization. Devoy was unlikely to have been able to give them the money they required, even if he had been willing to do so. But Clan na Gael probably regarded Sinn Féin as a rival group to the people they supported in Ireland whom they called the 'H.O.' These initials stood for 'Home Organization' and referred to that nebulous Irish body, the Irish Republican Brotherhood.

This assignment of Michael's was the first full-time commitment he had made to the Sinn Féin cause. He and Bulfin set off for New York six months after Michael's return from the US. They took the B&I ferry to Liverpool, where they embarked on a transatlantic liner for New York. While Michael was waiting for the liner to sail, he wrote to Nannie on 27 November 1909:

I wish you would pray for success, as I know no other method of influencing it. It was pathetic leaving the office last night and realising that so much depended on what we do. Don't forget to mention the name to advertisers when at all possible as every little helps.

In New York he stayed with his two unmarried sisters-in-law in an apartment on Park Avenue where they were living with their aunt. Michael wrote to Nannie from the apartment:

We are getting on fairly well and have a hopeful trail under way now. I am trying to combine the advertising proposition with the other and make a success that way. . . . I had a great reception from the Digest people who were very nice indeed.

Michael gives no clue about the sort of people or business groups he and Bulfin were trying to interest in the new Irish daily, but all their efforts came to nothing and they returned home empty-handed. The *Sinn Féin Daily* ceased publication early in January 1910, about six months after its first issue. This failure was a major setback for the

radical Irish nationalist movement and a bitter disappointment to all
those involved. The £8,000 that had been subscribed turned out to be
much less than was required, but it was still a substantial sum of
money. Shares were given to subscribers (there are a bundle of them
among O'Rahilly's papers) but those who invested knew that they had
little chance of getting a return on their money. Many, probably
most, of those who subscribed were not investors taking a chance on a
new speculation, but were nationalists who were giving money, which
they could ill afford to lose, in the hope of advancing the 'cause'.

Even for those who were running the paper, and who were
desperately anxious for it to succeed, it was as much a moral crusade
as a commercial enterprise. This fact can be seen in the decision of
the directors not to publish the horseracing results because of their
belief that it encouraged gambling.

The failure of the *Daily* dashed the high hopes of many radical
Irish nationalists, and the funds of Sinn Féin were so depleted by its
efforts to keep the *Daily* going that there was a danger that even the
Sinn Féin *Weekly* could not survive.

In an effort to ensure the survival of the *Weekly*, Michael wrote to
his friend James O'Mara on 10 January 1910:

My dear Jim,

As you are probably aware the Sinn Féin Daily is considerably
handicapped for lack of capital, and some of us are trying to get together
about five hundred pounds to ensure that the Weekly at least can be
maintained in order to prevent the set back the movement would
experience if it were to be left without an organ.

You doubtless realise the full meaning of the policy which is one that we
both approve.

I am guaranteeing them one hundred pounds and have got a promise of
another hundred. Can you make it three which would considerably
encourage me in my efforts to get the rest?

I cannot write all that could be said in favour of your helping us, which is
probably an advantage, as it would probably bore you vastly, but you know
that there is much more than the prosperity of a newspaper involved in the
question.

If you are compelled to refuse I shall thoroughly understand that it is not
from want of inclination, and in either case I want you to excuse the
comparative brusqueness of this request, which is compelled by the facts of
the situation.

Believe me your most sincere friend.

    Michael Joseph Rahilly

O'Mara was willing to help and on 18 January Michael wrote to thank him:

My dear Jim,

I received your favour this morning and it is scarcely necessary to say how much I appreciate your action in the matter. It contrasts so favourably with some other experiences that I have had that it is all the more impressive. We make the public appeal in to-day's issue and hope for some results from that.

Michael collected enough to keep the weekly paper going, but the money that had been lost on the *Daily* was a severe handicap to the party and a bad setback for those who had worked so hard to bring it into existence.

Shortly after Michael and Bulfin's return from the United States, Michael opened the paper one morning to read of William Bulfin's sudden death. This was a further setback for Sinn Féin, and a personal loss for Michael. They had become close friends on that trip to New York.

Soon after Michael and Nannie had settled in Dublin, he turned his mind to finding some activity that could provide him with an interest and that also would contribute to the economic development of Ireland. There was a widespread belief among Irish nationalists that the turf industry could be developed and become an important source of employment and economic activity.

A Christmas card from Laurence Ginnell, the Nationalist MP for Westmeath, was found among Michael's papers. He and Michael had become friendly in London. Ginnell was such a staunch defender of Ireland's rights that in Westminster he was given the soubriquet 'The member for Ireland'. The Christmas card was a small hand-painted watercolour of a rural cottage on the edge of a bog. Underneath was the caption:

> Irishmen search the world for gold.
> While in Ireland's bogs lives wealth untold.

Michael decided to investigate the possibility of developing a turf industry in Ireland. He wrote to the German firm Buchau Wolf, who made machinery for the Brown Coal and Turf Industries, and asked them to quote for a small plant to make turf briquettes. There was an extensive hand-turf production in Ireland at that time, but hand turf was a labour intensive operation and the quality of the fuel was unpredictable. If the drying season was good and the turf was of good black quality, well-harvested, it made an excellent fuel, but the quality varied so much that it was impossible to develop an industry on an unpredictable product. At that time turf briquettes had never been made in Ireland and possibly nowhere else either.

Buchau Wolf's reply was not encouraging. The firm said that it would cost about £20,000 to establish a small plant to make turf briquettes, but warned Michael that with good household coal selling in Dublin for £1.50 per ton (he had told them this), it would be impossible to make turf briquettes competitive. Michael accepted this and did not pursue the idea.

Michael O'Rahilly had not been long in Dublin when he became fully involved in the work of Sinn Féin. Countess Markievicz recalled that when he joined, the organization was moribund. His enthusiastic commitment gave them new life and hope, where before he joined there had been endless bickering between Arthur Griffith and Bulmer Hobson, with Hobson constantly reminding them that they must be true to the ideals of Tone and Davis.

Hobson was a Northerner who had come to Dublin and become involved in almost all the avant garde nationalist organizations. His first activity was to organize with Countess Markievicz the boy scouts, 'Fianna Eireann'. Later he joined the Irish Republican Brotherhood and became one of its leaders. He was the editor of the monthly *Irish Freedom*, which was subsidized by Clan na Gael. Hobson's main source of income was a stipend he received for a weekly contribution to the *Gaelic American*, published in New York.

The basic policy of Sinn Féin — that the Irish nationalist members should refuse to sit in Westminster, and instead set up their own mock parliament in Dublin — might have been effective before 1910, but was no longer sensible after the British general election of that year. In that election an equal number of MPs had been elected as Liberals and Conservatives, so the Irish Party, under John Redmond, held the balance of power and could decide which party was to form the government. The Liberal Party had previously given lukewarm support to the proposal to set up a parliament in Ireland, but now they had to give a firm commitment to the Irish Party that they would introduce a Home Rule Bill if they wanted the votes of the Irish members to enable them to form a government. They gave this commitment and it appeared reasonably certain that there would again be an Irish Parliament in Dublin with some control over matters of Irish interest. Nationalist Ireland had been waiting for more than a hundred years for this day. Yeats spelled it out when he said that we had been

> And planning plotting always that some morrow
> May set a stone upon ancestral Sorrow!

When Sinn Féin's policy of urging Irish MPs to leave Westminster was no longer relevant, their work was largely devoted to convincing the Irish people that they should support their own manufactures. To spread this message, an 'Aonach' was held every year in Dublin, shortly before Christmas, in the Mansion House or the Rotunda. The word 'Aonach' means a 'Selling Fair' and all Irish manufacturers were invited to take stalls and exhibit their goods to the public. Many of them were suitable for Christmas presents and the visitors could do their Christmas shopping at the Aonach.

Apart from the actual sale of goods, the Aonach was a social gathering of Irish Irelanders, and during the week there was a convivial atmosphere, with people discussing political and social developments. The organization of this Aonach was the main activity of Sinn Féin during those years when Home Rule appeared to be imminent.

When the Sinn Féin 'Party' is spoken of, it is difficult to estimate to what extent it had any real existence at that time. By 1910 the two presidents, John Sweetman and Edward Martyn, had resigned and there was just a small band of workers in Dublin, and some groups of supporters in parts of the country. The total numbers of active workers might have been a few hundred.

O'Rahilly was interested in the developments of aviation. In December 1903 the Wright Brothers in North Carolina had demonstrated that it was possible for a heavier than air machine to be airborne. Once this principle had been established, it seemed likely that commercial flying would become a new industry. Michael realized how important it would be for Ireland to play a part in the development of this industry. In the summer of 1910 the Slieve Donard Hotel of Newcastle, Co. Down offered a prize to any aviator who succeeded in flying a plane from Belfast to Newcastle. The hotel hoped to attract visitors, who would come to see aviators attempting this flight.

Michael's interest was aroused and he decided that the family would spend that summer holiday in Newcastle. The only pilot to make the attempt was a young mechanic named Harry Ferguson, who had built his own plane. The plane never succeeded in getting airborne and Ferguson put a seat on the front axle and gave people rides on it for a small charge, while he drove the plane at its maximum speed along the strand, probably about 30 or 40 mph.

About that time Michael organized an 'Irish Aero Club', so that people who shared his interest could meet and discuss aviation matters. He also decided that people would be attracted to the Aonach if an Irish-made plane (even one that had never got off the ground) were to be exhibited there. He had become friendly with Ferguson and arranged for him to bring his plane to Dublin. That Christmas the Aonach was held in the Rotunda, and the plane was put on view in a separate room. For a small charge, visitors were allowed in to see it. When a group of visitors had been assembled, the engine was started. Its deafening roar and the blast of wind from the propeller, which sent people's hats flying, added to the interest and excitement.

In a further effort to encourage interest in flying, model planes were sold at the Aonach that year. Their backbone was made from a light piece of timber which carried an elastic motor, enabling the plane to fly about 50 yards. The wings were of wood veneer, held in place by elastic bands. Michael made these up in his house and they were sold in the Aonach for one shilling. He also made a collection of photographs of every plane that had ever been built, including many pictures of planes that had crashed. These pictures were mounted on cardboard for display to members of the Irish Aero Club. The collection was later donated to the Aer Lingus Museum.

5

The Gaelic League

When Michael became involved in the work of the Gaelic League for the revival of Irish, his first move, to improve his own fluency, was his decision to spend the summer holidays of 1911 in the Irish-speaking Ballinskelligs, County Kerry. Later that year, on 11 November, another son was born and was christened Maolmuire (Myles in English).

The Gaelic League had been started by Douglas Hyde, Eoin MacNeill and Father Eugene O'Growney in 1893 and by 1911 had made remarkable progress. Previous societies had studied the Irish language but had done so as an academic exercise. The purpose of the Gaelic League was to revive it as the normal language of the Irish people.

It is uncertain how fluent in Irish Michael himself became, but in 1913, when Eoin MacNeill wrote him a note about the foundation of the Volunteers, he had no hesitation in writing to O'Rahilly in Irish.

It was about 1911 that Michael began signing himself O'Rahilly, rather than just Rahilly, which had been the family name until then. Many Irish families had dropped the 'O' from their names in an effort to renounce their 'Irishness' and conform to the anglicization of their country.

Michael's first contribution to the work of the League, apart from his own commitment to learn Irish, was his proposal to have flag days to collect money. It was probably an original idea which had not been tried before in Ireland. He reasoned that it would be easier to find 240 people to give one penny to support an activity of which they approved, than to find one person to give a pound. Michael believed that most Irish people approved of the idea of reviving the Irish language, and would be willing to give a penny and to wear the little Gaelic League flag, attached to a pin, to show their support. The flag, not much bigger than a postage stamp, was on green paper with the outline of Ireland in white.

To convince the League that the scheme was feasible, Michael said that he had seen such flag days in the United States. Maybe he had, but I doubt it. He organized the manufacture of collection boxes and the supply of the flags. The collections took place around St Patrick's Day and made a useful contribution to the League's funds. Since then flag days have been used to collect for many causes.

It was at this time that the National University of Ireland was formed to take control of the 'Queens Colleges' of Cork and Galway, and unite them with Dublin in a single organization. The fact that Irish citizens would now have control of the Irish universities raised the possibility of making a knowledge of Irish an essential requirement for Irish students entering these colleges. There was much opposition to this; many Irish people regarded Irish as a dead language and did not consider its revival to be desirable, even if it was possible. The low regard in which Irish was then held was demonstrated when Frank Rahilly won a scholarship to Blackrock College in Dublin. He said that he wanted to study Irish, but the college had no Irish teacher. He said that he would have to find another school. Frank was a brilliant scholar and they did not want to lose him, so they found him an Irish teacher.

The Gaelic League was in the forefront of the struggle to make Irish a compulsory subject, and O'Rahilly was fully involved in it. The Gaelic League won this struggle. O'Rahilly made a useful con-tribution to the revival of Irish when he designed a simplified form of spelling Irish, in which the long tails which had been attached to the letters 's' and 'r' were eliminated. This became the standard script for writing Irish, and was used for many years. He also did much work on a simplified form of spelling Irish words, and his papers contain many notes about how to achieve this. But it was a major task and it was not until the Irish state was set up in 1922 that this work was accomplished.

O'Rahilly initiated another move in the efforts to revive the Irish language. In those days the Post Office authorities would not accept letters addressed in Irish, so he decided to bring pressure on them to reverse their policy. First, he asked one of the Irish MPs to put down a question in the House of Commons seeking to learn why the language of a substantial proportion of the Irish people would not be accepted in addressing their letters. The Minister responsible had no difficulty explaining why this refusal was reasonable, and it was clear to O'Rahilly that more forcible pressures were necessary.

He organized about twenty people to go in a group to the GPO at a busy time of the afternoon when many people were handing in parcels. Each of the twenty had a parcel with the address in Irish. When the Post Office staff refused to accept these parcels, the twenty remained at the counter, arguing their rights to use the Irish language, and prevented anyone else from handing in parcels. They left only when the evening's parcel post had gone. When the same twenty appeared with their parcels the next afternoon, the Post Office authorities gave way and accepted the parcels.

This success gave rise to another problem. Most people did not know the Gaelic names of the streets because all street signs were in English. O'Rahilly began a campaign to have these replaced by bilingual signs. The local authorities were generally willing to co-operate, but often there was some doubt about the correct Irish name. In Dublin many of the principal streets were called to honour famous English people who had some connection with Ireland, such as Sackville Street, Westmoreland Street, Brunswick Street and Rutland Square.

Finding correct names for streets for which there was an Irish translation was a formidable task, and it was an even more difficult one to concoct Irish names for those that were basically English. According to Marcus Bourke's biography, O'Rahilly organized a team of Irish scholars to provide these names. The work had to be voluntary because there were no funds in the League to pay for it. The men and women doing this work believed that they were preparing for a time when the Irish language would again be widely spoken by the people of Ireland.

Another activity of the League was persuading banks to issue cheques in Irish. Not many members of the Gaelic League would have had bank accounts, but it was still considered important to have Irish cheques available. When O'Rahilly approached the banks, they were willing to help, knowing that if they did not provide this service, competitors might do so. But the banks raised the difficulty of finding a suitable design for the cheque with the words in Irish, so O'Rahilly himself made designs and supplied the banks with blocks for printing them.

These Gaelic League activities occupied much of Michael's time during the next three or four years, and he continued to improve his own proficiency in the language. About 1911 Michael was elected to the 'Coistegnoithe' of the Gaelic League. This status gave recognition to the energy and enthusiasm he showed in his work for the League. It was about this time that he wrote the manifesto urging the supreme importance of the revival of Irish. (See Appendix 1.) He also tried to ensure that his children became fluent. Irish was the language we usually spoke at home and Mother also became proficient. It was a pidgin Irish we all spoke, except for Michael, and a purist like Frank O'Rahilly did not like it.

Mother made a brave effort, even years after her husband's death, to keep up the use of Irish in the home. She did this out of loyalty to the cause to which he had been so committed and for which he had done so much.

From the time of his first efforts to teach himself Irish in Philadelphia, Michael was convinced that, if an independent Irish nation was to be restored, the revival of the Irish language was essential. In pursuit of this, he decided that the best help he could give his own children to become fluent *Gaelgeoirí* was for them to spend a month or two every summer in the heart of the Gaeltacht, where they would hear nothing but Irish spoken by the local people. They could also attend the local schools for some weeks because the holidays in these schools were shorter than those in the Dublin schools.

The Kerry Gaeltacht was his obvious choice in which to build a bungalow, and the end of the Dingle peninsula was the heart of Corca Dhuibhne, one of the last bastions of Irish. When searching for a place in which to build, the village of Ventry appeared to have everything to commend it. It was only about four miles from Dingle town, which was served by a narrow-gauge railway from Tralee, and it had a sheltered harbour and a fine strand. Michael did not know it, but Ventry did have a serious disadvantage in that there was more English spoken in this village than in any of the surrounding countryside. The explanation of this was that, in the Famine times, a 'colony' of about ten houses was built at one end of the village. These houses were given to people who were still known as 'Soupers' when we went there in 1912. During the Famine the antecedents of these people were given the houses and were kept alive with soup when people around them were dying of starvation. There was a condition to getting a house and being kept alive with soup: the recipients had to become Protestants and speak English. If there had been acrimony between these 'Soupers' and their neighbours at the time of the Famine, there was complete harmony by the time we came to Ventry. Nevertheless, the descendants of the original 'Soupers' continued to speak English, although they must have been fluent Irish speakers living in the heart of the Gaeltacht with Irish spoken all around them.

Michael decided to build a wooden bungalow rather than a stone house, which was the traditional method of building in Kerry at the time. He thought of it as a house that would last for fifteen or twenty years, until his children had grown up. However, his grandchildren are still using it regularly, more than seventy-five years after it was built. When he was dissatisfied with the contractor's progress and feared that the summer would be over before the bungalow was ready, he went down himself and gave a hand with the carpentry, which he could do as well as any tradesman.

The bungalow was finished and we received a telegram which said 'All ready come to-morrow.' From that time my brothers and I continued to enjoy a summer holiday in this bungalow until we were middle-aged. These Kerry holidays helped our Irish, but none of us became really fluent Irish speakers.

It was during a holiday in Kerry that Michael and Nannie first met Desmond and Mabel FitzGerald. The FitzGeralds were then living in a house outside Dingle, but later they moved to the old coastguard station on the opposite site of Ventry harbour to where we lived and only a few miles from our bungalow.

The families remained firm friends thereafter. Michael and Desmond were together in the GPO in 1916, and just as Michael was about to lead the twelve Volunteers in a charge against the British barricade at the end of Moore Street, he sought out Desmond to bid him farewell, as Desmond recalls in his memoirs. Nannie and Mabel remained close friends for the rest of their lives.

Another interest of Michael's was heraldry. It seems to have been a life-long preoccupation, with observations on the subject kept in his 'envelope file'. He believed that he could put this knowledge to use in the weekly paper *Sinn Féin* and each week he contributed an article on heraldry for this paper. He wrote an account of the part of Ireland in which a particular Irish family was prominent and gave details of historical events in which they had been involved.

Underneath he drew the family coat of arms.

Each week the shops that sold the *Sinn Féin Weekly* would exhibit large posters giving the name of the family in that week's issue. It was hoped that members of the family bearing the name would buy that particular issue and then might continue to buy subsequent issues and thus boost sales.

There was a footnote under each heraldry article, saying that hand-painted copies of the coat of arms could be ordered, at a cost of half-a-guinea for watercolour on paper or one guinea for oils on parchment. This commercial venture is the only known effort Michael O'Rahilly ever made to earn money, apart from the work he did in the family business in Ballylongford or what he was paid for working in the woollen mills in Pennsylvania. There is no record of how many coat of arms he painted, but I recall him doing this work at his desk. I was fascinated to see how he applied the gold leaf. It was so thin that it was supplied attached to a sheet of tissue paper. Michael kept up this series in the *Sinn Féin Weekly* for two years and gave it up only when his work for the Irish Volunteers occupied all his time.

Michael believed that a knowledge of the history of Ireland would spread his own conviction that the link with England was the basic cause of many Irish problems. It was his knowledge of Irish history which led him to this conclusion and he hoped that, if he could stimulate this historical interest, it would spread the desire to 'break the connection with England' (Wolfe Tone's famous words). In the early 1900s there were historical traditions still alive in many parts of Ireland, which Michael considered important to collect and record. He hoped that an Irish Topographical Society would record these historical traditions in an organized way.

To expound this proposal and stimulate interest, he gave a lecture on the subject, probably under the auspices of Sinn Féin, in their rooms in 11 O'Connell Street. The title of the lecture was 'How to make history popular'.

This first public address was an important occasion for Michael. He liked dressing up and spared no trouble for this lecture. When he emerged from the cab that brought him to the lecture hall, he was in full evening dress with a top hat and an evening cloak, 'just like any toff coming to a reception at Dublin Castle' as someone remarked. His purpose was to impress on the audience that well-dressed 'toffs' could be radical nationalists.

The lecture encouraged people in every locality to start researching and recording any local tradition of past events so that these traditions would not be lost to future generations. To do this systematically, Michael O'Rahilly formed the Irish Topographical Society. His hope was that those who joined would hold meetings, read papers and discuss matters of common interest.

About this time Michael became aware that there was a storehouse of place-names in the Ordnance Survey buildings in the Phoenix Park. The documents were stored in a wooden shed and could never be replaced if there was a fire.

It may seem strange that tiny, pauperized Ireland was the first country in the world to have a properly triangulated, detailed map, showing with precise accuracy every road, river, mountain and lake, with contour lines every 100 feet. The explanation is simple and is spelt out in the name Ordnance Survey. 'Ordnance' means 'Artillery' and the purpose of the survey was to produce detailed maps that would enable artillery to be used accurately and effectively.

In 1796 Britain came closer to losing her grip on Ireland than at any time since the Occupation began. The French expeditionary force, which was anchored in Bantry Bay in the midwinter of that year, delayed its landing to wait for the arrival of the vessel carrying the commander-in-chief, General Hoche. If the second-in-command, General Grouchy, had had the courage to grasp his opportunity and land his troops, there were no British forces in Ireland capable of resisting this French force supported by the United Irishmen. Wolfe Tone pleaded in vain with Grouchy to land his army. Grouchy hesitated and an easterly gale dispersed the fleet. The best opportunity the Irish ever had of getting rid of the British was lost.

In the next century the British assumed that there would be further wars against the French, Britain's traditional enemy. Army generals normally expect that future wars will be similar to the last war, and the British decided to take whatever steps they could to defeat a future French invasion of Ireland. They believed that a detailed survey of the country would be an advantage in fighting such a war, and so they proceeded to make an 'Ordnance Survey'.

A young Scottish engineer, Captain Drummond, who was placed in charge of the survey, which was begun about 1830, did an excellent job and developed surveying techniques that later were copied all over the world. It did not take him long to decide that a knowledge of Irish was essential for him to carry out the survey, and arrangements were made to have a scholar, John O'Donovan, give him lessons in the Irish language. Drummond soon realized that there was no possibility of his acquiring a fraction of O'Donovan's knowledge and he was given permission to put O'Donovan on his staff. When it became clear that O'Donovan could not cope with all the work, another scholar, Eugene O'Curry, was recruited.

These two scholars accompanied the survey teams all over Ireland and compiled a collection of place-names, which were then stored in the shed in the Ordnance Survey depot in the Phoenix Park. When O'Rahilly became aware of these place-names, he decided that it was essential to make a copy of each document, so that, in the event of a fire, the information they contained would not be lost.

Michael was uneasy that his activities with the Gaelic League and Sinn Féin had already come to the attention of the authorities in Dublin Castle and that an application from him to go into a British army barracks might not be well received. It may have been in anticipation of such a refusal that the Irish Topographical Society, with a secretary who was a student in Trinity College, was set up as a subterfuge to obtain access to the Ordnance Survey barracks.

When the Irish Topographical Society sought permission to have a group of its members visit the Ordnance Survey barracks one afternoon each week, the authorities agreed without question. The team consisted of O'Rahilly, his sister Anna, Arthur Griffith, and usually either Mrs Nancy Wyse Power or Michael's nephew Dick Humphreys. (It had been Mrs Wyse Power who reported on Michael's activities eight years earlier in the London branch of the UIL.) These copying sessions in the Survey depot continued every week for two or three years. Michael usually drove everyone out in his car, but if the car was not available they rode to the Phoenix Park on their bicycles.

Michael's car normally had a small green flag mounted on the radiator cap. I asked him one day why the flag was removed every Thursday. He laughed and expressed surprise that I had noticed this. Then he explained that every Thursday he and others went into a British army barracks and he doubted if they would be welcome if they had a green flag mounted on the automobile.

In those days there was no alternative to manual copying if the records were to be duplicated. It was labour in vain because the store did not get destroyed by fire and the place-names were never published. Among the papers, there were many sketches of items of an archaeological interest and Michael always brought a supply of tracing paper so that he could make tracings of these sketches. When the work was complete, the copies were stored in cardboard boxes in our house in Herbert Park. After 1916 the boxes were given to the Royal Irish Academy and are now believed to be in University College, Cork.

6

The Royal Visit

Edward VII died on 6 May 1910. His heir, George V, planned a visit to Ireland the next year. When Edward VII had come on a visit to Ireland in 1901, Dublin Corporation refused to present him with an address of welcome. In the eyes of Irish nationalists, it was imperative that the citizens of Dublin should also refuse to welcome George V, whose army of occupation still held them in subjection. O'Rahilly undertook the work of organizing those nationalist groups who were willing to help resist the pressures they knew would be brought to bear to ensure that the monarch was properly welcomed. He formed a body called the United Nationalist Societies and undertook to act as their honorary secretary. All those societies opposed to the King's visit were invited to join.

It was decided to hold a 'monster' meeting of the citizens of Dublin in Beresford Place, to demonstrate that many of them were opposed to any address of welcome to the British sovereign. The meeting was fixed for 22 June 1911, the same day as the new King was to be crowned in Westminster Abbey.

Meanwhile, all members of Dublin Corporation were canvassed and urged to resist agreeing to any motion approving an address of welcome. The United Nationalist Societies agreed that an appropriate gesture to show their disapproval of the King's visit would be to erect a large canvas scroll across Grafton Street which the King could not fail to observe as the Royal Cavalcade passed down this thoroughfare. The scroll would contain a disloyal message, making it clear that he was not welcome in Dublin. Michael O'Rahilly undertook to get this done.

He applied to the paving committee of the Corporation for permission to erect two poles across Grafton Street. The committee probably assumed that the poles would be used to carry some sycophantic message of welcome or loyalty to the new King. Michael took out a £1,000 insurance on the poles in case they fell or caused damage for which he could be held liable. Countess Markievicz was fully involved in the protest and has recorded what took place:

It was [Michael O'Rahilly] who gave us the motto and the war cry that inspired us in our exertions to counteract the effects of the Royal Visit. He took the well-known lines, 'Thou art not conquered yet, dear land' and wove them into a poem for the occasion. It was haunting and beautiful, and just put into words what we all felt. . . . His proposal to put the banner across Grafton Street was approved by the National Societies Committee and left to The O'Rahilly to carry out.

The Paving Committee gave the required permission, and their workmen lifted the pavement, and made the holes. We were busily engaged on the scroll; there was an immense amount of work to be done. The O'Rahilly was one of the neatest and best dressed men in Ireland, yet there he was down on his knees on a dusty floor, pencilling out the gigantic letters on the calico for us to fill in with printing ink. When we were finished he started cutting stencils out of the lines and printing from them on strips of white calico, to be cut into badges for distribution.

The scroll was finished at last and dry. It was carried secretly across to a small white-washed cottage standing in a yard among a lot of tall houses near Westland Row. The poles were being prepared there and the ropes and pulleys got ready.

At 11 pm a lorry arrived and we loaded up our burden, and started off in a drizzling rain. There were very few people about: two or three policemen looked at the strange little convoy and then followed us but they did not interfere. After some trouble the men got the poles firmly planted and the scroll into position. It made a splendid show.

Of course the enemy pulled it down, but not till quite late the next morning, and it had done its work. Half Dublin had seen it; it had been photographed and the papers had howled.

If the King did not see the message, he was probably told about it.

Among O'Rahilly's papers was the following message from Countess Markievicz, scribbled on the back of an envelope:

The poles etc are down; all the black torn off. Nothing left but white masts lying in the gutter. What can we do? Can we put them up again in Broad Daylight. I must go to my cottage to-day at two o'clock, but could work to-night or to-morrow. A wire would find me at Balally Cottage.

  C. de M.

Countess Markievicz said that O'Rahilly borrowed the well-known lines, 'Thou art not conquered yet, dear land'. Following the publicity about the poles and the message on them, there was a controversy about their origin. The ballad that he wrote for the occasion reads:

Thou are not conquered yet, dear land,
Thy spirit still is free.
Though long the Saxon's ruthless hand,
Has triumphed over thee.
Though oft obscured by clouds of woe,
Thy sun has never set,
Twill blaze again in golden glow,
Thou art not conquered yet.

Chorus
Thou are not conquered yet, dear land,
Thy sons must not forget,
The day shall be when all shall see,
Thou art not conquered yet.

Though knaves may scheme and slaves may crawl,
To win their master's smile,
And though thy best and bravest fall,
Undone by Saxon guile,
Yet some there be, still true to thee,
Who never shall forget,
That though in chains and slavery,
Thou art not conquered yet.

Through ages long of war and strife,
Of rapine and of woe,
We fought the bitter fight of life,
Against the Saxon foe,
Our fairest hopes to break thy chains,
Have died in vain regret,
But still the glorious truth remains,
Thou art not conquered yet.

The poles were taken down, but this illegal seizure aroused more publicity than if they had been left in place. The meeting in

Beresford Place was a huge success, with 30,000 people attending; it was claimed that it was the biggest gathering in Dublin since Parnell's meeting in Inchicore in 1891. Michael, as secretary of the committee, read letters and telegrams of regret for their inability to be present from many prominent people, including Willie Redmond MP and John Devoy, the Fenian, who lived in New York. The speakers included Major John MacBride, who had fought against England in the Boer War, Dr Paddy McCartan, Laurence Ginnell MP, the Hon. James O'Sullivan of New York, Countess Markievicz, Arthur Griffith, Cathal Brugha, who spoke in Irish, and James Connolly from Belfast.

Dublin Corporation did not vote an address of welcome to the King, nor did Pembroke Urban District Council, which was generally regarded as a Loyalist stronghold. The same pressures were exerted in Waterford, when it was proposed that they should send an address of loyalty. O'Rahilly spoke at the public meeting in that city, instead of Major MacBride, who was unable to attend. In his speech he said of MacBride, that 'he was a man who did more to uphold the cause of nationality than any of the men of the present generation, when he went out with his gun on his shoulder and fought the common enemy on the South African veldt.'

Some time later, when Countess Markievicz was thinking about the whole affair in her cottage in the Dublin Mountains, she made a rough drawing on a postcard of the police walking off with the poles and sent it to Michael. He was impressed by the idea and made a finished coloured drawing on a larger scale. Blocks were made, from which coloured postcards were printed and sent around the country. Hundreds, and possibly thousands, of these cards were printed and sold to let as many Irish people as possible know about the 'Capture of the Poles'. The postcards carried the caption 'Deeds that won the Empire'.

O'Rahilly's efforts to organize opposition to an address of welcome had an important side-effect. He had succeeded in bringing into one joint body all those Irish societies that had any aspiration to an independent Ireland. Nothing comparable happened again until 1918, when all Irish nationalist organizations united to oppose the conscription that the British government had decided to impose on Ireland.

O'Rahilly had demonstrated that if the Irish organizations – such as Sinn Féin, the Gaelic League, and the Ancient Order of

Caricature drawn by O'Rahilly from sketch by Countess Markievicz. The poles in Grafton Street were erected in protest against the planned royal visit.

A Volunteer parade, Kilrush, County Clare, c. 1914, before the split.

A Uí Raġallaiġ na gcarad

Is oċ liom nár ḃ'féidir liom ṗ an ...
tráċtas so do sgríoḃaḋ ní ba luaiṫe.
Ḃíoḋ mo ḋíċeall. Is eagal liom leiġ
go ḃfuil sé ro-fada, aċt b'fearr liom
go dtuigfiḋe mé 7 tá mórán daoine
ar fuḋ Éireann ná tuigeann cúrsaí
na Cúigiḋ úd Ulaḋ.

Rud eile, is é mo ḃaramail daingean
go gcaiṫfear raṁ-ḃuannas (Volunteers)
do ċur ar buḋ fearsa gan moill ar fuḋ na
tíre mar tá déanta i mbaile Áṫa luain.
Is mór an feall é, mara ndéantar ... Ní
tigleir an Réamonnaċ a ḋéanaṁ. Tá
sé ceangailte. Ní mó tigleir, 7 ní
ḋóċa gar ṁran leir, cuir 'na ċoṁne.
Slán 7 beannaċt leat
Eoin Mac Néill.

Tá súil agam go ḃfaiġir glan sollain arís, nó
mara ḃfaiġir, gur fearr tormo go mbaoir.

Hibernians – joined forces in a united front, the British would find their pressure difficult to resist. The United Nationalist Societies ensured that there was no address of welcome to the British sovereign. Michael was entitled to be pleased with his success in organizing this opposition.

7

A Call to Arms

About the time Michael Rahilly returned to Dublin, radical political changes were taking place in Britain. The changes had a profound impact on Irish political life because the only political power which the Irish people had was whatever influence a tiny minority of Irish members could exercise in Westminster.

In the early months of 1910 the Liberals under Herbert Asquith had an overall majority in the House of Commons, having won a victory in a general election during January. They proceeded to introduce a radical budget, based on their election manifesto. This included, for the first time, old-age pensions, and to pay for these and for other social reforms, a higher income tax was introduced, as well as increased taxes on drink and cigarettes. There was also, for the first time, a land tax. This tax was particularly resented by the hereditary peers, many of whom still had large landed estates.

This budget was passed by the Commons, but the House of Lords rejected it. The rejection of a finance bill by the Lords was unprecedented, and created a constitutional crisis. If the House of Commons and the government were to accept this veto by the House of Lords, it meant that this second chamber, dominated by hereditary peers, was now running the country. This made a mockery of democracy and could not be accepted by any government. Members of the establishment of both parties tried to work out a compromise, but they failed to reach agreement.

The situation was further complicated by the fact that the new King had not yet been crowned, and the government was reluctant to confront him with a crisis before he had even been installed.

There was one final pressure the Liberal government could bring to bear. The King was obliged to create new peers on the advice of the government. The government could use this power to flood the House of Lords with enough new peers to get the Home Rule Bill passed. This was a final threat that the Liberals were as reluctant to use as the Conservatives were anxious to avoid.

In order to confirm that he had a popular mandate, Asquith called another general election. The result was a stalemate, with the Liberals and Conservatives each getting 272 seats, yet now the Irish Party, under John Redmond, held the balance of power. This was the position that the Irish Party had always hoped to achieve and now it had come about fortuitously. It was heady wine for Redmond, who overnight became one of the most powerful political leaders in Britain. He was now in a position to decide which party would form the next government.

The Liberal Party, since Gladstone's day, had given a mild commitment to Home Rule for Ireland, but were not over-enthusiastic about it. Indeed, many leading Liberals were no more anxious than the Conservatives to loosen the British grip on Ireland. The situation now was very different. The Liberals would have to give a firm and specific commitment to introduce an Irish Home Rule Bill if they wanted to be in a position to form an administration.

Even with such a commitment from the Liberals, it would not have been possible to enact an Irish Home Rule Bill while the House of Lords retained its veto on any legislation passed by the Commons. This veto ended when Asquith threatened to fill the House of Lords with, as the Lords described them, upstart nominees of the Liberal government. The Lords then agreed to amend their absolute veto and to accept as an alternative the power to delay a Bill for two years. The Lords could now refuse to pass a Bill only twice, but if it was presented a third time, it became law whether they passed it or not.

All nationalist Ireland rejoiced. The country was to have its own Parliament again, a hundred years after the Irish Parliament had voted itself out of existence. Asquith introduced the Bill granting Home Rule to Ireland in the House of Commons in 1912, and it was passed by the combined Liberal and Irish Party votes.

The powers to be given to this Irish Parliament were derisory. It would have no power to raise revenue. This meant that its only source of finance depended on whatever funds the British government provided. Even worse, this Irish Parliament would have no armed forces under its control. In the last analysis, all government depends on its ability to command the loyalty of an armed force, but it was not even to have control of the police force for six years. Nevertheless, despite these shortcomings, it would be a start, and the Irish people would again be able to elect a government that would have some influence on matters that were important for the welfare of Ireland. The Irish Party hoped that this Home Rule was merely a start and that eventually an Irish Parliament could gain real power. Likewise, those in Britain who were totally opposed to Home Rule for Ireland, feared that once an Irish Parliament was set up in Dublin, it would end in complete separation.

When the House of Commons had passed the Home Rule Bill in 1912 and it was only a matter of time before it became law, Redmond decided to call a Convention in Dublin, to report progress to his supporters. The leaders of the Party outlined the functions that would be granted to the new Home Rule government. Redmond was conscious of how very limited the powers of this government would be. Fiscal autonomy was ruled out. The Irish Parliament would have no power to protect Irish industries by putting a tax on imports. At that time, nearly every country in the world, except Britain, imposed import taxes in order to encourage the development of their own manufactures. The Irish government would have no power to raise revenue through taxes; it would be dependent on British government subventions and would have no other source of revenue. Another defect was that if the Irish government became involved in any issues that might require negotiations or discussions with foreign governments, these would be handled by the British Foreign Office.

Alas, Redmond's Irish Party was so supine that there was no general expression of dissatisfaction at this Convention. There is no record that anyone even mentioned that the Irish government would never have control of an army, nor for six years would they even have control of the police force.

Soon after this Convention, Redmond decided to hold a mass meeting in O'Connell Street to welcome what had been achieved. At that time there was no electrical amplification of sound to enable all those who attended this celebratory meeting to hear the speeches, so four platforms were placed along the street, with a different group of speakers on each platform. Patrick Pearse spoke from one of the platforms in both Irish and English.

Many Irish people regarded this Home Rule Bill as the dawning of the day for which they had waited so long. They hoped that Ireland was about to become 'A Nation once again'. Michael O'Rahilly did not share this enthusiasm. He regarded a government without any armed force as a meaningless charade. In 1912 he wrote a series of articles for the monthly paper *Irish Freedom*, in which he argued that it was essential for Irishmen to be armed if they wanted their freedom. His friends knew of his firm conviction that the British would never release their grip on Ireland until the Irish were in a position to compel them to do so by armed force. Countess Markievicz recalled how O'Rahilly refused to join the IRB. This secret society had been in existence for many years, but he knew that in all that time it had achieved nothing. Everyone knew that such secret societies in Ireland were always riddled with British spies. O'Rahilly told the Countess that the only secret society he would join would be one in which every member was required to have a rifle and a thousand rounds of ammunition in his possession.

The first of O'Rahilly's *Irish Freedom* articles began:

In the last analysis the foundation on which all government rests is the possession of arms and the ability to use them; therefore it cannot fail to be instructive to us to consider the circumstances of the most recent occasion when any considerable body of Irish people appealed to arms . . . .

O'Rahilly then gave a detailed description of every action fought in the 1798 Rebellion, citing the names of the leaders on both sides, the tactics of the battles and the number of casualties. In the June issue of the paper he summed up:

The results of the Wexford campaign make it clearly evident that a simultaneous Rising in, say, one fourth of the Irish counties, would have defeated all the forces that the British and Irish Governments could have sent against them. Any considerable disturbance in even one of the mountainous counties like Kerry, Galway or Donegal might have turned the scale. Why was there no such disturbance?

The arrest of Lord Edward and the other leaders cannot be given as the reason, because after the 23 May there was no further occasion of secrecy and every man knew his duty. The charge of cowardice is disproved by the fact that such counties as Limerick, Cork, Kerry, Westmeath, Galway and Kildare provided scores of regiments which fought against their countrymen. It will hardly be asserted that they did not desire a change of Government, and the only tenable explanation is that the Irish counties had no arms. And why had they no arms? Had they not received 628 years previous notice that men who wish to be free must first arm themselves? Didn't they have sufficient commonsense to know that a man who is dissatisfied with his form of Government, and has not got a rifle and 1,000 rounds of ammunition in a place where he can get them when he wants them, is only playing at politics?

But, you may say, there were disarming Acts, Martial law, searches of houses and so forth, and it was impossible for the people to obtain arms. I refuse to accept this explanation. There are no disarming acts now. Rifles can be bought by anyone who has the price of them. Powder, while somewhat dearer, is as easy to obtain as sugar. Yet will anyone assert that Irishmen who desire a change of Government are armed to-day.

If you observe that conditions are different to-day and that there is no prospect of Ireland getting such a chance in our time as she had in 1798, I reply that Ireland never had such a chance in 1798 as she had 100 years later during the Boer war. By inaction the chance was missed in 1798; in the same way it was missed in 1900.

Let it be the work of all those who desire their country's freedom to prepare so that it shall not be missed when the opportunity comes again.

These articles contain the quintessence of the message O'Rahilly wished to deliver to his fellow countrymen. His advice to them was simple and direct: 'If you are serious in wanting freedom from British domination, get arms and be prepared to use them.' This was a far more forthright clarion call to the men of Ireland than MacNeill's article 'The North Began', which appeared eighteen months later.

O'Rahilly's articles in *Irish Freedom* produced no results. Trotsky, one of the leaders of the Russian Revolution, laid down as a guiding principle that 'Revolutions are not the products of our brains, but of ripe material conditions.' When O'Rahilly wrote his articles, the material conditions were not ripe. It was not until Carson had formed his Ulster Volunteers to resist Home Rule that conditions were ripe for the formation of the Irish Volunteers.

The only known result of O'Rahilly's exhortations was his subsequent formation of a rifle club. The members were trained in target practice and competitions in marksmanship were held. Little more is known of it, but probably it had only twenty or thirty members.

O'Rahilly's articles had nothing to do with Orangemen arming to oppose Home Rule. It was a year later before there was any suggestion of the formation of such an organization. But in 1912 there was already a general feeling that it was only a matter of time before the growing power of Germany would lead to a European war. Such a war would give the Irish the opportunity to win their freedom, but to do so they would need an armed force under the control of an Irish government.

O'Rahilly also realized that it would be difficult for the British government to suppress a body of armed Volunteers who were under the control of the Irish government. The force would have to be a Volunteer army because the British would not provide funds for a paid army, and the Irish government would have no funds, other than what they received from the British.

8

The Ulster Volunteers

The formation of the Ulster Volunteers to resist Home Rule, if necessary by force, evolved gradually during 1913. There was never a formal meeting of leading Orangemen in Ulster at which it was decided that a Volunteer Army would be recruited.

When the Home Rule Bill had been passed by the Commons, and the power of the Lords to veto it had been reduced to the power to delay it for two years, Orangemen in the North of Ireland and their supporters among the British Conservatives demanded a referendum on the issue. They insisted that Asquith had no power to break up the Empire since he had not included an Irish Home Rule Bill in the manifesto on which he had fought the election.

The Orangemen, led by the Dublin lawyer Sir Edward Carson, began their opposition by organizing a vast campaign to get signatories to an anti-Home Rule Covenant. There was an initial signing ceremony in the City Hall in Belfast, at which all the leading members of the Ulster Establishment signed. Carson was the first to do so and many of those who followed him signed with their own blood. Additional signatures were then sought all over Ireland, and eventually they claimed almost half-a-million signatures.

To add force to the signing of the Covenant, there were protest meetings across the North of Ireland. At one of these, a group of ex-soldiers decided to march in military formation. They looked so impressive in their disciplined ranks that the practice quickly caught on, and in a short time it became common for groups at these meetings to march as military units. Thus the idea of an Ulster Volunteer Force was born. Once the idea of an army to oppose Home Rule was adopted as basic policy, Carson was carried along with it, but it soon became a force that he could no longer control.

The practice of having bodies of men marching in military formation to the meetings opposing Home Rule spread rapidly through Ulster. The many military men among them realized that, to establish control, it would be necessary to organize the companies formed in different districts into battalions, and then the battalions into larger units.

Before long, many of the men who had rifles began to carry them on these parades. The possession of a rifle soon became a status symbol, and those who could afford it bought one. There were then no restrictions on the purchase or the ownership of a rifle. A single-shot weapon could be bought for thirty shillings, and many of the Ulster Volunteers could afford to buy one. When the ban on the importation of rifles into Ireland was imposed in November 1913, 25,000 of the Ulster Volunteers were armed.

The constitutional opposition to Home Rule, such as signing the Covenant and attending meetings of protest, developed into a determination by these Ulsterman that they would resist Home Rule by all the means in their power. If this involved an armed confrontation with the forces of the British Crown, then so be it. One of their slogans was: 'Ulster will fight and Ulster will be right'. Another was: 'Kaisers and Mausers and any King you like'.

These Ulstermen were determined not to submit to a Dublin 'Home Rule' Parliament. For them the ideal would be an independent Ulster linked to Britain, with Britain paying the bills. They obtained this later, but there was no sign of such a solution in 1913.

These Orangemen realized that an Ulster on its own embracing the 600,000 nationalists who were in the nine Ulster counties, with three million hostile Irish nationalists south of its border, was an impracticable political entity. Their leaders concluded that it was essential to form a link with a European country, which was largely Protestant, and which was strong enough to be able, if necessary, to face up to a showdown with Britain.

In 1913, imperial Germany was the only country in Europe that could meet these requirements. In those days it was normal for the European empires to use their military and naval strengths to carve up the world between them; the subject countries were not considered to have any rights of their own. The only restraints that the empires recognized was that a rival European power might object to a proposed annexation.

If it appears unrealistic today for one million British subjects to have contemplated breaking the connection with Britain to form a link with Germany, this appears so with the benefit of hindsight and the knowledge that in two World Wars, in which the British and the Germans were the principal antagonists, there were millions of British casualties. In 1913 there was little antagonism between Britain and Germany. The traditional enemies were France and Germany. There was trade rivalry between Britain and Germany, but this was a far cry from the war *à outrance* that began in 1914. The German Kaiser and the English King were first cousins and there were many other close connections between the two countries.

It will never be known if the people who threatened to set up an independent Ulster, linked to Germany, intended it as a bluff, or if it was a serious option. The danger of making such a bluff is that those making it may end up taking it seriously. Whether it was serious or a bluff, it had to be seen to be feasible if it was to have any credibility, and this is what the Orangemen proceeded to do.

The first priority for these Ulstermen, and for their supporters in Britain, was to enlist an army of Volunteers, numbering up to 100,000 men of military age, and to have them trained and disciplined, with a command structure of experienced officers, and to arm them with modern rifles.

There was no lack of funds from wealthy British Tories and no lack of retired British army officers to organize and train the Ulster Volunteers. An 'insurance' fund of one million pounds was established to support any Volunteer who might be wounded, or to give a pension to his dependants if he was killed. Carson himself guaranteed £10,000 to this fund, and many wealthy British people followed suit to raise the imaginary million pounds.

There were also substantial contributions of real cash. The writer Rudyard Kipling gave a cash donation of £30,000. These donations ensured that the Ulster Volunteers had adequate funds to buy arms, and they did this without any urgency since there did not appear to be any likelihood that the British government would prohibit the importation of arms into Ireland.

In A.T.Q. Stewart's book, *The Ulster Crisis*, he describes how Lord Milner, a prominent member of the British Establishment, gave enthusiastic support to Carson, and he also refers to the raising of the money:

The first step was the creation of a vast fund of money contributed by his wealthy friends to support the resistance. Documents marked 'Very Secret' among his papers indicate that Waldorf Astor (the son of an American millionaire) had subscribed his name for £30,000 and Lord Rothschild and Lord Iveagh and the Duke of Bedford for £10,000 each. As we shall see it is virtually certain that some of this money was used to purchase Crawford's rifles in Germany.

The second essential in giving credibility to the revolt was to form a liaison with the Imperial German government and to investigate the possibility of Ulster being made into a German colony, largely controlled by the Irish Protestant majority. To explore this proposal, Carson went to Germany in July 1913. He had lunch with the Kaiser and they discussed the possibility of such an association.

No official communiqué was issued following this lunch, at which Carson told the Kaiser that the Ulster Protestants were determined not to submit to domination by a largely Catholic Dublin Parliament. Rather than accept this humiliation, they would prefer to become a German colony.

The Kaiser would have been cautious about giving Carson a firm commitment. Britain would not stand idly by if they heard that such a link was being established. The most serious implications for the British would be that the Germans could station naval squadrons in the North of Ireland. This would end the British power to enforce a naval blockade on Europe. Carson was probably told that the matter would be given careful consideration, but it seems unlikely that any firm decision followed this exchange of views between himself and the Kaiser.

Carson's plan of campaign to defeat Home Rule required the achievement of three objectives. He needed a large body of Volunteers, armed, trained and led by experienced officers, and he was well on the way to achieving this by mid-1913. He needed a commitment from the Kaiser to make Ulster a German colony, but on this he had advanced no further than exploratory talks. Finally, he needed to suborn a sufficient number of senior British army officers so that if it came to a showdown, and the British army was ordered to suppress the Ulster Volunteers, these officers would refuse to obey the order. If Carson could achieve this third objective, it would be impossible for the British cabinet to enforce Home Rule on Ulster, no matter what Westminster decided.

Many senior British army officers, such as Sir Henry Wilson, an Irishman from County Longford, were bitterly opposed to Home

Rule and needed no suborning. Wilson was second-in-command of the British Expeditionary Force, which would be sent to Europe to help the French if there was a war in Europe.

The considerable influence of the Conservative establishment was enlisted to urge junior officers to resist any efforts by the Liberal government to suppress the Ulster Volunteers. When these officers were home from Ireland on leave and went into certain London clubs, senior figures of the utmost respectability pointed out to them that the Liberal government's policy would lead inevitably to the break-up of the Empire. If the Irish were given Home Rule, the Indians would want the same, and so on around the world.

These junior officers were persuaded that it was a sacred duty to preserve the Empire by blocking any efforts of the Liberal government to impose Home Rule on Ulster. They were told that the government had no mandate to break up the Empire, and so they were entitled to refuse to obey any commands that might lead to this, even to the point of resigning their commissions.

It emerged later, in what became known as the Curragh Mutiny, that this suborning of British army officers serving in Ireland had achieved its purpose. In March 1914 when the War Office, on the instructions of the cabinet, ordered a regiment stationed at the Curragh, in County Kildare, to move to Ulster to guard British army stores there, only two out of the sixty officers were willing to obey. The others said that they would resign their commissions rather than go to the North.

Not all the members of the British establishment were as irresponsible as Carson and his friends. There were senior figures in Britain who realized that the Orangemen's refusal to accept the decisions of the British Parliament could lead to anarchy. Winston Churchill, First Lord of the Admiralty in Asquith's government, was deeply concerned at what might happen if the Conservative Party refused to accept the government's authority. When he was told that the Ulster rebels were setting up a headquarters for their provisional government outside Belfast, Churchill ordered a flotilla of destroyers to proceed into Belfast Lough, with instructions to shell this headquarters if the rebels attempted to take over the province. Asquith heard of Churchill's order and lost his nerve, instructing the destroyers to return to base. Churchill made a speech in which he defended his decision: 'There are worse things than bloodshed, even on an extended scale, and anarchy is one of them.'

The German Foreign Office was watching every move in this British constitutional crisis. There was a general belief that a European war was inevitable. The German army was by far the most powerful military force in the world, and the German navy was fast approaching parity with Britain's. To defend themselves against this German menace, France, Russia and Britain had formed themselves into an alliance so that they could surround and overpower the rising German Empire. The Germans were as determined to break out of this stranglehold as the Allies were to maintain it. If war was inevitable, the Germans decided that they were not likely to find a more favourable opportunity to strike than when Britain was involved in such a constitutional crisis that regiments of its army were refusing to accept the orders of the War Office, issued on the cabinet's instructions.

The assassination of the Austrian Crown Prince at Sarajevo in July 1914 gave the Germans the pretence they needed to declare war on Russia. The ultimatum issued to Serbia by the Austrian-Hungarians could not have been issued without German clearance, and the Germans knew there was no possibility of the Russians allowing the Austrians to take over Serbia, which would have been the outcome if the Serbs had accepted the ultimatum. In the German Foreign Office records, World War I is called the 'Russian War', and the Germans knew that France inevitably must support her Russian ally.

The Germans hoped that Britain would remain aloof. They knew the serious problems the British were having in Ireland, and it seemed possible that Westminster might decide to let the European powers fight it out amongst themselves.

While the Ulster Rebellion may not have led directly to World War I, it was certainly a contributing factor. It led the Germans to hope that the crisis in Ireland would keep the British out of the war, but the Ulster crisis may also have contributed in a perverse way to Britain entering the war. The Asquith government may have regarded this 'foreign' war as a welcome alternative to the domestic crisis to which it could see no solution other than a bloody civil war.

9

The Irish Volunteers

There were obvious implications for Irish nationalists when the British government made no moves to interfere as the Orangemen were organizing an armed military force, whose declared purpose was to resist the decision of the British Parliament to confer a measure of Home Rule on Ireland. If the British allowed the Orangemen to do this, did they expect the men in the rest of Ireland who wanted Home Rule to ignore the Orangemen? What is surprising is that it took so long for the Irish nationalists to form their own Volunteers.

The Irish Party's success in getting the British government to pass a Bill granting Home Rule to Ireland was the starting point that made it possible for the radical Irish nationalists, the physical force men, to begin the armed struggle. Until the Home Rule Bill had been passed by the House of Commons, and the Ulster Volunteers had been formed to prevent its enactment, if necessary by armed resistance, there were no physical force men in Ireland. The Orange unionists were the people who initiated the policy that if you could not get what you wanted by constitutional means, then you took to the gun.

When O'Rahilly realized that the time was ripe to form the Irish Volunteers, he needed a vehicle in which to expound his proposal. He was heavily involved in the Gaelic League and knew that its paper, *An Claidheamh Soluis*, was doing badly and was a heavy drain on their finances. He offered to act as the paper's honorary manager, saying that he hoped to liven it up and so increase its circulation. His hope was that, by including more photographs, he could make the paper more interesting.

He made his offer conditional on the board agreeing that in

future the leading articles would carry a signature, as was usual in continental papers. His purpose in this precondition soon emerged. He realized that a leading article, signed by a prominent individual, would carry more weight than if the article was written anonymously. The board agreed to this proposal, although it was a basic principle of the Gaelic League that it was non-political.

O'Rahilly made some cosmetic changes to the paper and did include many more pictures, mainly taken from other papers, which did not object if the source was acknowledged. He also designed a new masthead, with a naked sword running through the letters (the English meaning of *An Claidheamh Soluis* is 'The Sword of Light'). This name block expressed more clearly than words what O'Rahilly had in mind when he offered to act as honorary manager of the paper. His basic strategy soon emerged.

John Redmond in 1913 was in an unassailable position to issue a proclamation to the manhood of Ireland to enrol in a volunteer force dedicated to defending the rights of the vast majority of the Irish people, who were now under serious threat from the Ulster Volunteers. Redmond was generally accepted as the leader of the Irish people. His status was then at an all-time high as a result of his success in obtaining the enactment of the Home Rule Bill. If he had come to Dublin and issued a public appeal to the men of Ireland to enlist in an Irish volunteer movement, Irishmen would have rushed to join in their tens of thousands. The British government could not have denied Redmond the right to make such a move when it had allowed Carson to organize the Orangemen of Ulster to oppose Home Rule with an armed body.

Redmond made no such move. In 1913 he was a middle-aged man who had been practising parliamentary politics all his life, and the thought of taking on the role of a military leader probably did not even occur to him.

In order to plant his idea in Redmond's mind, O'Rahilly knew that he would have to find an intermediary who would be granted an interview – someone known as a moderate constitutional nationalist and a dedicated supporter of the party. It did not take him long to decide that he was unlikely to find a better person than his Gaelic League colleague, Eoin MacNeill. The two men knew each other well from their work together on the Gaelic League.

O'Rahilly was confined to the house, recovering from the effects of a bad cold, and he asked MacNeill to come to see him in October

1913. My brother Mac can recall seeing his father and MacNeill talking earnestly in the drawing room. Subsequently he was told that this was the conversation in which his father had pointed out to MacNeill the opportunity they now had to found an Irish Volunteer force.

O'Rahilly wanted MacNeill to seek an interview with Redmond to convince him that the circumstances were now propitious for the formation of such a force, and to urge Redmond to take the initiative by issuing a call to the men of Ireland to enrol. O'Rahilly also asked MacNeill to contribute a signed leading article to *An Claidheamh Soluis*, advocating the formation of an Irish Volunteer Army. Some weeks later MacNeill sent O'Rahilly this leading article, apologizing for the delay, but his covering letter does not reveal if he saw Redmond himself or conveyed the message through an intermediary. MacNeill's letter was in Irish and reads in translation:

Dear O'Rahilly,

I regret I did not succeed in sending you this article sooner. I did my best. I am also afraid it is too long, but I would prefer to be understood, and there are many people throughout Ireland who do not understand about Ulster. Also I am convinced that Volunteers must be started throughout the country, just as has been done in Athlone. It will be a great blunder if it is not done. Redmond cannot do it. He is tied. But neither could he, and I doubt if he would want to, oppose them.

With kind regards, Eoin MacNeill

I hope you are quite well again and if you are not that you soon will be.

MacNeill said that Redmond himself could not be involved, the reason being 'Tá sé ceangalte' ('He is tied'), although MacNeill suggests that Redmond would not oppose the formation of such a force.

The leading article was written in English and was entitled 'The North Began'. It has now become famous as the first move in the steps that led to the formation of the Irish Volunteers. In view of its importance, it is worth examining in some detail. It contains 1,422 words, and is a tortuous account of the political situation in the North of Ireland and the relationship between the dying remnants of feudalism there and the still living feudalism of Britain. In his covering letter, MacNeill apologizes for its length, but says it was necessary to explain the political situation in Ulster. In the article MacNeill suggests that Carson and the Orange unionists are the real

Irish 'Home Rulers' because they are determined that nobody is going to push them around. In all this convoluted sophistry, there is no forthright message about the organization of a force of Irish Volunteers. The nearest MacNeill gets to such a suggestion is in this paragraph:

In any case it appears that the British army cannot now be used to prevent the enrolment, drilling, and reviewing of Volunteers in Ireland. There is nothing to prevent the other twenty-eight counties from calling into existence citizen forces to hold Ireland 'for the Empire'. It was precisely with this object that the Volunteers of 1782 were enrolled, and they became the instrument of establishing self-government and Irish prosperity. Their disbanding led to the destruction alike of self-government and of prosperity, and the opportunity of rectifying a capital error of this sort does not always come back again to nations.

If MacNeill did not explicitly urge the Irish to form a corps of Volunteers, he told them there was nothing to prevent them doing so. Yet if this article is regarded as a call to arms, it is necessary to state that the word 'arms' is mentioned only to pour scorn on the fictitious 'insurance fund' that the Ulster Volunteers had talked of setting up to provide compensation for casualties if fighting took place:

. . . but perhaps the crowning sham was the announcement of an insurance fund of £1,000,000. The real insurance fund for real war is fighting material, men, arms, ammunition, transport . . . and those who are in earnest about war will not devote a penny to any other sort of insurance.

If MacNeill had any ideas of expelling the British from Ireland by force of arms, he was keeping them strictly to himself.

MacNeill has said that when O'Rahilly asked him in October 1913 to accept the leadership of an Irish Volunteer movement, he had sought the advice of his friend George Sigerson, another distinguished Gaelic scholar. Sigerson had said, 'If you accept the leadership of such a movement, do you think that you will be able to control it?' MacNeill believed he could and he accepted the leadership.

Unfortunately MacNeill's letter is not dated, but the article was published in *An Claidheamh Soluis* on 1 November 1913, so we can assume that O'Rahilly probably received it about a week earlier. The fact that MacNeill apologized for his delay in sending it indicates that it must have been at least two weeks since he had been asked for it, so the meeting might have taken place in early October.

In his letter, MacNeill refers to the Athlone Volunteers. It was reported in the national newspapers, without much comment, but the local paper said that the meeting had concluded with the band playing 'God Save the King'. So whatever else these Athlone men had in mind, it was clearly very different from what the Dublin men intended. In O'Rahilly's *Secret History of the Irish Volunteers*, published in 1915, he had this to say about the Athlone Volunteers:

Previous to this, indeed, a journalist in West Meath, who is said to have conceived the possibility of a Midland Volunteer Force, had published a report of the inception of such a body in Athlone. Whether the Midland Volunteers had any real existence except in the news columns is much debated and is open to doubt; but there is no doubt that the organisers of the Irish Volunteers absolutely failed to discover any Volunteers, either in Athlone or the Midlands, until long after the Wynn's Hotel meeting.

If O'Rahilly was not too pleased with the moderate tone of MacNeill's article, nevertheless, coming from a well-known constitutional nationalist, it was a suitable opening gambit for the development he had in mind. The following week he asked Patrick Pearse to write the leader for the Gaelic League journal. Pearse called his article 'The Coming Revolution'. It is even longer than MacNeill's and is a moving exhortation to Irishmen to press ahead to the next stage in the regeneration of Ireland. Pearse believed that the Gaelic League had now fulfilled its purpose. His message was that Irishmen must prepare for the difficult task of achieving control of their own country. The Gaelic League is given full credit for the essential work it had done in making Irishmen aware of the task ahead. It was an inspiring appeal which few Irish nationalists could read without being moved, yet the article ends quite irresponsibly:

I am glad the North has 'begun'. I am glad that the Orangemen have armed, for it is a good thing to see arms in Irish hands. I should like to see the A.O.H. [Ancient Order of Hibernians] armed. I should like to see the Transport Workers armed. I should like to see any and every body of Irish citizens armed. We must accustom ourselves to the thought of arms, to the use of arms. We may make mistakes in the beginning and shoot the wrong people; but bloodshed is a cleansing and a sanctifying thing, and the nation which regards it as the final horror has lost its manhood. There are many things more horrible than bloodshed and slavery is one of them.

It is only fair to point out that Pearse was expressing these sentiments before the obscenity of modern warfare was widely known. There was still a belief, which Pearse shared, that war could bring out heroism, nobility and courage. John Ruskin, in an essay twenty years earlier, had expressed similar ideas, but few people could share these views after the appalling barbarity of World War I.

Pearse believed that Irishmen had to demonstrate that they were willing to die for their country, and he was prepared to sacrifice his own life to make his countrymen free citizens. His suggestion that every body of Irishmen should be armed, with the implication that if they were not given what they wanted, or what they believed they were entitled to, they could use their arms to enforce their desires, was scarcely to be taken seriously. If two of these armed groups were in conflict, was it then acceptable for them to fight it out and, if so, what sort of society would result?

Pearse's article was published on 8 November 1913. Two days later O'Rahilly sent out invitations to a meeting in Wynn's Hotel, Dublin for the next day. In his *Secret History of the Irish Volunteers* he gives us the details:

As the invitations to that meeting were written and issued by myself, I am in a position to know something of the personnel of the original Committee; and I say now that the men invited were deliberately selected not on Party, Political or Sectarian lines, but solely because they were amongst the sincerest Nationalists of my acquaintance in Dublin.

Among those whom O'Rahilly invited were Eoin MacNeill, Bulmer Hobson, Patrick Pearse, Seán Mac Diarmada, W.J. Ryan, Eamonn Ceannt, Seán Fitzgibbon, J.A. Deakin, Pierce Beasly, Joseph Campbell and D.P. Moran. MacNeill presided and O'Rahilly acted as secretary. The discussion was conducted in Irish until someone said that not all of those present were Irish speakers, so they changed to English.

O'Rahilly was conscious that history was in the making and he recorded the names of those who attended, and also the agreed objectives of the organization it was proposed to form. These were: 'to secure and maintain the rights and liberties common to all the people of Ireland, without distinction of class, creed or politics.'

The meeting concluded with a decision to call a public meeting, at which the Volunteers would be launched and the men of Ireland invited to join.

One of those who did not attend that first meeting was Bulmer Hobson. He gave several explanations, none of which was plausible, for his failure to be at Wynn's Hotel. The most likely reason is that he was secretary of that largely imaginary body, the IRB, funded by the American-Irish organization Clan na Gael. John Devoy was head of Clan na Gael and Hobson may have decided that it would not be wise to become involved until he had cleared the matter with Devoy.

The public meeting to launch the Volunteers took place on 25 November 1913 in the Rotunda. The numbers attending surpassed the most optimistic expectations of those who had called the meeting. A large overflow meeting outside the Rotunda was also addressed by several speakers. There were contingents from the trade unions and from the National University. The speakers represented all political views. One of those listed to speak was Larry Kettle, a brother of Tom who was an engineer working for Dublin Corporation. He was shouted down because his father had employed scab labour to break a strike of farm workers some time previously.

Another speaker who got a hostile reception was a young student named Michael Davitt, the son of the famous leader of the Land League. His father was revered all over rural Ireland in recognition of the part he had played in the land struggle more than thirty years before. The reason the son was shouted down was that he had done his utmost to discourage his fellow students at the university from coming in a body to the meeting. Young Davitt was a close friend of John Dillon, one of the three leaders of the Irish Party, and it was generally believed that he was acting on instructions from Dillon to do what he could to prevent the formation of the Volunteers.

Bulmer Hobson claimed in later years, when there was considerable kudos attached to having being involved, that both he personally and the IRB had played an important part in the formation of the Volunteers. This claim is refuted in the account given by Eamonn Ceannt (who was himself in the IRB) some months after the inaugural meeting. Ceannt's account was published in *An t-Óglach*, the Volunteer weekly paper, and would have been read by all those who were involved. It rules out any claim that Hobson or the IRB participated either in the original moves to launch the Volunteers or in the subsequent efforts to develop the organization:

The extraordinary development of the Irish Volunteers makes it a matter of some interest to set down now some of the facts of its origin. There is a little urgency too as already misleading statements are being widely circulated. The first meeting held in Dublin to consider the proposition to found a Volunteer force open to all Irishmen was called by Ua Rathghaille [The O'Rahilly] by a circular letter addressed to a small group of Nationalists. The circular was an invitation 'To meet Mr Eoin MacNeill to discuss the matter.'

The meeting was duly held, Eoin presiding, and the opening statement by him, as well as much of the subsequent discussion, was in Irish. The next and several subsequent meetings of the Provisional Committee was strengthened by the addition of others known to sympathise with the project. A certain city Rifle Club supplied quite a number of members. Messrs Eoin MacNeill (founder of the Gaelic League), and Laurence J. Kettle, son of the redoubtable 'A.J', agreed to act as secretaries. The meeting was publicly launched on Tuesday 25th November, in the Rotunda Rink, Dublin, amidst great enthusiasm. The speakers included Pearse, MacNeill, Alderman Kelly and Luke O'Toole (GAA).

The news that an organization of Irish Volunteers had been formed in Dublin spread across the country like a prairie fire. Radical Irish nationalists realized that this was what was needed as an opposition to Carson's Volunteers whose purpose was to block the enactment of the Home Rule Bill which Redmond had won fron the British Parliament. In every city and county, groups of such men came together to form Volunteer corps in their district. In most cases they wrote to Dublin or sent one of their members to enquire about the procedures to be adopted in the formation of a local Volunteer corps.

There was no one among the small group who had gathered in Wynn's Hotel who had any experience of creating an organization such as was now evolving. All those involved were unpaid Volunteers, so no one could be 'ordered' to do anything.

From the very beginning there were problems with the senior executive, whose function should have been to decide policy and to see that it was observed. When meetings were called of the small organizing group, many of them brought along friends who were anxious to help and these were immediately co-opted to the executive. Nobody in the original group had the authority or the resolution to insist that, however it was constituted, the supreme executive should consist of only half-a-dozen dedicated men.

Since anyone was free to come along and be co-opted to the executive, this body was enlarged soon to twenty-five, all Dublin men. It should have been obvious to them that meetings of this size could achieve little, but there was no one with the authority to devise some means by which the twenty-five could be reduced to six, without offending anyone.

Meanwhile, those who had joined did all they could to help and their numbers grew rapidly. Some of the early recruits were of special importance. Sir Roger Casement and Colonel Maurice Moore were living in London when the Volunteers were formed and both, independently, decided to come to Dublin to offer their services. Both of these men played important roles in the development of the Volunteers. Maurice Moore was a retired British army officer who understood the nature of the command structure necessary in a military organization, and he undertook the role of 'Inspector General'.

Sir Roger Casement's involvement gave the Volunteers a great boost. He had already acquired an international reputation, and a knighthood, in recognition of his work in Africa and South America on behalf of the natives who were being cruelly exploited in the search for rubber. He had retired from the colonial service in 1912 and threw himself into the Volunteer movement with the utmost enthusiasm. The news of his involvement gave the organization considerable credibility. The Irish Volunteers could no longer be dismissed as just the silly antics of some Sinn Féin soreheads.

The movement grew as groups of radical nationalists came together to form local corps. Their first move was usually to send to Dublin and ask for one of the leaders to address a public meeting to help form the local branch. Such a meeting was organized for Cork City and MacNeill and Casement went down to speak at it. MacNeill considered it important to emphasize that the Irish Volunteers, of which he was president, had not been set up in opposition to the Ulster Volunteers. In his efforts to make this point forcibly, MacNeill began his address by calling for three cheers for Carson. This provoked a near riot. Indignant members of the audience mounted the platform and MacNeill might have been physically assaulted if it had not been for the stewards.

MacNeill's purpose was to stress that the Ulster Volunteers and the Irish Volunteers were not enemies and to express his horror at the thought of rival bodies of Irishmen becoming embroiled in a conflict that might lead to civil war. In his view, the Irish people should have been grateful to the Orangemen of the North for having shown them that the way to deal with the British was to recruit an army.

This casuistry was too subtle for the nationalists of Cork, who could see nothing but evil in Carson's army. They knew that the purpose of the Ulster Volunteers was to maintain the Protestant Ascendancy of the province, whereas the declared aim of the Irish Volunteers was 'to secure and maintain the rights and liberties common to all the people of Ireland, without distinction of class, creed or politics.'

It would be difficult to imagine any objectives more radically contrary to those of Carson's Volunteers, even if these had been clearly spelled out.

Order was restored at the Cork meeting when someone explained to the audience that what MacNeill had in mind was that Carson's modus operandi was to be welcomed, even if they did not approve of his objective. In Limerick later, MacNeill made the same mistake of praising Carson, with the same result. After that he decided to leave Carson out of his speeches.

In the early months of 1914, the Irish Volunteers grew rapidly. About this time there was a serious concern that the Catholics of Derry might be the victims of an Orange pogrom, and Colonel Moore was sent there to organize the Volunteers to defend the Catholics if this were to happen.

10

Redmond Becomes Involved

While Colonel Moore was in Derry, he wrote to his friend Stephen Gwynn in London, asking him to find out from Redmond what he thought of the growth of the Volunteers. Both Moore and Gwynn were prominent and influential supporters of the Irish Party and Gwynn had no trouble in securing an interview with Redmond. His reply was much the same as the response MacNeill had received, either directly or through a third party, when he, at O'Rahilly's behest, had asked Redmond to participate in the launch of an Irish volunteer force. Gwynn replied that Redmond was well-disposed to the Irish Volunteers but gave no hint that he had, at that time, decided to become involved with them.

Some weeks later Moore had a meeting with Redmond and Dillon in the House of Commons. He was asked how many men had enlisted in the Volunteer movement. The leaders of the Irish Party were getting uneasy that this new radical organization might become a serious competitor for the allegiance of Irish nationalists. In reply to the question, Moore said that their record-keeping was not up to date but they estimated that they had already enrolled about 20,000 members and that the numbers were increasing at the rate of about a thousand men per week.

Redmond found it difficult to believe that so many had enrolled in such a short time, but Dillon confirmed Moore's estimate. If this new organization, without funds, and without any well-known influential political leader to guide it, had made such rapid progress, Redmond and the leaders of the Irish Party had every reason to be worried.

If the leaders of the Irish Party were concerned at the growth of the Volunteers and the effect that this might have on the grip of the party on the allegiance of Irish nationalists, it is certain that Dublin Castle was also concerned at the prospect of radical Irish separatists building up an armed organization whose declared objective was to eject the British from Ireland. Even if these Irish Volunteers were now drilling with dummy rifles, how long would it be before they obtained real weapons? The importation of arms had been banned within a week of the meeting in the Rotunda to launch the Irish Volunteers, but there was no certainty that the leaders would not find a means of evading the ban.

When the concern of Dublin Castle was conveyed to the British cabinet, it put them in a serious dilemma. There were obvious and serious risks in allowing the newly formed Irish Volunteers to expand, but they could not ban the Irish Volunteers without also banning the Ulster Volunteers. The government knew that to attempt to ban the Ulster Volunteer Force, in which some of the top members of the British Conservative establishment were heavily involved, would be political dynamite.

If the government had decided to ban both organizations, and to apply punitive sanctions to any group disobeying this ban, they knew that they had no armed forces either willing or able to enforce such a decision. This emerged some months later when the cabinet decided to instruct the War Office to place military guards on army stores in Ulster. It led immediately to 'the Curragh Mutiny'. If the British army could not even place a guard on its own stores, there was no possible chance of it undertaking an armed confrontation with the Ulster Volunteers.

The cabinet may have decided that its best hope was to render the new Irish Volunteers innocuous. They knew that Redmond had no subversive ideas and they may have asked him to exert his great influence in Ireland to obtain control of the Irish Volunteers.

Whether or not they were prompted by the British cabinet, the leaders of the Irish Party realized by April 1914 that the widespread enthusiasm for the Irish Volunteers, and the numbers that were joining, made it imperative for the party to have an important influence on, if not outright control of, this new body. Most of the Volunteer executive also accepted this. A number of meetings were held to discuss a united force, some in the House of Commons and others in the Gresham Hotel in Dublin, and at one time it seemed possible that an acceptable arrangement had been achieved. There were intransigent individuals on both sides: men like Pearse and

Tom Clarke, who wanted no link with the Irish Party, and there were those who did not want any association with the radical men of the Irish Volunteers.

At one meeting in London, Eoin MacNeill was accompanied by Professor Tom Kettle, a prominent supporter of the Irish Party. He had offered to accompany MacNeill, ostensibly to impress on Redmond the supreme importance of ensuring that the ban on the import of arms into Ireland was revoked, thus enabling the Volunteers to become a serious armed force, rather than a group of men marching with dummy rifles. In London Kettle made no effort to urge this: he had come under false pretences. At the meeting with Redmond, he never made any reference to having the ban on the import of rifles lifted, but kept impressing on Redmond that the Volunteers were being strongly influenced by irresponsible, physical force Irish nationalists. This meeting achieved nothing, but just as MacNeill and Kettle were parting company back in Dublin, Kettle remarked that MacNeill could expect an ultimatum from Redmond within a few days. This was an insulting and unexpected slap in the face for MacNeill.

There were other meetings at which third parties tried to suggest an acceptable arrangement, but such meddling was futile and even harmful.

During these negotiations, Redmond several times made the point that the composition of the Provisional Committee, which consisted of twenty-five self-appointed individuals, was unworkable. This was true, and it reflected no credit on MacNeill that he had allowed such a committee to develop. It was clearly going to be difficult to reduce the committee to a manageable size. A new governing executive would have to be appointed and most of these twenty-five, who had initiated the movement, would be asked to stand down. This was a difficult nettle for MacNeill to grasp.

No matter how unpleasant it was going to be to inform most of the twenty-five that they must now take back seats, it had to be done if a united body of Irish Volunteers was to be formed, with the Irish Party having an important influence in the organization.

At one of their meetings Redmond proposed to MacNeill that there would be an executive council of five, two from the men who had formed the Volunteers, two from the Irish Party, with MacNeill as chairman. This was an opportunity that MacNeill should have grasped. If he had, the Volunteers would have been supported by

Redmond and the Irish Party, and there would have been no limit to the numbers who would have joined. It would also have been possible for Redmond to refuse to keep Asquith in office unless the ban on the import of rifles was lifted. But MacNeill dithered and the chance was lost.

After one meeting, Colonel Moore was convinced that a solution had been worked out. This proposal was for a committee of seven, three from the Volunteers, with three from the Irish Party and again MacNeill as chairman. Redmond's two most senior supporters in the party were John Dillon and Joseph Devlin. All three were to nominate the Irish Party members of the new committee. Redmond chose his brother Willie, whom the original committee were happy to accept. Willie Redmond was one of the unsung heroes of that period. When it came to urging Irishmen to join the British army in the autumn of 1914, he said that he would not ask any man to join until he himself had enlisted. He did enlist and did not get a safe assignment behind the lines. He was sent into the front line and was killed in action in June 1917.

Joseph Devlin picked himself as a member of the new executive. As a Belfast man, he was an ideal person to have as one of the seven. But then came the stumbling block. John Dillon wanted young Michael Davitt, the student who had been shouted down at the Rotunda meeting because he had tried to stop the students from marching to the meeting. Davitt was a political nonentity, with nothing to contribute except his father's name. Indeed, he was little more than a schoolboy.

It is easy now to see that MacNeill should have asked for an urgent meeting with Redmond or Dillon, to point out that Davitt would not be acceptable. If Redmond had insisted that no one else would satisfy him, MacNeill should have given way. One nonentity on a committee of seven was something they could live with. Again MacNeill missed his opportunity. Redmond could wait no longer and sent MacNeill the following letter:

As the matter is very urgent, I beg you to let me have a definite reply by return. The members of the Irish Party will be leaving London on Wednesday next, to visit their constituencies during the Whitsuntide recess [of 1914] and they must have a clear understanding before leaving here as to whether, on the basis of it, the full support and co-operation may be given to the Volunteer movement, as at present constituted.

Colonel Moore wrote in his book: 'This brought matters to a crisis which could not be delayed for a day, and as a Committee could not be called, MacNeill came to consult us at Buswell's. Both Casement and I agreed that it would be better to accept these terms, and I was asked to go to London and negotiate for a settlement on the basis of the six names already mentioned, two more to be nominated by Mr Redmond, and Colonel Moore as Inspector General to be added.'

On 23 May 1914 MacNeill wrote to Moore:

My dear Colonel Moore,
    Read the enclosed, and if you wish, add anything that occurs to you.
    When you are over, ask Redmond to get a leading man, his brother or Mr Devlin, to see me at Whitsuntide. I believe if one of these men came to our Committee, spoke generously to them and in support of the Volunteers, we could have the most wonderful development on National Unity and Strength.
        Yours sincerely
        Eoin MacNeill

The meeting between Moore and Redmond took place on the same day, and on the 26th Redmond wrote to MacNeill:

Dear Mr MacNeill,
    I have your letter of the 23rd of May and I am greatly gratified that you agree to my suggested addition to the new governing body which is proposed. As the matter now stands the proposed new body would consist of,
1. The present four officers, that is yourself, Mr L. Kettle, Mr John Gore and The O'Rahilly.
2. Mr W. Redmond M.P. and Sir Roger Casement.
3. The men nominated by me. I would be inclined to nominate Mr Joseph Devlin M.P. and Mr Michael Davitt, but I have not as yet asked them to act. Further I approve your suggestion to add Colonel Moore as a ninth member.

Colonel Moore thought after this meeting that all had been settled amicably, but he was not aware of Redmond's choice of Davitt:

I left London on the 29th May in the firm conviction that no more conflict would arise; there seemed to be perfect peace and agreement . . . .
    On the 1st June I was back in Dublin, and learned that Mr Dillon had been over: that the Party representatives were Mr William Redmond, Mr Devlin and young Mr Davitt . . . . About the first two there could be no difference of opinion; they fulfilled in every way the proposals we had ourselves made; indeed, I think that William Redmond was probably the most acceptable member of the Party that could have been selected as we

would have chosen him ourselves if we had been asked . . . . But the nomination of Mr Davitt caused much resentment; he had attended the first meeting of the Volunteers but had not been allowed to speak, as it was believed that he was against the movement; he had taken the most prominent part in opposing the establishment of a Volunteer Corps in the National University . . . . It was generally supposed that of the three Party leaders Mr Redmond had nominated his brother, and Mr Dillon, always preferring to sit in the dark background pulling the strings of an automaton, had named Mr Davitt to represent himself.

Redmond made a tragic blunder in nominating Davitt, but the Provisional Committee made a worse one in not accepting him. The benefits that would have accrued from a united Volunteer Force would have been dazzling. The number of those enlisting would have doubled or trebled in a few months. Money would have been available to buy arms. Possibly Redmond could have compelled Asquith to lift the arms embargo, since it was common knowledge that the Ulster Volunteers had been allowed to defy it. With money and the arms embargo lifted, there would soon have been a real Volunteer Force, which could not have been coerced by the British government, even if it had a mind to do so.

But there would still have been the nightmare of two armed and trained Volunteer armies in Ireland, one of them committed to achieving Home Rule for the whole of Ireland and the other determined to oppose being a minority in any Home Rule government.

On 16 May Redmond showed his impatience in a letter to MacNeill:

I am extremely anxious that we should come to some understanding on this matter, as I am of the opinion that it would be the greatest misfortune if a disagreement should result in the possible establishment of a second body of Irish Volunteers. It is clearly in the interests of the country that the Volunteer movement should be a united one, and under a single guidance.

When MacNeill said that Davitt was not acceptable to the committee, Redmond lost no time in issuing his ultimatum, which was published on 10 June 1914 (see Appendix 2).

Redmond's criticisms of the Volunteer executive were valid. They were self-elected and there were too many of them. They all should have realized that if Redmond set up a rival organization, 90 per cent of those who had enlisted with the MacNeill group would leave and join Redmond's body. This should have convinced them that there was no alternative to accepting the Redmond nominees if they wished to create a united powerful force of Volunteers. However, to achieve this, it was essential that Redmond's nominees were firmly committed to the idea of having an armed body under the control of the Irish Party, who were, in effect, the 'Government in waiting'. O'Rahilly knew of another imperative reason why unity should be preserved, although he could not disclose it, even to the members of the Volunteer executive. A cargo of rifles had been purchased abroad and was on its way to Ireland; if there had been a split in the Volunteers, and most of those who had enlisted with MacNeill had left to follow Redmond, O'Rahilly could not be sure there would even be enough men left to carry the rifles back to Dublin from Howth, a small fishing port on the north arm of Dublin Bay. When it came to making a decision, the arguments were bitter and, in the vote, twelve were for the admission of the Redmond nominees and eight were against. These eight issued a minority report explaining the reasons for their opposition. O'Rahilly wrote a long letter to Devoy, telling him the agonizing choice they had faced and giving his reasons for deciding to vote for the admission of the Irish Party men.

The Volunteer executive's acceptance of the Redmond nominees resulted in a vast influx of new members. These were mainly Irish nationalists who were active supporters of the Irish Party: men who had been reluctant to join until the Volunteers had been given Redmond's approval. Then the massacre on Bachelor's Walk gave rise to a wave of 'savage indignation' throughout Ireland and caused a further surge of additional recruits.

As the numbers grew, the Dublin headquarters formed adjoining companies into battalions and the battalions into larger units. Colonel Maurice Moore, the Volunteer's inspector general, has described the formation of the Volunteers:

Every county in Ireland had already a number of Volunteer corps within its boundaries; in some, of course, the movement spread more than in others, because our missionaries were few, our means limited, and we had not been able to go everywhere in so short a time . . . but corps were springing up with such increasing rapidity in different centres that no correct role could be given. I cannot however estimate the number at this time throughout Ireland as less than thirty-five or forty thousand; there may have been forty-five thousand men.

In another estimate Moore later said that, after the split, the number who followed Redmond might have been 120,000, while the MacNeillites, as they were known, did not exceed 10,000. He then goes on:

An enumeration of the Volunteers . . . was published in the 'National Volunteer', and was roughly correct. It will be seen that dissenters were strong in the city, and very weak in the outlying districts; in the provinces the proportion was even more negligible than in Dublin County.

	National Volunteers	Irish Volunteers
Dublin County	3,509	210
Dublin City	2,375	1,103
Total	5,884	1,313

The Dublin total was over 7,000, and of these almost 6,000 sided with Redmond.

Moore prepared other figures, which are now in the National Library. These were written on House of Commons notepaper and give a detailed analysis of the number of Volunteers in the whole country. Not only does Moore give the number of men who opted for Redmond and MacNeill, he enumerates the meetings that were held in each county when they made their decisions and records the attendance at each of these meetings.

These lists were compiled so meticulously it suggests that word was sent to every company in the 32 counties to hold a meeting to decide whether to support Redmond or MacNeill. The totals amounted to 158,300 for Redmond and 12,306 for MacNeill. These figures show the extraordinary influx of recruits into the Volunteers during the four months up to October 1914, when membership increased from about 40,000 to 170,000. When O'Rahilly called the meeting at Wynn's Hotel, he could scarcely have imagined that, in less than a year, there would be so many recruits.

11

Arming the Volunteers

Most of those invited by O'Rahilly to come to the meeting in Wynn's Hotel, to discuss with MacNeill the formation of an Irish Volunteer Force, took it for granted that it would be an armed body. Unless they were armed, they would not be taken seriously; indeed, they knew that with dummy rifles they were only playing a game of charades. The Ulster Volunteers were well supplied with rifles, and, despite MacNeill's casuistry that there was no rivalry between them, everyone knew that the objective of the Ulster Volunteers was to obstruct Home Rule, and the aim of the Irish Volunteers was to achieve it.

In the years before World War I, an army consisted largely of men armed with rifles. They had to be well-trained and disciplined in obeying orders and to be led by competent officers. Artillery was desirable when buildings were being attacked, but the infantryman with a rifle was the backbone of an army.

When O'Rahilly made his appeal in 1912, urging Irishmen to arm themselves if they wanted freedom from British domination, there were no restrictions on the purchase of arms or ammunition in Ireland. At the time the Ulster Volunteers were formed at the beginning of 1913, they could legally obtain all the weapons they could afford, and the British government must have known that they were acquiring large numbers of weapons, yet Asquith's government made no effort to prevent the Ulstermen buying arms.

Within a week of the Rotunda meeting to form the Irish Volunteers, the same British government placed a ban on the import of rifles into Ireland. The formation of the Irish Volunteers was for the British an entirely new situation. The Ulster Volunteers

Lafayette portraits of Nannie and Michael O'Rahilly, c. 1915.

Mary Spring-Rice, prime mover of Howth gun-running in July 1914.

O'Rahilly and his sister Nell Humphreys, with her collie dog Dash.

O'Rahilly with his wife, Nannie, and three children, Mac (seated), Niall (below left) and Egan (author).

The author (centre), his brother Mac (left) and cousin Emmett Humphreys in their Fianna uniforms at 54 Northumberland Road, c. 1915.

were organized and financed by several of the leading members of the British establishment, some of them Ulstermen but many others British Conservatives. The government's inaction in allowing them to acquire arms was an entirely different matter from allowing radical Irish nationalists to acquire them.

This ban on the import of arms into Ireland probably was made in consultation with John Redmond, because the Asquith government could remain in office only with his support.

The tasks facing O'Rahilly when he accepted responsibility for arming the Volunteers were formidable. The legal ban meant that arms had to be imported without the knowledge of Dublin Castle. There was the problem of finding the money for the purchase of suitable weapons; and, finally, the problem of delivering them into the hands of the Volunteers.

The Irish Volunteers had no wealthy patrons and the fundamental problem was to find the money to import an initial supply of rifles. O'Rahilly believed that many of those who had joined the Volunteers were both willing and able to buy their own weapons. If an initial shipment were available, their sale would enable a second supply to be bought, and so on. The difficult decision about delivering the rifles was whether this should be done secretly, or openly, in defiance of the ban.

Among O'Rahilly's papers is a letter he wrote to the Irish newspapers, in which he sets out the general situation in Ireland. It begins with an account of the landing of the arms at Larne, and the refusal of British troops in the Curragh to obey an order from the War Office to guard British army stores in Ulster. The Curragh Mutiny was the most serious political development arising from the passage of the Home Rule Bill. The government now realized that British troops in Ireland were no longer under its control.

The Curragh Mutiny was welcome news to the German government. It was an important consideration in their assessment of the forces that could be mobilized against them in the European conflict which was then imminent, and may well have been the decisive influence in Germany's decision to launch World War I some months later.

In his letter to the press, O'Rahilly points out that the native Irish were the only group in Ireland who were then defenceless, and he urges them to subscribe funds to arm the Volunteers:

A Chara,

Although we have read comment ad nauseam on certain recent political incidents I don't think that the Irish public yet realises the full significance of these events; they do not appear to appreciate the moral of them nor to understand how vitally the situation concerns themselves.

Until recently Ireland was understood to be in the Military Occupation of an army directed by and obedient to the British Government. The several Parties in Ireland assumed that England controlled this army, and they shaped their policies accordingly, none of them contemplating a resort to the decision of war. But the Curragh incident, which shows that the Army of Occupation (like Kipling's Raw Recruit), 'won't obey no orders unless they are its own', has rudely shattered that delusion and the importance of the discovery is heightened ten-fold by the remarkable coup by which the army of Ulster has provided itself with arms and ammunition despite the combined efforts of the British Army, Navy, and Police.

This means that the only party in Ireland which is not fully armed are the 'old Irish', i.e. the Celtic and native population of this country, in which you Sir, have the honour to be included. It leaves you in the pleasant position of being largely without effective arms and forbidden to obtain them by a proclamation which prevents their being landed at Dublin while permitting their delivery in Belfast. In this position you are confronted by the Armed Garrison of England, a garrison which detests you so cordially that it will not maintain even the laws of England when these laws are such as you desire to be maintained. At the same time you are confronted with another well equipped and considerable army of Irregulars, which army has openly threatened to invade your territory and presumably to desolate it on its march to Cork. In other words the soundness of your sleep during these nights past was entirely due to the forbearance of Sir Edward Carson. Had his disposition been more belligerent and had the humour seized him to march on Cork earlier, we have the fullest grounds for supposing that the English popinjays of the Curragh and elsewhere would have done nothing to prevent him. Be you ever so valorous, without a modern weapon in your hand you are absolutely helpless, and I write to ask you how long do you purpose to remain so.

There is fortunately one force in sight upon which you can rely for the defence of your life and property. That is the Irish Volunteers. But the Irish Volunteers although their growth and progress is nothing less than phenomenal are not yet fully equipped for active service. May I also, Sir, ask what you and your readers are doing to equip them? It can hardly be that you still doubt that their equipment is desirable and possible. The Curragh incident has made it clear to you that you may not rely upon the scarlet warriors of England, and the unimpeded discharge of the Fanny [a vessel] has left your party the only considerably unarmed section in Ireland. The

112

balance of power has not only been disturbed but destroyed and the status quo can only be restored by the immediate extension of the Irish Volunteers, and by their being armed as an efficient defensive force. This is the obvious National duty of your readers, and for those of them to whom the sense of National duty does not appeal may I point out that it is an urgent and necessary measure for their personal protection to busy themselves in the work.

The Proclamation need worry nobody. The latest decision of the Government has proved that the Proclamation only forbids the entry of small quantities of sporting goods. Military Rifles in lots of 50,000 and cartridges by the million are freely admissible without interference, prosecution, or punishment.

Let us profit by these remarkable conditions. Provide the money and the Irish Volunteers will procure themselves arms.

      Is mise, do chara,
        Ua Rathgaille
40 Pairc Herbert,
Ath Cliath.
4th May, 1914

O'Rahilly tells in his *Secret History of the Irish Volunteers* of his efforts to get funds to arm the Volunteers: 'Curiously enough our utmost efforts failed to secure any assistance from the Irish people on the Continent, the very people who could most easily and effectively have helped us.' Who were these Irish people on the Continent? Irish emigration to the Continent had been widespread up to the time of the American Revolution, but then the United States became more attractive than mainland Europe for Irish emigrants. Irish Americans, with their more recent memories of the ruin that the British occupation had inflicted on Ireland, would have seemed the most likely people from whom to solicit help. Yet it was not until April 1914 that O'Rahilly wrote to John Devoy, the veteran leader of Clan na Gael. The Clan regarded the IRB as its home organization and subsidized the radical Irish monthly, *Irish Freedom.*

O'Rahilly may have delayed so long before asking the Clan for help because he did not want the Volunteers to be too dependent on this American organization. A basic principle of the Irish Volunteers was that they were to be independent. They wanted to build a new movement, which members of others groups were free to join, but which would not be dominated by any other organization.

Another important conclusion to be drawn from O'Rahilly's

appeal to Devoy is that it rules out any suggestion that either Clan na Gael in the USA or the IRB in Ireland had any part, or indeed any interest, in the formation of the Volunteers or in the subsequent moves to develop and arm them. If the IRB had been involved in the formation of the Volunteers, their members surely would have approached their controlling body in America and solicited help from them for the new movement. Yet it was not until six months after the formation of the Volunteers that O'Rahilly requested help from the Clan and he had no connection with the IRB and had several times refused to join them. He wrote to Devoy on 6 April 1914:

Dear Mr Devoy,

Though I have not had the pleasure of meeting you my subject justifies me in writing.

You have heard of the Irish Volunteers (not the Ulster but the other), and you will be glad to hear that the situation is more hopeful than it has ever been in my time. We have reached the stage of having a body of men, drilling and training themselves in the open as soldiers and without interference. They already number about 25,000 and are increasing at the rate of perhaps 1,000 a week. The permanence of this depends *absolutely* on our being able to provide the essential features of their equipment at once, that is before any new development changes the conditions. In other words if we are able to provide rifles etc. for the men that we can rely on, there is nothing else to prevent us from creating an efficient army of, say, 200,000 Volunteers within a measurable period. The incalculable importance of this both for Ireland and the 'Empire' you can readily understand. It is the biggest movement of modern times.

Now the present position is that it is not the Proclamation which prevents us going ahead, but the lack of funds. And we don't want any colossal sum, or such sum, for instance, as you might imagine was needed to equip 200,000 men. Provided that buying in large quantities were possible, it would be found that a fairly modern rifle would be available in Ireland for our members to purchase at say, three dollars apiece. At this price they would sell like hot cakes, and the original capital would be available to pay for another lot, which would in turn pay for the next supply and so on.

Most important of all, the distribution of even the first thousand would prevent the possibility of disarmament, except in actual warfare, say, by an enemy using artillery.

If the sincere Irish in America will not help us they will have neglected the greatest opportunity of a century. The wealthy Irish here will not subscribe. They are intensively thick-skulled, and are so bewildered by the complexity of political conditions that they don't even know which side they are on, to say nothing of appreciating the present opportunity. If you prefer it that way I don't want a single cent in cash. What I want is the purchase, anywhere, by anyone you like of a large quantity of workable equipment, standard in pattern, which can be retailed at popular prices.

Address your reply to me under cover to Miss Dora French, St. Annes, Donnybrook, Dublin, or get someone to call on me. There never was such an opportunity in our time, and if we don't grasp it, the next political development may destroy the chance.

> Is mise do chara,
> Ua Rathghaille

Devoy was undecided whether Clan na Gael should give financial support. The formation of an open organization was an entirely new concept to the Clan, which had always assumed that an Irish revolutionary body would be secret, with oath-bound members and surreptitious meetings. Devoy sent O'Rahilly's letter to leading members of the Clan, asking for their opinion about whether the Clan should help arm the Volunteers. Some replied that, since there was now in existence an Ulster Volunteer Force determined to resist Home Rule, if necessary by armed force, the creation of a rival armed body, determined to achieve Home Rule, would inevitably lead to civil war, and they advised that the Clan should not give O'Rahilly any funds. Others believed that monies should be sent because the objective of the Irish Volunteers was to achieve freedom from British rule. At least one of the leaders thought it likely that if the Clan did not give financial aid, the Volunteers would start a rival body to the Clan in the United States to collect money themselves. He advised Devoy to give the Volunteers support.

When a month had passed and O'Rahilly had not heard from Devoy, he decided to enlist the support of Tom Clarke, a former member of Clan na Gael. Clarke had served fifteen years in prison for planting bombs in England in 1899. Some time after his release, he went to the US where he became friendly with Devoy. Clarke returned to Ireland in 1907 and opened a tobacconist's shop in Parnell Street. He was one of the leading members of the IRB.

Clarke was highly regarded by Clan na Gael and O'Rahilly believed that if the veteran revolutionist endorsed his plea to Devoy, it would enhance his chances of getting the help he needed. Among O'Rahilly's papers there is a letter from Clarke in which he says that he would like to have a further talk with O'Rahilly about the matter they had discussed recently. Clarke was not officially connected with the Volunteers. He was a 'ticket of leave' man, which meant that he had been released from jail before the completion of his sentence, but if he was convicted of any form of illegal activity, he could be sent back to jail to serve out the rest of his sentence. This constrained him to at least appear to be law-abiding.

If Clarke wanted a further talk with O'Rahilly to endorse his appeal to Devoy, it was successful. About a month after Devoy received O'Rahilly's letter (to which he had not replied), he got a letter from Clarke. While this letter did not explicitly refer to the request for help to arm the Volunteers, Clarke said that there had been a transformation in nationalist Ireland since the formation of the Volunteers:

The country is electrified with the Volunteering business. Never have I known in any former movement anything to compare with the spontaneous rush to start drill and get hold of a rifle. . . . And the change that has come over the young men of the country who are volunteering. Erect heads up in the air; the glint in the eye and then the talent and the ability that had been latent and is now being discovered. Young fellows who had been regarded as something like wastrels now changed to energetic soldiers.

Some days after Devoy received this letter from Clarke, he got a letter from Major John MacBride. MacBride and Devoy had met in New York when MacBride had been on an American lecture tour. In his letter to Devoy, MacBride said:

The Volunteer movement will be a tremendous force in National life over here if properly handled. The country people are at last coming to kick against the Home Rule bluffers.

It was scarcely a coincidence that these two veterans of earlier struggles should have written to Devoy at the same time, effectively endorsing O'Rahilly's plea for help. The strategy bore fruit. Clan na Gael had been uncertain how to respond, but these letters ended their doubts. Devoy sent O'Rahilly a draft for $5,000, and on 25 June 1914 O'Rahilly acknowledged the money:

I have just received advice from the Bank of your magnificent subscription which you have cabled to our credit, and on behalf of the Volunteers and ourselves personally I wish to convey our deep and heartfelt gratitude for the noble way in which you have helped in our work.

In the meantime, even before the money arrived from the US, other developments, in connection with arming the Volunteers, were taking place in Dublin.

One morning in April 1914, O'Rahilly received a letter from an unknown writer, who turned out to be a young woman:

A Chara,

I shall be in Dublin for a couple of nights next week, Wed. and Thurs., and again in Easter week for a couple of nights 15th and 16th. If you will be in Dublin either of these times, perhaps we could meet and have a talk about the Volunteers at the Arts Club for instance. Conor O'Brien tells me he has being seeing you about rifles.

They seem to be going well ahead with the movement in Limerick city.

Mise le meas,

Mary Spring Rice

There is no suggestion here that the writer had ever met O'Rahilly. Her only introduction was that Conor O'Brien (her cousin) had been organizing the Volunteers in Limerick, and that he had been discussing the supply of rifles with O'Rahilly. The only answer O'Rahilly could have given O'Brien, when he asked for rifles, was that, although O'Rahilly was director of arms for the Volunteers, he did not have any rifles to give him.

This young woman, a modern Joan of Arc, then went to work. She spent a fair amount of her time in London, where she was friendly with Erskine Childers and his wife and with Mrs Alice Stopford Green, the Irish historian. She discussed the problem with Childers, whose main interest was sailing in his yacht. Mary Spring Rice had been born in Foynes, Co. Limerick and had spent much of her life there, and since her cousin, Conor O'Brien, was also an enthusiastic yachtsman, she probably had some experience of sailing in the Shannon estuary.

Mary Spring Rice would have known the difficulties of financing any shipment of arms, and must have got encouragement from Mrs Green that there were London Liberals who were strong Home Rulers, and who could and would provide funds for a gun-running operation.

Her next move was to write to O'Rahilly, the member of the Volunteer executive responsible for the procurement of arms. They met and she unfolded her plan for importing a cargo of rifles in a sailing vessel. She told O'Rahilly of a fishing vessel that was lying unused at Foynes, which she knew could be bought cheaply. She thought the price would not be more than £80. She told O'Rahilly that it would not cost much to make this vessel seaworthy and fitted

117

out to take a cargo of rifles. Mary Spring Rice was convinced that a gun-running operation could be successfully carried out in this vessel, but she stressed to O'Rahilly that one condition was of fundamental importance if the operation was to succeed. This was that Erskine Childers would have to be in charge of the project. She went out of her way to impress on O'Rahilly that Conor O'Brien could not be given charge of the operation; in her opinion, he was too liable to panic.

At that time O'Rahilly had probably never met Erskine Childers and maybe had never even heard of him, unless he had read the novel that Childers had written about ten years previously. *The Riddle of the Sands* was about a yachting trip along the Dutch coast in which the yachtsman came across German preparations to carry out an invasion of England by embarking an army in barges that would be towed across the Channel. Although it was only fiction, it was taken seriously by many top people in England and played an important part in the pressures building up in Britain to have the size of its fleet increased, to ensure that there was no possibility that the Germans could achieve the naval victory that would make such an invasion possible.

There is no record of when O'Rahilly and Childers had their first meeting, but over the next few months both Mary Spring Rice and Childers wrote frequently to O'Rahilly. He kept the letters he received, but his own letters have not survived.

In her first letter to O'Rahilly, Mary Spring Rice suggested a meeting on 8 or 9 April. This letter probably reached him about the time he wrote his first letter to Devoy, which was on 6 April, and may even have inspired him to write it. O'Rahilly asked Devoy to buy anywhere a consignment of suitable weapons, and he would take delivery. It would have been a simple matter for Devoy to have bought a consignment of rifles in the US or elsewhere and to have shipped them to the free port of Hamburg, and then to have left it to the Dublin men to organize delivery to an Irish port.

O'Rahilly had written that letter to Devoy before there was any news of the Larne gun-running, although it was about this time that the Larne rifles were being transshipped in the Baltic from the lighter to the coastal vessel that would bring them to Ireland.

The first move in the Howth gun-running was a visit by Childers to Foynes to see the disused fishing vessel. Childers wrote a full report of what he found in a letter to his wife after he had inspected the vessel. He decided against using it for a number of reasons: it would take a long time to get it seaworthy, and probably would cost a lot of money. Furthermore, he had no knowledge of the availability of good tradesmen in the area to carry out the necessary repairs. Another reason for not using the vessel was that it was lying within sight of the local police barracks, and the police would surely be curious to know why this old fishing boat was being repaired. Childers's final reason was that the gun-running route would take them along the south coast of England at the height of the yachting season, and many local people would be curious to know what this old fishing vessel was doing, sailing along the south coast of England, when it was not fishing.

Childers decided instead to use his own yacht. The *Asgard* would excite no interest going around the English coast during the yachting season and it could be made ready much sooner. Childers demonstrated his total dedication to the project by his willingness to use his own yacht, his great source of recreation and pleasure.

The letters in O'Rahilly's papers give us some information about the various operations and the people who performed them, but much of what went on has to be interpolated. Secrecy was a fundamental consideration. Only three of the most senior members of the Volunteer executive were informed of what was taking place.

It is now a fact of history that the landing of the arms at Howth, on 26 July 1914, in open defiance of the British government's ban on the importation of arms into Ireland, was the opening move leading to the rebellion which ejected the British from 26 of the 32 counties of Ireland. This landing was comparable to the storming of the Bastille in the events leading up to the French Revolution, and deserves to be as fondly cherished in the memories of Irishmen who value their country's freedom from British rule, as Bastille Day is among Frenchmen.

Pride of place in the operation goes to Erskine Childers. He was one of the few men in Ireland who had the technical skill, the dedication, the courage, the integrity and the commitment to carry out this self-imposed duty. He undertook it without any regard for the risks and hardships involved. It must also be acknowledged that Mary Spring Rice suggested the basic concept. The key role she played was spelled out by O'Rahilly when he met her in Buswell's

Hotel on the morning after the landing and introduced her to Colonel Moore saying, 'she is the young woman who originated the whole operation.'

The three people involved in carrying out the plan were Mary Spring Rice, Erskine Childers and O'Rahilly. Mrs Green organized a group of English Liberals who provided some of the finance by subscriptions, and who also undertook to provide funds as a repayable advance, which O'Rahilly personally guaranteed.

It is not recorded how O'Rahilly found the weapons firm of Moritz Magnum of Hamburg; he may have just picked the name from a trade directory. He went to Hamburg to examine the rifles on offer. He selected samples of those he considered suitable, but then thought it best to test-fire them. To do this, he joined a London rifle club, and had two specimen rifles sent to this club where he test-fired and passed them as suitable for the Volunteers. The gun-running could now go ahead.

MacNeill, Casement and Hobson were the only other members of the Provisional Committee who knew of the plans to import the rifles, although none of them was actively involved in carrying out the arrangements. The rifles were stored in Liège in Belgium and Darrell Figgis, a freelance journalist, agreed to undertake the important role of examining every rifle before they were sent by train to Hamburg. At that port he had them loaded on the tug which delivered them to the rendez-vous with two yachts in the English Channel, outside the estuary leading to Antwerp. The yachts were the *Asgard*, owned by Childers, and the *Kelpie*, owned by Conor O'Brien.

When these plans had been made, Childers and Figgis went to the Continent to close the deal and to make the financial arrangements. The money was lodged in a German bank, and a letter of credit was given to Moritz Magnum under which the money would be paid to them when the captain of the tug-boat certified that he had delivered the rifles to the buyer's yachts. It was a normal commercial transaction, but Childers was nervous that there might be some loophole. Figgis recalled how Childers spent the evening mulling over the contract, while he himself went off to the opera. When Childers had signed the contract, he wrote to O'Rahilly to say that he had bought 1,000 rifles at 12/6 (62 pence in today's currency):

We have not enough cash. (Total required is 800 pounds and of this 175 pounds is freight) and Mrs Green will advance a considerable balance, but would you kindly on receipt of this send her your guarantee as you stipulated when you were over here. It is only right, don't you think, that she should have it in a proper form before proceeding on a heavy liability.

Even before the money arrived from the US, there had been some new development which made the guarantee no longer necessary. On 19 June Childers wrote to O'Rahilly to say that he was coming to Dublin and wanted urgently to see him. In a postscript to this letter he said: 'Have just seen Mrs Green and have important things to say to you, inter-alia, the guarantee which we think is, happily, no longer necessary.'

The most likely explanation is that some new subscriptions had been received which made O'Rahilly's guarantee no longer necessary.

A few days later the £1,000 arrived from the US and this extra money enabled the order for the rifles to be increased from 1,000 to 1,500. The total cost, including ammunition and freight, was £1,500. Of this, £1,000 was Volunteer money, including some of the Clan na Gael finance, and £500 was money that had been raised by Mrs Green, and most of which was repaid to her when the rifles were sold. It emerges from one of the letters which Childers wrote that O'Rahilly had given Childers a personal contribution of £100 to help defray expenses.

At the end of June, everything seemed set for the gun-running, but then a difference of opinion arose between Childers and O'Rahilly as to how the rifles should be landed in Ireland. O'Rahilly wanted seven different landing points. His idea was that mock funerals would be arranged in each of these places to take away the rifles. Childers said that it would not be possible to arrange such a timetable with a sailing yacht. If the wind was unsuitable or if there was bad weather, it would be impossible to maintain the schedule. In the letter Childers wrote explaining this, it appeared to O'Rahilly that Childers was losing heart in the whole operation.

O'Rahilly appears to have written to express his dismay that Childers was not going ahead with the gun-running, but this letter has not been preserved. Childers answered that nothing was further from his thoughts than bailing out of the project. In this letter he confirms his total commitment, and says how much work he has already put into it, emphasizing that he has no intention of giving up:

I don't know how you read into my last letter such gloomy significance. It comes, I suppose, inevitably from the form one has to write in. I have been working incessantly at this business for a considerable time with all my strength and think of nothing else and foresee much harder and more responsible work to come . . . all of which it never occurs to me to grudge for the sake of the cause, and my wife is doing and thinking the same. We are also committed financially as deeply as means permit. Please do not think for a moment that I should turn back or lose hope, unless failure were certain, which is far from being the case.

Their differences were sorted out and the Childers plan was then put into effect. Two yachts were to bring the weapons to Ireland. The *Asgard* was to land them openly at Howth and the Irish Volunteers would march brazenly with them through Dublin, just as armed Ulster Volunteers were frequently marching through Belfast. If anything went wrong with the cargo carried by the *Asgard*, such as the British getting word of the operation and having a naval vessel at Howth to seize the yacht, then the other yacht, bringing the rest of the rifles secretly at night into Kilcoole, Co. Wicklow, would ensure that at least half the rifles were in the hands of the Volunteers.

Bulmer Hobson claimed later, when all those who could refute his claim were dead, that he was responsible for the decision to defy the British proclamation by marching openly with the rifles into Dublin. It is unlikely in the extreme to have been Hobson's decision. He was paralyzed with pusillanimity in every crisis or emergency.

The *Asgard* and the *Kelpie* were to meet at Cowes in the Isle of Wight where they were to settle the final details and send word to Figgis telling him of the timetable that had been arranged. Figgis, having inspected and passed the rifles, was to send them to Hamburg by train and then go there himself and charter a tug to take the rifles to the rendezvous. It has never been explained why the rifles were not sent to Antwerp from Liège, quite a short rail journey, instead of railing them several hundred miles north to Hamburg, and then having to carry them back the same distance by sea to the rendezvous in the English Channel.

The decision to ship them to Hamburg may have been because the Irish believed that, if the British got word of the gun-running, they would find it easier to put pressure on the Belgian government to seize the rifles than if they were in the free port of Hamburg.

An essential part of the plan was that Figgis was to come back to

Ireland and to be outside Howth harbour in a motor boat, to tell Childers if the Volunteers were ready to take the rifles and if the *Asgard* was to come in at the scheduled time of 12 noon on 26 July 1914.

Conor O'Brien's yacht, the *Kelpie*, was to bring half the rifles to the Welsh coast where they were to be transferred to a motor yacht owned by Sir Thomas Myles, who would bring them to Kilcoole and land them at midnight. The reason for the transfer to Myles's yacht was that a sailing vessel would find it difficult to meet an exact arrival time, but this would not be a problem with a motor yacht.

Sir Thomas Myles was a Limerick surgeon who was one of the most eminent in his profession. He had been elected president of the Royal College of Surgeons, and this position was normally honoured with a knighthood. He was a keen Irish nationalist, as he showed by bringing in this cargo of rifles. He also helped during the 1916 Rising. He knew of a Volunteer who had been wounded with a bullet through his lung and was in the Richmond hospital. Myles was afraid that the British would come to arrest him and decided to take him away. Sir Thomas was in some British medical organization which entitled him to wear a British army officer's uniform. He put on this uniform and was able to bring the wounded Volunteer, Eamon Martin, in his car through all the British army checkpoints.

The plans for the gun-running were simple and seemed to be foolproof, but nothing is certain when dealing with sailing boats. It took Childers longer than he expected to get his yacht ready, and there was delay in getting out of Conway Harbour, a port in North Wales, where he moored the *Asgard*. Mary Spring Rice and Molly Childers, who was crippled, were on board. When they finally did get started, they were battling against headwinds day after day along the Welsh coast. At one time the weather was so bad that they headed in towards Fishguard to take shelter. The weather improved and they were able to carry on, but Childers reproached himself for even having contemplated seeking a haven, and wasting time in the attempt. He regarded it as a sacrifice of duty for comfort.

The headwinds were so severe that the *Asgard*'s sails were damaged, and they were several days late arriving at Cowes. Conor O'Brien was in a towering rage at the delay. He complained that he had spent all his money while waiting for them and that he had been sending off telegrams to try to find out where they were.

There was further delay while repairs were made in Cowes and the *Asgard* sailed for the rendezvous a day later than the *Kelpie.* The weather was again unfavourable, with little wind, as they set out. The British navy was holding a major review of the fleet because of the mounting tension in Central Europe and the realization that it might lead to war. There were British battleships all around the yachts as they sailed through the English Channel.

By a miracle of navigation, Childers brought his yacht on time to meet the tug, only to be dismayed by the news that O'Brien's yacht had already come and gone, but had taken on board only 600 rifles, instead of the agreed 750. This meant that the *Asgard*, which was the same size as the *Kelpie*, had to take 900 rifles.

Before the *Asgard* arrived at the rendezvous, the crew had jettisoned most of the furniture from the main cabin, so this was then half-filled with rifles and everyone had to crawl over them in great discomfort. The yacht was heavily overloaded and low in the water. The last two boxes of ammunition had to be carried on deck, but the next morning Childers realized that they were not safe there and he dumped them overboard.

As they were setting out on the return journey, Childers had a sudden uneasy thought. They had never checked whether the ammunition fitted the rifles. Nervously he got a box open and was greatly relieved when he was able to fire a round to check the fit.

The journey back in the grossly overloaded yacht was uneventful, but on the last leg from Holyhead to Howth they had to contend with gale force winds. Childers spent the whole of that atrocious night at the helm and demonstrated his competence as a navigator when dawn broke next morning and he was dead on course for Howth.

The *Asgard* cruised around Lambay Island on that Sunday morning, waiting for the entry at noon and looking anxiously for the motor boat with Darrell Figgis on board, but there was no sign of it. Figgis's failure to meet them could not have been due to bad weather: the photograph of the *Asgard* sailing away after discharging her cargo shows clearly that the storm had abated, the wind was offshore and the sea was calm.

Most of the arrangements for the Howth gun-running were observed faithfully, and the 1,500 rifles were collected and delivered as planned (apart from O'Brien's failure to take his quota). The only serious snag was the failure of the motor boat to meet the *Asgard.* If Childers had decided not to come into Howth without the agreed clearance from Figgis, the whole operation would have ended as a fiasco. There has never been an explanation for the failure of Figgis to meet the *Asgard*. It raises the suspicion that some of the Volunteer leaders decided that the gun-running was too risky and hoped to abort it by not sending out the motor boat.

The yacht which brought the cargo of rifles that Sunday was described by O'Rahilly in his *Secret History* as the 'Harbinger of Liberty'. As soon as it had been unloaded, the Volunteers set off on the road back to Dublin. It was an historic occasion and men like MacNeill and O'Rahilly, who were familiar with Irish history, were elated at the thought that armed Irishmen, under Irish command, were about to march through the streets of Dublin for the first time since the Volunteers of 1782. Each man had a rifle on his shoulder, but they might just as well have been dummy rifles because no ammunition was issued to the Volunteers.

Hobson explained the strange decision to give the men rifles, but no means of defending themselves if an attempt was made to disarm them, when he said that the men were not sufficiently familiar with the use of firearms to entrust them with live rounds for their rifles. Hobson took responsibility for this decision, but since MacNeill was the commander-in-chief, he must have known and approved of Hobson's decision.

The Ulster Volunteers had different ideas. When their rifles were issued at Larne, every bundle of five rifles had its quota of ammunition wrapped up with it, so that each man getting a rifle was in a position to use it to defend himself. The essential difference was that the Ulster Volunteers were determined that no one would push them around, whereas the Irish Volunteers were the conquered people, making their first tentative attempts to regain their freedom.

Hobson halted the Volunteers at Raheny and was still there, half-an-hour later, when MacNeill, having had lunch at Howth, came along in a tram on his way back to Dublin. MacNeill wrote a long account of the Howth gun-running. It was addressed to Roger Casement and seemingly was given to Hobson to send to Casement in the United States. It was never sent to Casement but was found among Hobson's papers after his death in 1969. Probably Hobson was fearful about sending it to Casement because he was named as the person in charge of the Volunteers who had brought the rifles home from Howth.

In MacNeill's account, he says that when he saw the column halted at Raheny, he 'requested' Hobson to resume the march into Dublin. The halt at Raheny was not just for a rest and a smoke. They were halted there for half-an-hour. It seems likely that Hobson lost his courage as they approached the city and was afraid to proceed until MacNeill 'requested' them to do so. MacNeill marched some distance with them and then was given a lift in a car to Nelson's Pillar. From there he took a tram home.

MacNeill wrote to Casement that when the car in which he was driven into the city was passing through Clontarf, there was no sign of any police or military. However, when the column of Volunteers reached Clontarf about an hour later, the police and soldiers were drawn across the road and would not let it pass. There was a parallel road into Dublin which some of the Volunteers thought of using, but when the police saw this move, they quickly deployed some of their men and soldiers to block this road also.

When the Volunteers came face to face with the police and soldiers, the police officer said that the armed Volunteers would not be allowed to march into Dublin, and he demanded that they surrender their rifles. Thomas MacDonagh was at the head of the Volunteer column and he argued that there was no law compelling them to surrender their rifles. He pointed out that armed Ulster Volunteers were parading regularly through Belfast and asked how could there be one law for Belfast and a different one for Dublin.

The police officer made it quite clear that he had no intention of allowing them to proceed any further, and he ordered his men to disarm the Volunteers. This led to scuffles in which some Volunteers were hurt, but not seriously. A number of policemen refused to obey the order to seize the arms and they were dismissed from the force on the spot. However, they were reinstated the next day.

The soldiers, with fixed bayonets, assisted the police in their efforts to seize the rifles and they managed to get sixteen rifles, which were returned the following day. One of the Volunteer leaders, a man named Judd (or Judge), was knocked to the ground and received a bayonet wound in the shoulder. I recall this man visiting our house some weeks later and being asked to lift back his shirt to show us his wound. It was the first wound inflicted by the occupation forces in the struggle which ended with the withdrawal of the British army from most of Ireland.

While this confrontation was going on at the head of the column, the Volunteers at the rear quietly dispersed and dumped their rifles in houses and gardens beside the road along which they had come. The Citizen Army managed to secure some of these rifles before the Volunteers came back to retrieve them and these were the weapons which armed that body.

A fleet of cars and taxis, including O'Rahilly's scar, were at the Howth pier at noon on that Sunday, to bring back to Dublin the ammunition and any rifles that could not be carried by the Volunteers. O'Rahilly was in civilian clothes and he brought his two sisters with him to allay suspicion. When he reached the city on the return journey, with the car loaded with boxes of ammunition, the engine stalled and he could not get it restarted. Policemen looked on as the munitions he was carrying were transferred to another vehicle, but they did not interfere. All the ammunition that was carried in the cars and taxis was stored in safe houses in the city.

The commissioner in charge of the police at Clontarf was a Mr Harrel. When he saw the Volunteers disappear and dispose of their rifles, he sent the police and the soldiers back to their depots and barracks. The story went around Dublin that there had been trouble and one of the hurt Volunteers had been taken through the city in a motor cycle sidecar with a bandage around his head. This relatively minor encounter became magnified in the telling to a major confrontation, with rumours that the soldiers had bayoneted many of the Volunteers.

A crowd of men, women and children followed the soldiers, members of the King's Own Scottish Borderers, as they made their way through the city back to their barracks. The crowd were shouting insults at the soldiers; it was alleged that stones were thrown; but none of the soldiers suffered any injury.

When the soldiers reached O'Connell Bridge, they turned to the right along Bachelor's Walk and then trouble began. The official enquiry stated later that it was unfortunate that the police had not marched with the soldiers, because a small body of police would have had no trouble dispersing the crowd. The official report continued:

By this time Major Haig, who had heard of the disturbances, had joined the force, and being the senior officer took command. The crowd were occasionally kept in check by the action of the rear-guard turning and making feints with fixed bayonets: upon which occasions the crowd dispersed, gathering again in a little time and still continuing its course of unjustifiable and mischievous misconduct.

Upon the other hand the Commissioners do not doubt that the soldiers, through great provocation, got out of temper and partly out of hand. Sometimes they would pursue the crowd for some distance, chase people into shops and in one case a soldier drove a bayonet through a shop door. We do not think that the officers could have failed to observe this . . . .

A particularly unfortunate incident of the situation was that Major Haig — from his arrival until the occurrence of the firing on the crowd by a large body of men — was not aware that the rifles of these men were loaded.

At about the corner of Liffey St. that officer [Major Haig] being of the opinion that the conduct of the crowd was past endurance, told off about 30 men, who turned and lined across the road with fixed bayonets, four or five men kneeling. To five or six of the men Major Craig spoke hurriedly, asking each one if he were loaded, and to be ready to fire if he gave the order. We are not satisfied, upon the evidence, that there was any particular excess of violence by the crowd at this point, although the throwing of stones and other missiles was continuing. A laundaulette passed on quietly through troops and crowd without injury.

Some witnesses say that there was no more than throwing of banana skins, others that the stone throwing was severe. We think that one soldier, in a tussle with civilians, was knocked down. On the whole our opinion was that the fracas was of such a kind and dimension as a small force of police would have quickly settled. We are of the opinion that no occasion had actually arisen for using loaded firearms. These were the circumstances in which Major Craig lined up his men and instructed them as mentioned.

That officer stated, in evidence, that first his intention was to warn the crowd, and secondly, in the event of the threatening and the stone throwing of the crowd continuing, he would have asked that those men so spoken to shoot two particular ring-leaders to be pointed out by himself. He plainly disapproved, in his evidence of the action, any notion of an order given to troops in general to fire indiscriminately upon a crowd.

This, however, is what occurred. We are satisfied that neither Major Craig, nor any of his fellow-officers, did give an order to fire. But not only did firing take without an order, but it was indiscriminate firing. Twenty-one men discharged their rifles at the crowd. Twenty-nine shots were fired. Three people were killed; at least thirty-eight were injured, and fifteen of these so seriously as to be detained in hospital. It is a feature also of the transaction that one of the dead and some of the injured appeared to have had upon their bodies, not only bullet but bayonet wounds . . . . The firing, in short, was at large, without distinction of age or sex, and was at short range.

This was the massacre of civilians, by the King's Own Scottish Borderers, on Bachelor's Walk, on 26 July 1914. This Major Haig could not abide the idea that a crowd of rabble in a colony should have dared to shout insulting remarks at British soldiers: it was a classic example of the arrogance of the 'master race' towards the conquered helots. The crowd were told, in no uncertain terms, 'Croppy lie down'. Major Haig would show them who was the 'master race' and he did. It was the first time in over a hundred years that British soldiers had fired on a crowd of civilians in a part of what was then called the British Isles.

Three people were killed and thirty-eight more injured. The only explanation as to why there were not more casualties is that the crowd dispersed so completely and so rapidly that the soldiers could not shoot or bayonet any more people. It is quite clear, from the official report, that it was not just soldiers firing from a distance at a crowd of civilians, which would have been bad enough. What obviously happened was that the soldiers charged with fixed bayonets at the crowd and, in many cases, having inflicted bayonet wounds, the soldier, while his bayonet was still stuck in his victim, then fired his rifle. One witness said that an officer deliberately shot a woman at point-blank range. Even on Major Haig's own evidence to the enquiry, he admitted that he had decided to inflict summary sentence of death on one or two of the ringleaders in the crowd.

When the outrage of Bachelor's Walk was raised in the House of Commons some days later, it was a matter of grave embarrassment to the government and to Asquith, the Prime Minister. He promised a full enquiry into the shooting and in the meantime said that the importation of arms into Ireland was not in itself a serious matter, adding that the proclamation had 'exhausted itself'. It is not clear what he meant by this phrase. He may have had in mind that, when it was imposed in November 1913, it was hoped that it would end the importation of arms into Ireland, but since it had not done so, it served no further purpose. The legal validity of the ban was also being challenged in the courts.

During the first eight months of 1913, before the ban was imposed, the gunsmiths of Belfast had been having a bonanza selling rifles to the Ulster Volunteers. The Royal Irish Constabulary estimated that, by the middle of 1914, these men had over 50,000 rifles. Since half of these had been imported at the Larne gun-running, the Ulster Volunteers had purchased 25,000 rifles legally from the gunsmiths of Belfast. These gunsmiths were reluctant to forego this lucrative trade and started legal proceedings in the Four

Courts in Dublin, to question the validity of a law which differentiated Ireland from Britain when they were supposed to be a single legal entity. Two of the Dublin judges in the High Court ruled that the ban was legal, but the third said that it was not. This judgment was to be appealed.

The British government may have decided that the easiest way out of this legal tangle was to revoke the ban and this was done early in August 1914. They may also have decided that, if the ban could not be enforced in the North of Ireland, it was not possible to maintain it in the South.

A final reason may have been that, because Redmond now had control of the Irish Volunteers, Asquith wanted to do everything possible to get his support, so that if the threatened war in Europe did take place, he would have Redmond on his side. Asquith may have decided that removing the ban on the import of arms was a small price to pay for this support. There was also the consideration that, if there was war in Europe, there was little possibility of rifles being available, whether or not a ban was in force. Whatever the British government's reasons for lifting the ban, the net result was that it again became legal, from early in August 1914, to import arms into Ireland.

If the leaders of the Volunteers (or rather the small number who had made the plans for the Howth gun-running) had been trying to arrange matters so that the importation of this small cargo of arms, in defiance of the British ban, would have the maximum possible effect in awakening Irish national spirit and pride, they could not, in their most optimistic dreams, have thought of anything so effective as what Major Haig did for them that Sunday afternoon on Bachelor's Walk.

There were few people in Ireland, either Catholic or Protestant, nationalist or unionist, who were not in a frenzy of 'savage indignation' at what the Scottish Borderers had done. The average Irishman had only one way of expressing his resentment and that was by joining the Irish Volunteers. It is estimated that, within a month of the Bachelor's Walk atrocity, the numbers enrolled had doubled to about 150,000. The killings that Sunday also resulted in the ban on the importation of rifles being removed and this was the means of getting a really sizeable supply of arms for the Volunteers.

O'Rahilly knew that there would be no chance that the enlarged executive of the Volunteers would be willing to agree to the purchase of any substantial quantity of weapons, so he decided to get approval by means of subterfuge. He proposed to the executive that they should decide on a standard bore rifle and purchase only weapons of this calibre. He suggested the British army bore of ·303 and this was agreed. O'Rahilly then said that he supposed he was entitled to purchase any weapons of this bore which became available and no one dissented.

With this approval, he went to Birmingham and arranged to buy the entire output of Martini Enfield rifles made by the firm of Greener & Company. This was a single shot weapon of ·303 bore and was available in two models, a short and a long version. The output of this firm has been estimated at 800 rifles per week. Since this purchase went on for three months, it provided the Volunteers with about 10,000 modern rifles.

The lifting of the ban enabled these Martini Enfield rifles to be imported legally. Most of them went to Redmond's National Volunteers, but it was those in the hands of the Irish Volunteers that made the 1916 Rising possible.

O'Rahilly said that the supply of these rifles ceased when the British government ordered the plant making them to be dismantled. What seems likely to have happened is that, when the War Office was recruiting Kitchener's New Army of one million men, they needed the whole rifle-making capacity of Britain to supply them with weapons. All these weapons had to be of the same pattern and so all the rifle-making firms in Britain were ordered to retool to make the short Lee Enfield magazine rifle.

The total cost of both the Howth and the Greener rifles with ammunition would have been about £15,000, which was much in excess of any money available to the executive. Most of this money was provided by individual Volunteers out of their own, mostly scant, funds. The men who could not pay in full were allowed to buy on a hire purchase basis. This may have been the first known sale of goods by hire purchase. If so, it was another original contribution made by O'Rahilly.

When O'Rahilly had disposed of the boxes of ammunition in a safe house, he went back to his sister's home on Northumberland Road. He was staying there while his own family were in the Kerry bungalow. His cousin Frank came in to talk about the events of the day. Frank had been on a tram going across O'Connell Bridge as the shooting was taking place, but he attached no significance to it because he had assumed that blank cartridges were being fired to disperse the crowd.

It is not known how O'Rahilly got word of the shooting in Bachelor's Walk, but the news of such an atrocity would have spread quickly in a city the size of Dublin. When he was told about it, O'Rahilly lost no time in getting his Mauser pistol, 'Peter the Painter', and boarding a tram for the city centre. If there were soldiers still on the rampage, they would find that someone was shooting back at them.

In the tram he realized that he had papers in his pocket which he would not want the British to get if he was killed or wounded. The only way to dispose of them was to burn them, and this he proceeded to do. He lit matches to burn each piece of paper, while his fellow passengers looked on, wondering what it was all about.

When O'Rahilly reached O'Connell Bridge, all was quiet and peaceful. The dead had been removed to the city morgue, and the wounded to various hospitals. He walked on down to the GPO and sent a telegram to his wife, which she received the following morning: 'Fierce shooting here to-day. I was not hit at all.' The message almost implied a disappointment that he was unscathed.

Pearse was on holiday in his Connemara cottage on that July Sunday. When he heard about Howth, he was clearly resentful that an event of such fundamental importance in the fight for Irish freedom should have taken place without his having been involved or even told about it.

He wrote to Joe McGarrity, with whom he had stayed in Philadelphia during his long visit to the US earlier that year. This letter reflects no credit on Pearse. In it he complains about the quality of the imported rifles, and says that the ammunition is dum-dum, outlawed by all civilized nations. This was nonsense. He had not seen one of the rifles and, even if he had, he was not competent to assess them.

The rifles were not modern. It would have been easy for O'Rahilly to have bought 200 or 300 modern magazine rifles for the same money. The rifles were obsolete in the sense that no European army would have equipped their soldiers with them at that time. But Childers, who had been in the British army and had expertise in such matters, had examined an alternative source of supply and had decided that the weapons chosen by O'Rahilly were more suitable.

It was essential for the leaders of the Volunteers to be able to give weapons to as many of their men as possible. If a man has a weapon, it gives him a feeling of confidence, an essential requirement for a soldier. The range or accuracy of the weapon has little to do with the confidence it inspires.

A recent historian has quoted Pearse's assessment of the Howth munitions as though it should be taken seriously because Pearse wrote it. Pearse was writing about a weapon he had not seen, and on a subject of which he had no knowledge. The lead bullets were identical to those used in every British army officer's revolver. They were not dum-dum bullets.

Another point of interest in Pearse's letter is his request for one thousand rifles to be sent to what he refers as 'Our People'. It is clear that, even at that time, only eight months after the formation of the Volunteers, Pearse already had begun to regard himself as the leader of a small group of 'sea green incorruptibles'. He was mentally rejecting the notion of a united movement of all Irish nationalists, who might have had some chance of expelling the British from Ireland. Instead of which, he was to become the leader of a small body of these 'ultras', who would sacrifice themselves even if they achieved nothing.

It is also worth noting that Pearse had been with Devoy, as well as McGarrity, during his lengthy stay in the US. He knew there were no restrictions on the purchase or export of weapons from there. Yet neither he nor Hobson, both of whom had stayed with McGarrity, had made any effort to persuade the Irish Americans to send a consignment of arms to Ireland. As far as is known, Pearse's plea to McGarrity for a supply of rifles did not produce any response.

The 600 rifles that Conor O'Brien had handed over to Sir Thomas Myles's yacht, off the coast of Wales, were landed safely later that week, in the middle of the night, at Kilcoole, Co. Wicklow. This operation was under the control of Seán Fitzgibbon, and it all went smoothly until the lorry bringing the rifles to Dublin broke down at Bray. It was then necessary to organize a fleet of private cars and taxis to take them to various safe dumps in the city.

When the Provisional Committee of the Volunteers, which now contained a majority of Redmondites, heard of the secret landing at Kilcoole, they also wanted those rifles to be sent to the North of Ireland. They ordered an enquiry to find out what had become of them, but the rifles could not be found; the Volunteers who had secured them had no intention of parting with them. The reason the committee insisted that all the rifles should be sent to the North was to enable the nationalists there to defend themselves if they were attacked by the Ulster Volunteers. Most of the Howth rifles were sent to the North, while most of those landed in Kilcoole were kept in Dublin.

The Howth gun-running was the first step in the 'physical force' movement which led to the British deciding to move out of the twenty-six counties. Those who played an active part in this operation were Mary Spring Rice, Alice Stopford Green, Erskine and Molly Childers, Conor O'Brien, Darrell Figgis, Mr Gordon, Sir Thomas Myles and O'Rahilly. Eoin MacNeill and Bulmer Hobson were aware of the plans, but did not play an active part. It is of interest to note that all those actively involved were Protestants, with the exception of O'Rahilly. One of those who helped to crew the *Asgard* was a 'Mr Gordon'. This is how Mary Spring Rice always referred to him. He was a British army officer who was a yachting friend of the Childers. On the return journey, he had had to leave the yacht at a Welsh port to rejoin his regiment, but he was at Howth the following Sunday for the landing.

The landing of arms at Howth and the purchase of the Greener rifles meant that O'Rahilly had achieved his objective of a body of Irishmen, able and willing to fight, and if necessary to die, to end the British occupatioin of their country. Without this supply of arms, the Rising of 1916 and the Declaration of the Republic would not have been possible.

A small incident in connection with the Howth gun-running will give an idea of life in Dublin during the occupation. When O'Rahilly was making plans for the landing of the rifles, he needed to make a thorough inspection of the pier at Howth and the surrounding area. He was constantly watched and followed by 'G' men, plain clothes men of the Dublin Metropolitan Police, so one Saturday, to allay suspicion, he announced that we were going for a drive. With his three children and two Humphreys children in the car, he set off for Portmarnock, giving the impression he was just bringing us out for an afternoon drive.

He left us all at Portmarnock and drove to Howth alone. That afternoon there was an outing of Baden-Powell boy scouts at Portmarnock. They were a British group and at their camp had put up a flagpole from which a Union Jack was flying. We watched our chance and, when there was no one around, we rushed in and removed the flag which we either buried or burnt.

When my father returned, we could not wait to tell him the good afternoon's work we had done for Ireland. He was very upset and scolded us. We were deflated and could not understand how it could have been anything but a heroic deed to have captured the flag. His niece Sighle was the eldest of the five children and, after the gun-running, he apologized to her, explaining that he had gone off to reconnoitre Howth. If the police had caught us, they might well have wanted to know where he had gone and what he had been doing while his children had been stealing other people's property. But all was well and the scouts never knew the identity of the gang, average age about ten or eleven, who had captured their Union Jack.

In his *Secret History of the Irish Volunteers*, O'Rahilly said that the Volunteers had missed their best opportunity of getting a supply of arms when Laurence Kettle received an offer of 27,000 modern magazine rifles, with a supply of ammunition, at a price of £4 each. Kettle did not inform O'Rahilly, who was responsible for the procurement of arms, of this offer. The reference O'Rahilly made to Kettle's failure to tell him implies that it was within their capacity to have financed such a purchase, but does not indicate where he would have found the funds. He may have had in mind that the improved status given to the Volunteers by the admission of the Redmond nominees would somehow have made such a purchase possible. He was certainly entitled to resent that he had not been informed of the offer.

When O'Rahilly wrote this pamphlet, he was not aware of an altogether better offer that had been within their grasp but had been missed. In November 1914 the German ambassador in the US, Count von Bernstorff, sent a wireless message to his Foreign Office in Berlin:

There have been purchased for India eleven thousand rifles, four million cartridges, two hundred and fifty Mauser pistols, five hundred revolvers with ammunition. Devoy does not think it possible to ship them to Ireland.

In his youth Devoy had played an active part in the Irish revolutionary movement, and had organized an expedition to Australia with the *Catalpa* sailing vessel to rescue Irish political prisoners. Since then he had kept alive the Irish revolutionary tradition in the United States, both as head of Clan na Gael and as editor of the *Gaelic American.*

Devoy wrote several books dealing with that period and kept many of the documents relating to the various events in which he had played a part, but in none of these is there any reference to this German offer of a substantial armament of modern weapons, at no cost, which could have been imported legally into Ireland.

It is clear from the German ambassador's message that, having bought these weapons for India, and having found they could not be shipped there, they had been offered to Ireland and Devoy had refused them. There was never any restriction on the export of arms from the US, so there was no danger of Devoy getting into trouble with the authorities for shipping out rifles. He would have been sufficiently in touch with events in Ireland to have known that, following the 'massacre of Bachelor's Walk', the British had lifted the ban on the import of arms into Ireland. This cargo of weapons, offered by the Germans, could have been loaded legally on a small steamer, or a large fishing vessel, at any American port, and she could legally have sailed into an Irish port to discharge her cargo.

No one will ever know what the British might have done to block such a shipment. If the cargo had been kept a secret, or if the vessel had left the US ostensibly bound for some port in South America, and if a monster parade of all the Irish Volunteers had been organized in Dublin, it might have been possible to repeat the Howth gun-running, but on a scale more than ten times larger.

The very least that Devoy should have done, when he received this offer, was to have sent a messenger urgently to Dublin to enquire from the Volunteer leaders what to do about it. It has never been suggested that Devoy was a pacifist or had any objection to the shedding of human blood. He put on record a bitter criticism of Roger Casement for having come to Ireland from Germany to endeavour to have the Rising cancelled. From this we can only conclude that, while Devoy wanted the young men of Ireland to rise in rebellion, he rejected an offer which would have given them adequate equipment. Devoy was clearly ashamed of this refusal and he never made any reference to it in anything he wrote subsequently. The facts did not come to light until the British published their *Documents Relative to the Sinn Féin Movement* pamphlet in the early 1920s (see Appendix 7).

If a motive is sought for Devoy's refusal of the German offer of weapons, the only one which comes to mind is that he realized that if such an arsenal of weapons had been sent to Ireland and distributed to the Volunteers, an Irish Rising might succeed in driving out the British. If this had been achieved, it would have finished his political existence. The end of the British occupation of Ireland would also have meant the end of Clan na Gael.

The British in room 40 of the Admiralty in London read and decoded this message from von Bernstorff to his Foreign Office and knew what a good turn Devoy had done them: they had narrowly escaped a situation in which they might have had to deal with a large force of well-armed Irish Volunteers. On the morning following the decoding of the message, the British reimposed the ban on the importation of arms into Ireland, in case Devoy might change his mind.

However, the ban now applied only to arms for the Irish Volunteers. Both Redmond's 'National Volunteers' and Carson's 'Ulster Volunteers' were doing everything they could to get recruits for Kitchener's army, and the British did not want to make any move which might antagonize either organization.

It is sad to have to report this damning indictment of this man in his old age. As a young man Devoy had done much to help the fight for Irish independence, but there is no honourable explanation for his refusal of this offer which would have transformed the effectiveness of the Irish Volunteers.

Devoy's refusal to accept this large consignment of modern weapons ended any hope of a significant supply of rifles for the Irish Volunteers. Redmond had promised to supply rifles when he had control of the Volunteers, but he did not honour this promise. The few that did arrive were worthless scrap metal and there was no ammunition for them.

The result of the efforts to arm the Volunteers in Ireland was recorded by the Royal Irish Constabulary, who knew the where-abouts of every rifle and the political affiliation of every owner. Their assessment of the situation at the time of the 1916 Rising was as follows:

Ulster Volunteers	51,539
Redmond's National Volunteers	8,834
Irish Volunteers	2,534
Total	62,907

The 11,368 in the hands of the National and the Irish Volunteers included both the Howth and the Greener rifles.

12

World War I

In the week following the Bachelor's Walk atrocity, there was a growing realization that Ireland had more things to worry about than the dead and wounded of that day. The assassination of the Austrian Crown Prince at Sarajevo led to an Austrian ultimatum to Serbia, which no country could accept. It was, in effect, a German ultimatum to Russia, which meant a German declaration of war on France, a country allied to Russia. This was the war which was generally expected for more than ten years during which the Germans had been building up the greatest army the world had ever known, and the European powers surrounding Germany had built up their own armies in the hope of being able to contain German expansion. Many people believed war to be inevitable.

It was the war O'Rahilly had in mind when he ended his series of articles in 1912 with his exhortation to Irish nationalists: 'Let it be the duty of all those who desire their country's freedom, that if such an opportunity occurs again, we are in a position to avail of it.' If many saw this war as the unavoidable climax to the tensions that had been building up in Europe since Bismarck had united the German states, no one could foresee the nature of the conflict which would result when the vast manpower of most of the states of Europe was harnessed to the potential armament production of the industrialized Western world. It was commonly believed that it would be a short intensive war and would be over in a few months. Many of the young men of Britain who rushed to join up were worried that the war would be over before they had seen any action. There was no general awareness that the defensive power of the machine gun in a concrete 'pill box' had transformed the nature of warfare.

Irish nationalists had always believed that 'England's difficulty is Ireland's opportunity'. Yet in August 1914 only a tiny minority of these nationalists regarded the war in which England was about to embark as the opportunity for which Ireland had been waiting. The sympathy of most Irish people was with England, and they had no desire to use her difficulty for Ireland's benefit. This change of sympathy appeared to have been justified when Redmond got the Irish Home Rule Bill passed by the British Parliament. The enactment of this Bill produced in Ireland a groundswell of goodwill towards the British. From the day the war started, the sympathy of most Irish nationalist MPs was for the Allies. Indeed, many of them had become mentally British subjects. If Irish nationalists were looking for guidance from the Irish Party, to know which side to support, there would have been no doubt as to the advice they would get.

No one could be certain whether Ireland would be better, or worse off, if Germany won the war. It was unrealistic to imagine, as some Irish people did, that the Germans were knights in shining armour, who were concerned about the welfare of the Irish. But it might suit Germany to have an independent and prosperous Ireland, whereas the British interest was in an Ireland subservient and undeveloped.

Even among those who were undecided, the ruthless jack-boot methods of the Germans in overrunning Belgium were not calculated to arouse any sympathy for their war aims, but what cannot be explained or excused is that Redmond and his party did not see that, regardless of where their sympathies lay, the war gave Ireland a bargaining power of enormous potential. It was the duty of the Redmondites to have used this power for the benefit of Ireland, and this they failed to do.

The British were keenly aware of the power that England's difficulty gave Redmond. It was clearly spelled out in Mrs Asquith's autobiography. She was the wife of the British Prime Minister and this is how she described the events leading up to the declaration of war:

We were still worried over the Irish question, and after dinner I wrote a letter to Mr Redmond, telling him that he had the opportunity of his life of setting an unforgettable example to the Carsonites, if he would go to the House of Commons on the Monday, and in a great speech offer all his soldiers to the Government; or, if he preferred it, to the King.

It appeared to me that it would be a dramatic thing to do at such a moment, and might strengthen the claim of Ireland on the gratitude of the English people.

Redmond replied the next day, 2 August: 'I received your letter late last night. I am very grateful to you for it. I hope to see the Prime Minister to-morrow, before the House meets, if only for a few moments, and I hope I may be able to follow your advice.'

One assumes that Redmond demanded some commitment from Asquith as the price for his support; but since Asquith was already willing to concede Home Rule, surely Redmond should have demanded a commitment from Bonar Law, the Conservative leader; he was supporting Carson and the Orangemen who were opposing Home Rule.

The next day in Parliament, Sir Edward Grey, the Foreign Secretary, made his speech announcing the declaration of war. He was at pains to emphasize the terrible consequences of the war for Britain, 'whether we are in it or whether we stand aside'. Then with a sudden lift in his voice, he added, 'One thing I would say. The one bright spot in a very dreadful situation is Ireland. The position in Ireland — and this I should like to be clearly understood abroad — is not a consideration in the things we have to take into account now.'

We do not know what assurances Redmond gave Asquith when he saw him, which enabled Grey to tell the House that Ireland would make no trouble. More importantly, it has not emerged what commitment, if any, Redmond was given in return.

It does not seem to have occurred to Redmond that this was his chance to hold the British up to ransom. The least he should have insisted on, if the Irish promised not to make any trouble, was a written assurance from Carson and Bonar Law that, in return for this commitment, they would accept the Irish Home Rule Bill which had been passed by Westminster.

If such a written commitment had not been forthcoming, as it may well not have been, and if, as a result, Britain had decided not to go to war, and if France had then been defeated in a short war with few casualties, Redmond would have done more for humanity than he could ever have hoped it would be in his power to accomplish.

When Grey told the House, and the world was listening, that the 'one bright spot in a very dreadful situation is Ireland', Redmond was elated and, having consulted two of his colleagues, got up to address the House. He pointed out the analogy with the situation at the time of the American Revolution when British power was at its lowest ebb, and the Irish Volunteers of those days were recruited to repel a possible invasion of Ireland; Redmond said that the British 'may take their troops away, and that if it be allowed to us, in comradeship with our brothers in the North, we will ourselves defend the coasts of our country.'

During the first month of the war, it seemed possible that France would be overrun by the Germans, just as she had been in 1870, and that Britain might be left to fight alone, with whatever help Russia could give. The British even thought of arming the Irish Volunteers, which Redmond promised in a speech at Maryborough in mid-August. However, when the French succeeded in halting the German advance, and the possibility of a German invasion of Ireland was remote, then any question of arming the Volunteers for the defence of Ireland was no longer considered. What the British needed were troops from Ireland for the war in Europe, and the War Office could not get enough of them.

The campaign for recruits began when Sir Bryan Mahon came to Ireland and inspected Volunteer companies in many parts of the country. At the end of each review he asked the men if they would join the British army to fight for the 'freedom of small nations'. The irony of asking the Irish to fight in the British army for the freedom of other small nations, a freedom that the British were denying to Ireland, does not seem to have occurred to Mahon. The reply he got after every meeting was that it depended on what Mr Redmond advised. When Mahon reported this back in London, Redmond came under intense pressure to advise the Volunteers to enlist.

Redmond held out for a few weeks, and he may have demanded some quid pro quo. What seems most likely is that he wanted Asquith to carry out his promise to put the Home Rule Bill on the statute book. This was a meaningless gesture, but Asquith may have been reluctant to do it to avoid antagonizing Carson any further.

Those who were close to Redmond knew that he was wavering on the question of advising the Volunteers to join the British army. The issue was discussed at a meeting in the House of Commons attended by Colonel Maurice Moore, Willie Redmond and some others. Most of those present urged Redmond not to advise the Irish Volunteers to enlist. However, when he was leaving the meeting, he said that he had made up his mind to support recruiting. Moore asked Willie Redmond to try to dissuade his brother from taking this radical and irrevocable decision, but Willie Redmond said that he did not think he could influence him and he advised Moore to write to Redmond. Moore did write, but the letter did not arrive until after Redmond had left for Ireland.

Redmond's supporters had presented him with a motor car as a token of their appreciation of his success in getting the Home Rule Bill passed, and he set out for Ireland in this car. Moore met him on his way down to Waterford, and they stopped to have lunch somewhere in County Wicklow. During lunch they were told that there was to be a Volunteer parade in Woodenbridge, and the local people were most anxious to have Redmond inspect the parade and make a short speech. Redmond told them that he had decided that his first public speech, following the passage of the Home Rule Bill, would be in his own constituency of Waterford; but the local people pressed him and he could not refuse.

Redmond then made the most famous, and the most disastrous, speech of his political career. It came to be recognized as the speech that brought the Irish Party to an inglorious end. It is not known, to this day, what Redmond got from Asquith to induce him to advise the Volunteers to enlist. It is probable that all he got for taking on the role of a recruiting sergeant for the British army was that Asquith had carried out his promise by putting the Home Rule Bill on the statute book the previous Friday. This formality added nothing to the enactment by the British Parliament of the Irish Home Rule Bill. Carson described it correctly when he said 'It is a scrap of paper which could be torn up.'

Colonel Moore considered it utterly irresponsible for Redmond to have delivered a political harangue to men on parade. They were soldiers under discipline and could not answer back or express a contrary opinion. Moore blamed himself later that he had not, there and then, spoken to the men, and told them that what they heard was merely a personal political opinion, and one which he himself did not share.

When it emerged several years later that the Woodenbridge speech had been a disaster for the Irish Party, many of the leading Irish MPs resented the fact that Redmond should have taken it on himself to make this speech without consulting his colleagues.

However, there is no record that any one of them had publicly found fault with Redmond for urging the Volunteers to join the British army. F.S.L. Lyons, in his biography of John Dillon, notes that, while Dillon several years later was critical of Redmond's recruiting speech, there was no evidence in anything Dillon said or wrote at the time to suggest that he disapproved of what Redmond had said at Woodenbridge.

The following is generally given as the substance of Redmond's Woodenbridge speech on 21 September 1914, but it is probably an abridged version of what he said:

Wicklow Volunteers, in spite of the peaceful happiness and beauty of the scene in which we stand, remember this country at this moment is in a state of war, and your duty is a twofold duty. The duty of the manhood of Ireland is twofold. Its duty is, at all costs, to defend the shores of Ireland against foreign invasion. It is a duty more than that of taking care that Irish valour proves itself; on the field of war it has always proved itself in the past. The interests of Ireland, of the whole of Ireland, are at stake in this war. This war is undertaken in defence of the highest principles of religion and morality and right, and it would be a disgrace for ever to our country, a reproach to her manhood, and a denial of the lessons of her history, if young Ireland confined their efforts to remaining at home to defend the shores of Ireland from an unlikely invasion, and shrunk from the duty of proving on the field of battle that gallantry and courage which have distinguished our race all through its history. I say to you, therefore, your duty is twofold. I am glad to see such magnificent material for soldiers around me, and I say to you – Go on drilling and make yourselves efficient for the work, and then account yourselves as men, not only in Ireland itself, but wherever the firing line extends, in defence of right, of freedom, and religion in this war.

In accounts of the speech it is usually suggested that Redmond gave a spontaneous impromptu address; but it is most unlikely that a politician of his experience would have made a statement of such fundamental importance without careful consideration. It seems most likely that the speech, well thought out and memorized, was to have been delivered at Waterford, but when he was urged to say a few words at Woodenbridge he decided to make his recruiting speech there instead.

The reaction of the men who had formed the Volunteers was predictable. Redmond's speech in the House of Commons on the declaration of war was entirely acceptable to them. These Volunteer leaders welcomed the proposal he then made to have the British army withdraw from Ireland, and the defence of the country left to the Volunteers. Radical nationalists would have hoped that if the British left, there would be good prospects of preventing them ever returning.

But when Redmond advised the Volunteers to join the British army, to fight on the side of, instead of against, the only enemy Ireland ever had, they were outraged. Most of them were out and out pro-German in their views. Their only desire was to see Britain and her empire utterly defeated and they were prepared to take a chance on the outcome for Ireland of such a British defeat.

I recall my mother and father talking about how the outcome of the war might affect them. Many of the investments on which they lived were in British companies, yet, despite this, O'Rahilly's lifelong hope was to see Britain defeated, even if it meant the destruction of those companies that supplied their income. Mother took a more pragmatic view, pointing out that a British defeat would be financially disastrous to them since they would have no income. But no such consideration worried Michael. 'We will meet that situation when it comes', he said, 'I can always make a living running a garage.'

Redmond could claim that his nominees and supporters on the Provisional Committee were at that time in a majority and that he spoke for that majority, even though they had not been consulted. But whether majority or minority, there was no possibility that men like O'Rahilly, and most of those who had started the Volunteers, were going to remain in an organization whose declared objective was to encourage recruiting for the British army.

The men who had founded the Irish Volunteers called a meeting and repudiated Redmond's advice to enlist. They also expelled all the Redmond nominees from the executive committee, and the movement which might have broken the British grip on Ireland, without the shedding of a single drop of human blood, was now divided into a 90 per cent majority who followed Redmond and a 10 per cent minority who followed MacNeill. Redmond called his followers the 'National Volunteers' and this body gradually faded out of existence. The men who opted for Redmond, if they remained active, were subject to all kinds of pressures to enlist in the British army, which most of them did. If they were not willing to enlist, there was little point in attending parades. However, in the funeral procession at the burial of Jeremiah O'Donovan Rossa in

Dublin on 1 August 1915, both Redmond's National Volunteers and the small minority of Irish Volunteers joined forces. This minority continued to drill and train and whenever possible to obtain arms, and these were the men who staged the Rising of 1916.

13

England's Difficulty, Ireland's Opportunity

From the time of the Woodenbridge speech until the end of the war, the main activity of the Irish Party was giving all possible assistance to the British drive for recruits. They organized a vast propaganda campaign for the hearts and minds of the Irish people. It went on for the four years of the war. No matter how many enlisted, the demand was insatiable. There were recruiting meetings in every city, town and village. British army bands marched through the streets to gather crowds for these meetings, in the knowledge that people would be attracted by the marshal music.

The result of this recruiting campaign was that 250,000 Irishmen enlisted in a foreign army to fight in a foreign war. It is not possible to compare the percentage who joined up in Ireland with other countries because in all other countries involved in the war, the men were conscripted.

In this drive to get voluntary recruits, no effort or pressure was spared. The press gave its wholehearted support. The public bodies made their own contribution. The Catholic Church may not have given active support, but it did nothing to discourage the campaign. I recall my father walking out of Mass when the priest said that some young man who had been killed in France had given his life for 'King and Country'. Employers discharged any workers they could spare to put pressure on them to enlist. Girls went around the streets pinning white feathers to the jackets of young men of military age in civilian clothing.

Young men from every category of Irish family enlisted. The first to join were the Anglo-Irish. In many of these families there was a tradition of service in the British armed forces, so that only the strong-minded or the very cowardly failed to join. Young men of this tradition had their own Officers Training Corps at Trinity College, Dublin. This corps and their instructors held the Trinity College area for the British during the 1916 Rebellion.

Then there were the Catholic bourgeoisie, the boys from schools like Belvedere and Clongowes. They would have had an Irish Party background and would have taken Redmond's advice. The extent to which they did so emerged when the war was over and the Clongowian magazine was able to boast that, pro rata with school numbers, more of its ex-pupils were killed in the war than old Etonians. (Not all Irish people regarded this as a matter for boasting.)

At the other end of the social scale were the 'sans coulottes' of the cities and towns, many of whom were unemployed or earning miserable wages. The chance to earn something was tempting to unemployed single men: if they were married, the separation allowance for their families might well be more than they had been able to provide when working.

One category of young men whom the War Office was most anxious to recruit were the young men from the small farms and country cottages. They were strong, active and healthy, used to hardship and to outdoor work in all weathers. They were generally adept in the use of shot guns for fowling, and quickly become crack-shots with a service rifle. However, the food shortages resulted in good returns for agricultural produce, and items like pigeons and rabbits were plentiful and fetched high prices, so these young men were under no pressure to enlist.

The British were so desperate to get Irish recruits that they even contemplated offering the Volunteers captured in the 1916 Rising a free pardon if they would enlist in the army they had just been fighting against. Wiser counsels prevailed and the offer was never made.

When every pressure and inducement had been exhausted, the British decided in 1918 that there was no alternative to the imposition of conscription, and a Bill to compel all able-bodied Irishmen to serve was passed by the House of Commons. This was more than even Redmond and his party were prepared to swallow. They walked out of the House of Commons and organized monster anti-conscription meetings all over Ireland. Even though the Irish Party did not support this conscription Bill, the resentment that it had even been passed added to the growing disillusion with the Irish Party at Westminster. At the general election following the German surrender in 1918, the Irish Party was swept aside ignominiously and went down to oblivion, unwept, unhonoured and unsung.

There has never been an official British record of the number of Irishmen who served in the British army during World War I. The number who were killed is well known. When a man was killed or reported missing, believed dead, there was no possibility of keeping this a secret. His next of kin had to be informed. These numbered in round figures 50,000. Every month during more than four years of that futile and incompetently managed 'old man's war', a thousand Irishmen were killed in a conflict that in no way concerned them.

The RIC kept a record of the number of soldiers demobilized in Ireland, and these amounted to about 150,000. Finally, there were those who remained in the British army after the war and those who were demobilized in Britain, which gives a grand total of about 250,000.

The ratio of the Irish killed to the total serving is one in five. The *Encyclopaedia Britannica* gives a ratio of one killed to every ten serving, as an average for all armies in the Great War. The explanation for the Irish ratio being double this average is that in all armies there are many safe jobs which do not involve getting close to the firing line. The Irish did not get these safe assignments. They were the cannon fodder.

The irrelevance of the whole ghastly bloodbath for the Irish is aptly summed up in W.B. Yeats's poem 'An Irish Airman Forsees His Death':

> I know that I shall meet my fate
> Somewhere among the clouds above;
> Those that I fight I do not hate,
> Those that I guard I do not love;
> My country is Kiltartan Cross
> My countrymen Kiltartan's poor,
> No likely end could bring them loss
> Or leave them happier than before.

When the war that O'Rahilly had been expecting erupted in August 1914, just a week after the landing of the arms at Howth, his only concern was to avail of it for Ireland's benefit. He was firmly convinced that a German victory was in Ireland's best interests.

His first move is likely to have been made in the weeks just before the declaration of war, after the Austrian ultimatum appeared to make war inevitable, but while it was still possible to travel to Germany. He knew a young man named Ernest Blythe who was working as a farm labourer in the Kerry Gaeltacht while learning Irish. Blythe had become friendly with Desmond FitzGerald, who had introduced him to O'Rahilly. Blythe was not prominent politically and would not have been subject to police surveillance. Having decided that Blythe was a suitable emissary to send to Germany, O'Rahilly went down to Kerry to see him and brought £100 in gold sovereigns and notes, for Blythe's travelling expenses to Germany. His mission was to make contact with the German government.

The most likely message that O'Rahilly wished Blythe to convey was that, if war came, the Volunteers were determined to stage a rebellion and wanted help from Germany. Blythe refused to undertake the mission. The reason he gives for his refusal in his autobiography, *Trasna na Boinne*, is that if it had been the correct thing to do he would have been told to go by 'na Braithre' (the Brethren) by which he meant the IRB. This is the only mention of this organization in his book, so it does not seem to have played an important part in his life, but it was useful as an excuse for refusing O'Rahilly's mission to Germany.

Blythe says that O'Rahilly bitterly resented his refusal; so much so that he would not talk to him after this any time they met. But some time later Blythe purged himself by serving a six months' jail sentence for some political offence (probably an anti-recruiting speech) and O'Rahilly forgave him.

O'Rahilly's next move, immediately war was declared, was to plan a coup d'état. The proposal was for the Volunteers to seize Dublin Castle and proclaim that the Home Rule government, which had been enacted by the Westminster Parliament, was now taking over the defence of Ireland. Their proclamation would announce that this government, which since the passage of the Home Rule Bill had been *de jure*, was now *de facto*.

As a military operation, it was simplicity itself. The Castle was unguarded except for a policeman at the gate. Dublin Castle was, in fact and reputation, the headquarters of the British administration in Ireland, and to have this citadel of British power in Ireland occupied by an armed body of Irish Volunteers would give a dazzling boost to every nationalist in the land. Immediately the Castle was occupied, a provisional Home Rule government would issue a proclamation to the people of Ireland. John Redmond, as the recognized leader of the Irish people, would be invited to Dublin to act as provisional president of the Home Rule government. A general election to elect a new Parliament would be promised as soon as this could be arranged.

If Redmond had been faced with this situation, he would probably have sought advice from Asquith. We can only surmise what advice Asquith might have given him. He might have urged Redmond to have nothing to do with this illegal coup d'état, and then have instructed the War Office to retake Dublin Castle. The War Office might have told Asquith that it was fully committed to mobilizing the British Expeditionary Force to send to France, to help stem the German advance which was already moving into Belgium, and to divert these efforts, in order to mobilize a second force to conduct hostilities in Ireland, might jeopardize the main war effort.

No one can be sure what the British might have done. A sensible move for them would have been to send Redmond over to Dublin, in the hope that his influence would cool down the hotheads and prevent any rash actions until the situation in Europe was stabilized or the war against Germany had been won.

O'Rahilly's proposal may have been a desperate gamble, but the radical nationalists at that time had a unique opportunity and it did conform to the principle advocated by Danton of the French Revolutionary Directory: ' Il nous faut de l'audace, encore de l'audace, toujours de l'audace.' For the first time since the Volunteers of 1782, a body of armed Irishmen could march legally through the streets of Dublin, at a time when the major powers of Europe were plunged into a war in which no one could foretell the outcome.

If the Castle had been occupied and the British did order immediate military measures to retake it and outlaw the Volunteers, and if the Volunteers had put up a serious resistance, just as they were to do in 1916, the British would have been seriously embarrassed. They would then have been faced with the propaganda problem of explaining to the world how they had two expeditionary forces in action; one was in Belgium fighting for the freedom of small nations, while the other was in Ireland, fighting for the suppression of the freedom of small nations.

Nothing came of O'Rahilly's plan. The only one of his colleagues who mattered was MacNeill, the president and chief of staff, and he was probably the sole person whom O'Rahilly consulted. If MacNeill had given his approval, the military operation would be no problem. A route march, such as was common in those days, would be organized and would excite no interest. The column of Volunteers, led by O'Rahilly, would make its way up Dame Street. However, there would be a fundamental difference between this march and any previous march of Volunteers in Dublin. As a result of the Howth gun-running a few days before the declaration of war, the Volunteers on this march would have real rifles on their shoulders and live ammunition in their bandoleers.

The Castle was unguarded except for a lone policeman on the gate. When the column reached this gate, O'Rahilly would give the order 'left turn' and he would lead the Volunteers into the Castle, as he led them into the GPO in 1916.

O'Rahilly's eldest son often recalled how his father had bitterly regretted that this chance of seizing the Castle had been missed. This was not a case of hindsight on O'Rahilly's part. He was not thinking of something which might have been done when it was already too late. His sister Nell wrote to Nannie, who was in Kerry at that time, and said that they now had a marvellous chance to seize control. Nell here was clearly stating the views her brother was advocating.

To be successful, this opportunity of seizing the Castle had to be taken during the first few weeks of the war, when the Allies were fully stretched in their efforts to stem the German advance. There was then the very real possibility of a quick German victory, as they envisaged in their Schlieffen Plan, and nearly achieved. In such a situation the existence of an Irish Home Rule government in office in Dublin would have been of incalculable benefit to Ireland when a peace treaty was being negotiated.

Alas, as so often has happened in the tragic history of Ireland's missed opportunities, the leaders either lacked the courage to seize, or the brains to understand, the opportunity that was then within their grasp.

Since the opportunity to seize Dublin Castle had not been taken, there was little for the Irish Volunteers to do during the first months of the war. When the followers of Redmond were expelled, the organization was reduced to a tiny fraction of what it had been, and in most parts of the country it had ceased to exist.

However, during these first few months, when O'Rahilly had received permission from the enlarged committee to purchase any rifles of .303 bore which became available, and he had booked the entire output of their Martini Enfield rifles from the Birmingham firm of Greener & Co, there was an estimated flow of 800 rifles per week to Ireland. This went on for three months until this source dried up. During these months O'Rahilly's main activity was taking delivery and distributing these rifles and collecting payment for them. The RIC records show that most of these rifles, in addition to nearly all the Howth rifles, went to Redmond's National Volunteers.

The major activity of the Irish Volunteers, from that time until the Easter Rising, was to do all they could, surreptitiously, to discourage recruiting for the British army. Any overt expression of opposition was given immediate punishment of six months' jail sentence. It was for expressing such an anti-recruiting sentiment that Desmond FitzGerald was given six months' hard labour in Mountjoy.

14

Casement Abroad

If there was little for the Volunteers to do in Ireland, there was considerable activity in the United States and Germany. Some weeks before the outbreak of war, Roger Casement had travelled to the United States. He had been active in the work of organizing the Volunteers from the time he arrived in Dublin shortly after the inaugural meeting in the Rotunda in November 1913. He was involved in the preparations for the Howth gun-running, but may not have known of the $5,000 that Clan na Gael had sent to O'Rahilly, because he may have already left for the US.

Casement's mission there was to collect funds to buy arms for the Volunteers. He knew that large sums were necessary, although, as O'Rahilly made clear in his letter to Devoy, they did not require the sort of money that could buy 100,000 rifles.

The Volunteers could not hope for the sums of money that British millionaires had given to the Ulster Volunteers, but there were millions of people of Irish descent in the US and many of them would have subscribed whatever they could afford to help drive out the British. There were various ways in which this fund of goodwill could be tapped, and there was no better man to do it than Casement.

In the spring of 1914 I recall being with my father in the garden of MacNeill's house at 14 Herbert Park. There were a number of men in earnest conversation, including MacNeill, my father and a tall man with a black beard. Later that evening I asked my father who was the tall man with the beard, and he told me that his name was Sir Roger Casement. This may have been the meeting at which it was decided to send Casement to the US.

When Casement arrived in New York, he got in touch with Devoy and then with McGarrity in Philadelphia. He was staying with McGarrity when word came of the successful landing at Howth. Both men were jubilant, but the next day came news of the killings at Bachelor's Walk.

Casement wanted to keep a low profile in the US but Clan na Gael was anxious to get the benefit of his reputation and he agreed to address public meetings organized by them. He was received with enthusiasm by the Irish Americans. He discussed with the leaders of the Clan the possibility of collecting money for the Volunteers, but no serious effort was made to start such a collection. In a letter home, Casement said he could have collected $50,000 if it had not been for the war. All interest in the Irish Volunteers died within a few days of the Howth gun-running, when World War I was declared and Europe became a battlefield.

The German ambassador to the US was then Count von Bernstorff. Devoy had spoken to him at a reception in New York in early August 1914, when the tension between the European powers was reaching a crisis. Devoy wanted to know if the Germans could give help to the Irish in the event of a European war. The German ambassador could not give a positive answer and the Irish Americans decided that it was necessary to send an envoy to Germany to seek a formal commitment from the German government in support of Irish independence. Von Bernstorff agreed to recommend to his government that it receive such an envoy.

Casement, with his international reputation as a humanitarian, was an ideal person to represent the Irish cause and he was willing to make the journey. It was a desperate and irrevocable decision for him to make and he was well aware that he was putting his neck on the hangman's noose in so doing, but he was fully committed to the cause of Irish independence and was willing to do anything he could to advance that cause, regardless of his own interests or safety.

About this time Casement wrote a letter to an Irish newspaper urging Irishmen not to enlist in the British army. At the same time he told the British Foreign Office that he did not intend in future to draw the pension to which he was entitled, and which was his only income.

The German Embassy in Washington made arrangements for Casement's reception in Berlin, and a passage was booked for him on a Norwegian passenger liner running to Oslo. The passage was booked in the name of an American citizen who was legally entitled to make this journey, and this individual came to the cabin along with Casement, who had shaved off his beard and washed his face in milk to whiten his sun-tanned complexion. Casement posed as a visitor to see off his friend, but when the visitors were told that it was time for them to leave the vessel, it was the American citizen who left and Casement who remained on board and travelled to Norway.

Casement made a disastrous blunder before leaving New York. He tells in his diary how he had 'befriended' a young destitute Norwegian whose name was Adler Christensen. This man spoke German and was willing to travel to Germany with Casement, who engaged him as a servant. It may have been useful for Casement to have such a 'servant' and interpreter with him, but the former diplomat had travelled extensively around the world and would not have had any trouble in making his way alone.

Christensen turned out to be a consummate scoundrel, and for Casement to have engaged a complete stranger, whom he had picked up on the streets of New York, when he was about to embark on a mission of such secrecy and importance, was utter folly. It is simply not credible that this pick-up was an innocent act of befriending an individual who was destitute.

When the vessel was stopped by a British warship and brought into Stornaway to be searched, Casement threw some of his papers overboard and gave others to Christensen to keep safely for him. This man was in no danger of being searched because he was a Norwegian citizen on a Norwegian vessel. The British were looking for Germans who were hoping to get back to Germany to contribute to the war effort. They found and arrested six of them and kept them in concentration camps for the duration of the war. The search party did not suspect Casement on account of his impeccable, upper-class English accent.

Christensen steamed open the papers he was given and discovered that his 'master' was a member of an Irish revolutionary organization. He proceeded to devise a plot to use this information for his own advantage.

As soon as they arrived at their hotel in Oslo, Christensen found some excuse to absent himself and went off to the British Embassy. The aide who saw him sent a report to the British Foreign Office. He said a young man speaking bad English with an American accent informed him that he was employed by an English aristocrat, and that he could give them useful information about his 'master' if he was well paid for it. The aide said that he got the impression that the visitor was hinting that he had had unnatural relations with his master, but the aide could not be sure of this.

This was the start of a futile intrigue which continued for months. When Christensen went back to the hotel, he told Casement that he had been accosted by a stranger in the hotel lobby. The stranger told him that if he would accompany him to a certain address in Oslo, he would be well rewarded. Casement and Christensen looked up this address and found that it was the British Embassy, and Casement foolishly agreed to allow his servant to go to the address to see what was afoot.

Christensen made frequent trips back to the United States and, on his trips through Oslo, kept in touch with the British Embassy. He gave the ambassador a letter sent by Casement to Eoin MacNeill, which was enclosed in a letter addressed to Alice Stopford Green. Christensen had undertaken to post this letter in New York when he arrived there. He also gave the Embassy all kinds of false and misleading information, such as imaginary plans of German minefields, and a story about a wealthy American who was lending his yacht to Casement to travel to Ireland.

The result of all these lies and deceptions was a handwritten letter from the British ambassador in Norway, offering Christiansen £5,000 for the apprehension of Casement. Although it did not explicitly say so, the letter implied that it could be dead or alive. When Casement received this note, he thought and hoped that it would be an extreme embarrassment to the British. He sent photos of it to all the embassies in Berlin. Most of them did not even acknowledge having received the photographs.

The British Foreign Office had warned their ambassador in Oslo not to give anything in writing to Christensen which might compromise them, but this warning did not arrive until after the ambassador had made his offer for Casement's capture. This letter may well have contributed to the pressures on the British to kill Casement when they had the opportunity.

There is no record of what happened to Christensen. It was stated in some of Devoy's papers that, when Casement was being tried in London, Christensen offered to go to the trial as a prosecution witness. The British State papers giving details of Casement's trial do not record any such offer. Commenting on this offer, Devoy said: 'We saw to it that he was prevented giving such evidence.' If Devoy's statement is true, it could mean that Christensen was assassinated in the US or, more likely, that the Clan made him a better financial offer to stay away than he was likely to get from the British.

When Casement arrived in Berlin, his introductions enabled him to secure interviews with some of the most senior officials in the German Foreign Office. Within weeks of his arrival, he was success-ful in getting from the German government a 'declaration of intent' with regard to Ireland. The essence of this document, which Casement liked to call a treaty, was that the Germans pledged that if their troops were to land in Ireland in the course of the war, they would not come as an invading army with the object of annexing Ireland, but as liberators, to free Ireland from British domination.

This was a remarkable achievement by Casement, and put the Germans under an obligation, if they won the war, or if it ended in a negotiated peace, to use their influence to secure an independent Ireland. This declaration helped the Germans in their efforts to win support among Irish Americans. It was also a matter of some embarrassment to the British, whose war propaganda was aimed at convincing the world that they were fighting it for the freedom of small nations such as Belgium. Now the Germans were announcing that they had no intention of annexing a small country like Ireland, which they pledged to liberate from British domination.

Casement also decided to form an 'Irish Brigade' from the Irish soldiers who were prisoners of war in Germany. John MacBride had done this in South Africa during the Boer War and he then led them in the fight against the British. Casement never spelled out how he hoped to use his 'Brigade', but if thousands or even hundreds had defected, it would have embarrassed the British and would have discouraged recruiting in Ireland.

The Germans thought it a good idea to recruit such a brigade from the Irish POWs, and, to facilitate Casement, they assembled many of the Irish prisoners in a camp in Limburg. Casement gave a binding commitment to the men he was asking to join the brigade that they would not be asked to fight against their former comrades on the Western Front. If they were not going to fight for the Germans, it was reasonable to ask what purpose they could serve. While it was not formally spelled out, what may have been in Casement's mind was that the Germans were going to be victorious in a short war. If this happened, and if contingents of the German army were sent to occupy Ireland, it would be desirable to have a contingent of such an Irish brigade to accompany them. The whole project was a fiasco when only fifty-five POWs joined the brigade.

Then, some time in the autumn of 1915, the Germans decided to take these fifty-five men from the large camp at Limburg and billet them in a small camp of their own at Zossen, not far from Berlin. The Germans may have already been thinking of sending them to Ireland, and if they were to take them out of the Limburg camp for such an expedition, it would have become known that some operation was being planned.

By this time the brigade was a headache to everyone. They were no longer prisoners of war who could be ordered around, nor were they serving soldiers subject to German military discipline. The Germans had no idea what to do with them. The failure of Casement's brigade project must have severely shaken any confidence in his judgment the Germans may have had.

In the early summer of 1915, while he was still hoping to get a significant number of recruits for the brigade, Casement received a letter posted in Berne, Switzerland. It was signed by 'James Malcolm', and informed Casement that the writer was on his way to Berlin. James Malcolm turned out to be Joe Plunkett, the eldest of Count Plunkett's sons. He was suffering from tuberculosis and had been allowed to go to Switzerland to seek a cure for his ailment.

He came to Germany to inform Casement and the Germans that the Irish Volunteers intended rising in a rebellion against the British army of occupation, and he wanted to find out what help the Germans could give them. There is no record of what the Germans promised in the way of help, but it is clear from the message the Irish sent to Germany, early in 1916, that help had been promised. This Irish message did not ask if help could be given, but specified when it should arrive.

Unfortunately, Casement kept no regular diary during most of 1915. He was disillusioned by the failure of the brigade and pre-occupied with his efforts to trap the British ambassador in Norway. When eventually he obtained the ambassador's letter, the affair turned out to be such an anti-climax that he became a bitterly disappointed man. However, he did keep some notes about a meeting that he and Plunkett had with some of the German High Command officers. At this meeting Plunkett spoke about the plans for an Irish rebellion. The officers said that Germany could provide no help and, if help in the way of armaments was required, these would have to be provided from the US. Casement says that when Plunkett heard this, he said to him, 'In that case I will have to see the Minister for War'. Commenting on this remark of Plunkett's, Casement's scornful diary entry reads: 'he might as well ask to see the Emperor'.

Perhaps Plunkett did succeed in getting an interview with the Minister for War, and was able to convince him that an Irish rebellion would be of such benefit to the Germans that it was worthwhile for them to do everything possible to send help to Ireland. Whatever persuasion Plunkett was able to apply, there is no doubt that he left Germany with a commitment from the German High Command to supply help for an Irish Rising.

Plunkett had brought with him a detailed account of the British occupation forces in Ireland. He began with Dublin and continued right around the country, describing every barracks, with the number of troops and the amount of artillery in each of them. This record speculated on the reception that German troops were likely to get in each part of Ireland. It was a meticulously detailed account and would have taken many months to prepare. Plunkett managed to bring this information through Europe by carrying it in a hollowed-out walking stick. There is no record that he discussed the possibility of a German expeditionary force landing in Ireland.

The Germans do not seem to have realized that, if there had been a Rising and if a large area of the West of Ireland came under the control of the rebels, they would have had an ideal opportunity to create a 'second front' in Ireland, by sending an expeditionary force there. It was the sort of outcome Casement dreaded; he was appalled at the thought of Ireland being turned into a cockpit in which British and German forces would slug it out and devastate his country in the process. In his heart of hearts, Casement was a pacifist and hated the thought of war or fighting. He hoped for a German victory that would enable Ireland to regain her freedom without having to endure the horrors of war.

In 1913, Robert Monteith was a British soldier working in the army stores in the Phoenix Park in Dublin. As soon as he heard of the formation of the Irish Volunteers, he offered his services to drill them. This offer was welcomed by the men who were trying to create a Volunteer army; Monteith's military training was an asset they badly needed. When the authorities became aware that he was drilling the Volunteers, he was dismissed from the army.

The Volunteers then employed him as a full-time instructor, and he was so employed until he was deported from Ireland, in the middle of 1915, under the Defence of the Realm Act. Most of those deported under this act elected to live in Britain, but Monteith decided to go with his wife and family to the USA. It is not known if this was a personal decision or if it was suggested by the Volunteer executive that he should go to New York and, with Devoy's help, travel to Germany.

Christensen, Casement's disastrous choice as a servant, was back in New York and Devoy enlisted his assistance in getting Monteith to Germany. Christensen, as a Norwegian citizen, was free to travel from America to Norway with Monteith and to smuggle him past the security check in Oslo.

It is possible, but unlikely, that Monteith had met Casement in Ireland. Whether he had or not, they were not long together in Berlin before Monteith developed a respect and admiration for Casement 'this side idolatry'. Monteith was able to give Casement recent information about events in Ireland and about the progress in arming and training the small minority who had remained in the Irish Volunteers, but would not have been able to give Casement any information about plans for a Rising at Easter, which were unlikely to have been made when Monteith left Ireland.

Casement put Monteith in charge of the Irish Brigade and sent him into the camp at Zossen in which the men were billeted. His duty was to enforce discipline and to see to it that the men did not get out of hand. Monteith brought the brigade on long route marches to keep them occupied and fit, and when Casement accompanied them, as he sometimes did, he took such long strides and walked so fast that the two of them often found themselves far ahead of the rest. During these walks, Monteith came to realize Casement's single-minded dedication to end the British domination of Ireland.

In December 1915, Casement received word that an Irish American had arrived in Hamburg to join the brigade. This man had been cleared as reliable by Franz von Papen, then a military attaché on von Bernstorff's staff in Washington. Von Papen was relying on clearance by Joe McGarrity. Casement asked the Germans to send this man to Berlin, although he knew that additional recruits for the brigade would serve no useful purpose.

This man's name was McGeoy, a name which is difficult to pronounce, so much so that he was usually referred to as McGoey. When he arrived in Berlin, Casement explained to him that nothing would be achieved by his joining the brigade and that he had better return to the US. McGeoy said that he had come from Chicago for the express purpose of joining and he insisted on going through with it. Casement could not refuse him but, before sending him to Zossen, he took the precaution of getting an agreement in writing from the Germans that this man was not to be regarded as a prisoner of war. He was volunteering to join the brigade and was to be under Casement's control, and free to leave if he so wished.

McGeoy had joined Clan na Gael in Chicago, which anyone could so, and it seems likely he had been a British spy in that organization for a number of years. It would be strange if the British had not put spies in Clan na Gael to keep them informed of developments. The most likely explanation of McGeoy's coming to Germany is that the British wanted to be kept fully informed about the brigade. When the brigade was in Limburg, the British were given all the details they required by the wounded prisoners who were exchanged, but this source of information dried up when the brigade was moved to Zossen. McGoey's mission was to keep the British informed of what went on in that camp.

The story McGeoy told was that he had come to Europe on a tanker, with no assistance from the Clan. This should have aroused suspicion, because the crews of tankers would not have found it easy to leave their ship and come ashore in Europe. He alleged that his family had emigrated from Ireland to Glasgow and from there had gone to Chicago. If he had said that his family had come from Ireland, there was the possibility that one of the prisoners might have come from the same part of Ireland. His name is unknown in Ireland and in some of his own papers which were found in the German archives it is spelt with an 'r' as McGeory. McGeoy was sent to Zossen and lived and trained in that camp, with the rest of the Irish Brigade, as though he were an ordinary POW.

When the fiftieth anniversary of the Rising was being celebrated in Dublin in 1966, the German who was the führer of the brigade was invited to come to Ireland and was questioned about McGeoy. The führer, whose name was Zerhausen, said he could barely re-member McGeoy because he had been only a short time with them, but he had been nicknamed the 'Cowboy', probably because he was from the American Mid-West.

15

The Die Is Cast

Early in 1916, Casement's doctor in Berlin told him that he was physically and mentally exhausted and needed a complete rest. Three years previously he had been in poor health, living in semi-retirement in London, but when he heard in November 1913 of the formation of the Irish Volunteers, he immediately came to Dublin and offered any help he could give to this new body. Since that time, the anxieties and frustrations to which he had been subject had taken their toll of his nerves and health and he was exhausted. He had taken his doctor's advice and was living in a nursing home in Munich when word was received by the German High Command that the Rising in Ireland had been fixed for Easter 1916.

The Volunteer executive had reached this decision early in 1916. The members of the executive who made this essentially foolhardy decision knew that they were putting their own heads on the block. It would be strange if it had been a unanimous decision. They all realized that, in addition to the hazards involved in the fighting, they were unlikely, in the event of a military defeat, to get prisoner of war treatment from the British. The British practice in Ireland, from time immemorial, was to punish revolt by putting the leaders to death.

As soon as World War I had started, most of the top men in the Volunteer movement became convinced that a Rising must take place before the war was over. Many reasons led them to this conclusion. If the Germans were victorious and the Irish had made no effort to assert in arms their right to independence, they could not expect any help from the Germans when they came to impose peace terms on the Allies. If the war ended in a negotiated peace, which seemed the most likely outcome, and the Irish had not staged a Rising, how could they expect any help from the Germans in their claim to be an independent nation?

It was self-evident that if there was to be a Rising, it should be when the British were using all their resources in the European war, and when some help from Germany could be expected. There was an age-old tradition that it was the duty of every generation to keep the flag flying and if necessary to seal with their blood the Irish claim to independence. It was a cause of shame that the British were able to boast that they had withdrawn all their troops from Ireland during the Boer War and that not a shot had been fired there.

There was also the risk that the British would decide to round up the leaders and disarm the Volunteers. The first message to Berlin spelled out this danger when it said: 'The arrest of our leaders would hamper us severely.' All the leaders, about 50 men and one woman, lived at home and could have been picked up any day in a dawn raid. When they had been arrested, or killed or wounded if they resisted arrest, the possession of arms would be made illegal and all the arms in the hands of the Volunteers would be collected. Thus would end for this war and most likely for this generation any possibility of an armed Rising against the British occupation.

These were logical and indeed coercive arguments for taking the initiative, and were accepted as such by the majority of the Volunteer leaders. Bulmer Hobson rejected them and argued that the Volunteers should 'keep their heads down' and not give the British any excuse for a confrontation. He dismissed any hope that the Volunteers might drive out the British in a successful Rising and he urged the importance of retaining an armed body to resist conscription if the British decided to impose it. Hobson could not have known it, but his policy was endorsed by the British War Office. They wanted a Rising in which they could defeat the Volunteers and then impose conscription when the Volunteers were eliminated. If the British wanted a Rising, it was clearly not in the Irish interest to oblige them.

Hobson's arguments had to be taken seriously on account of his considerable influence, as secretary of both the Volunteers and the IRB. But there was always the suspicion, both then and since, that Hobson and the people who supported him were not in the business of risking their lives for the achievement of Irish freedom.

When the decision for an Easter Rising had been made, the first essential move was to inform the Germans, to ensure that the help the Volunteers expected was despatched and arrived on time. The message sent to Germany on 2 February 1916 implied that such help had been promised to Joe Plunkett when he had visited Germany the previous spring.

Communications between Dublin and Berlin involved sending a courier to New York with the message written in a code that had been agreed between the Volunteers and Clan na Gael in New York. The courier who brought this coded message to John Devoy was Philomena Plunkett, one of Joe Plunkett's sisters. The wireless message received in Berlin read:

Unanimous opinion that action cannot be postponed much longer. Delay disadvantageous to us. We can now put up an effective fight. Our enemies cannot allow us much more time. Arrest of our leaders would hamper us severely. Initiative on our part is necessary. The Irish regiments which are in sympathy with us are being gradually replaced with English regiments.

We have therefore decided to begin action on Easter Saturday. Unless entirely new circumstances arise we must have your arms and ammunition in Limerick, between Good Friday and Easter Saturday. We expect German help immediately after beginning action. We may be compelled to begin sooner.

The German ambassador in Washington added a footnote:

The Confidential Agent [this was how the Germans described Devoy] will advise the Irish, if at all possible, to wait, and will point out the difficulties of our giving help, but nevertheless believes the circumstances make delay impossible.

There are several points worth noting in this first message from the Volunteer executive to the German High Command. The date for the Rising to commence is given as Easter Saturday, although it has always been assumed that Easter Sunday was the day it was intended that the Rising was to start. The message also asked for the arms to be delivered to Limerick between Good Friday and Saturday. The Volunteers may have wanted to convey that if the arms vessel had arrived on one of those days in the Shannon estuary, it could have remained there until the Rising had started on Sunday and then, when Limerick port was controlled by the Volunteers, the discharge could take place. The Volunteers would have realized that no discharge could take place until the Rising was under way. This first message makes no mention of German officers coming, yet later messages said German officers were 'imperative'.

This first message from the Volunteers came to light in 1921, when the British published a pamphlet entitled *Documents Relative to the Sinn Féin Movement.* This is one of the most important sources of information in connection with the Rising plans and the liaison between the Volunteers and the German High Command. The British published it during the propaganda war against Sinn Féin in the US, to show the close links between Sinn Féin and the Germans. At that time, immediately following the Great War, in which many Americans had been killed, there was much anti-German sentiment in the United States. Until this document was published, it was not generally known that the British were reading all the secret coded wireless messages between the German Embassy in Washington and their Foreign Office in Berlin.

The British have never given an official account of how they obtained this German code. They may have obtained it by bribing some venal German official. A semi-official account is that, during a naval engagement in the Baltic between German and Russian warships, a German vessel was sunk and the Russians picked up the body of a German sailor. He turned out to be the signal officer and they found the German code on his person which they sent to their British allies. The German code book was described by Winston Churchill, at that time First Lord of the Admiralty, as a 'priceless water-stained document'. This story is a fantasy.

It was essential for the British, while the war lasted, not only to keep all knowledge of their possession of this code book from the Germans, but to keep such knowledge from their own top people. If all the cabinet knew British intelligence officers in the Admiralty were reading secret German messages, it might have leaked back to the Germans, and the only way to ensure that there was no leak was to tell no one.

The British in room 40 of the Admiralty Building, who decoded the message from Ireland to say that the Rising was to start at Easter, were eagerly awaiting the German reply. This came three weeks later and read:

Foreign Office Berlin to German Embassy Washington. 4th March 1916.
In reply to telegram 675 of 17th February. Between 20th and 23rd April in the evening, two or three steam trawlers could land 20,000 rifles and 10 machine guns, with ammunition and explosives at Fenit Pier in Tralee Bay,

Irish pilot boat to await trawlers at dusk, north of the Island of Inistooskert at the entrance of Tralee Bay, and show two green lights close to each other at short intervals. Please write whether the necessary arrangements in Ireland can be made secretly through Devoy. Success can only be assured through the most vigorous efforts.

It will never be known, unless it emerges from the German military archives, if the Germans ever really intended to send the arms in steam trawlers. It may have been a deliberate German attempt to mislead the British. The Germans did not suspect that the British were intercepting and decoding the secret wireless messages between their Foreign Office and their embassies; but they knew of all the agencies through which this message to Ireland had to pass. If the British had a spy in any of these places, or if there was a leak through carelessness, the British might be alerted to the fact that a consignment of arms was on its way from Germany to Ireland. If the message that the arms were being sent in three steam trawlers was deliberate 'disinformation', then the Germans would have hoped that the British would be looking for steam trawlers and would pay no attention to what looked like a Norwegian tramp steamer on her lawful occasions.

There was disagreement from the start between the Irish and the Germans about the port in Ireland where the munitions were to be delivered. The Irish asked for them to be landed at Limerick, but the Germans ignored this and decided to land them at Fenit. The Germans may have decided on Fenit in the hope that if a quick discharge of the arms ship could be achieved there, it might be possible for the vessel to escape and reach the open sea, before the British could send a warship to sink or capture it.

There was further confusion when the Volunteers realized that it would not be possible to discharge the arms until the Rising was under way and the port of discharge was in the hands of the Volunteers. They then sent Philomena Plunkett back to New York with a further message to Germany, in which they gave urgent and explicit instructions not to land the arms until Sunday, when the Rising was under way and the port was under the control of the Volunteers. When this message reached Germany, the gun-running vessel had already left, but she did not have a wireless receiver and so could not be advised of the change of date.

The first essential for the Germans, when they set about making plans for the despatch of the arms, was to find a vessel in Germany which resembled an existing Norwegian vessel, and to check that it was away on some voyage which would ensure that the British blockade vessels did not report two different Norwegian vessels of the same name at about the same time.

The Germans found they had a British vessel called the *Castro* lying in a German port. She closely resembled a Norwegian vessel called the *Aud* and it was a simple matter to modify her so that there was no noticeable difference between them. The Germans also checked that the *Aud* was away on a long voyage outside European waters.

As Easter approached, final preparations were being made by the four major participants in the Rising: the Irish Volunteers, the German High Command, the top people in the British War Office, and Roger Casement. The Volunteer executive could make no final decisions until Philomena Plunkett arrived back in Dublin with the wireless message sent from Berlin on 4 March saying that 20,000 rifles and other munitions would be arriving in two or three steam trawlers in time for Easter. She received this message on 5 or 6 March, and if the Atlantic crossing took seven days, she would have delivered her message to the executive in Dublin not later than 15 March.

The executive then summoned a meeting in Dublin of all the senior officers, probably thirty or forty, to advise them that the Rising was to start at Easter, and to tell them what was expected of them. These instructions were verbal, but among Michael O'Rahilly's papers was the notice convening this meeting and stressing the importance of attending it. The officers who turned up for it would not have been surprised to be told that the Rising was to take place at Easter. All the officers and most of the rank and file accepted that a rebellion was the purpose of the Volunteers, and any members who did not intend to participate would have dropped out. These officers were told of the expected arrival of rifles from Germany, and of the critical importance of keeping a low profile so as not to arouse any suspicion among the British authorities that anything unusual was underway.

The decision to send help to Ireland had to be taken at a senior level of the German High Command in Berlin. The actual quantity of munitions was trifling, but the proposal to send help to stir up trouble in a British colony would require sanction by the Foreign

Secretary, possibly even by the Kaiser himself. At whatever level it was made, the promise to despatch a shipment of munitions to Ireland was sent to New York three weeks after Count von Bernstorff's request had been received. When von Bernstorff received the reply in code, he decoded it into clear and sent it to Devoy, who gave it to Philomena Plunkett in the Irish code.

When the decision was made to send help to Ireland, the German High Command should have, in common courtesy, sent word to Casement, who was ill in a Munich nursing home, but at that time his relations with the High Command officers were so strained that they were scarcely civil to one another.

The original intention may have been to send the arms in steam trawlers, but the Germans then decided to use a tramp steamer, disguised as a neutral. With such a vessel, they could also get rid of the fifty-five men of the Irish Brigade, who were now a nuisance in Germany. Arrangements had to be made to train the most reliable of them in the use of the German machine gun. The intention was to have a secret compartment in the vessel, large enough to house the brigade, and when the vessel tied up at the docks in Fenit, Co. Kerry, the men would take up defensive positions around the place where the vessel was to be discharged. With the approaches covered by ten machine guns, there was no possibility than any local British forces would be able to interfere with the discharge of the *Aud*.

When the Germans decided to use the *Castro*, disguised as the *Aud*, to send the weapons for the Irish Rising, they set about organizing the expedition. They appointed a Captain Spindler to take charge of the mission, and also selected a professional mate and two engineers. The remainder of the crew was recruited from criminals serving sentences in German prisons. If the mission was a success and they returned safely, they would be free men. There was no lack of applicants.

Spindler wrote a book some years after the war about sailing the *Aud* through the British blockade. Unfortunately, he was more concerned with making his book into a bestseller than in giving a truthful account of the voyage. Every item of information given in the book, if it can be checked, turns out to be false.

The *Castro* sailed from Hamburg to Wilhelmshaven where changes were made to make her resemble the *Aud*. Secret accommodation was made in the bottom hold for fifty-five men. The name

Castro was painted out in the middle of the night and she sailed back north with a new name, the *Libau*. She went through the Kiel Canal into the Baltic and docked at the port of Lübeck, where she was loaded with her cargo of arms and munitions and with her fake cargo of merchandise. Again in the middle of the night, her name was changed to the *Aud*. The double name change was considered necessary in case there were spies around who could report that a vessel called either the *Castro* or the *Libau* was involved in something suspicious. The British blockade might then be alerted to be on the lookout for a vessel of either name, but would pay no attention to a Norwegian vessel named the *Aud*.

While this part of the arms delivery plan was being carried out, the Germans were training the most reliable men of the Irish Brigade to use the German machine-gun and Monteith was informed that the brigade was to be sent to Ireland, on the arms ship, to help in the Irish Rising.

When Monteith was told this, he sent a telegram to Casement, urging him to come to Berlin. Casement wired back to say that he was too ill to travel and that if Monteith wanted to see him he would have to come to Munich. Monteith took the overnight express to Munich and saw Casement the next morning. He told him that a Rising was to take place and that a large cargo of arms was to be sent to Ireland, and also that the Irish brigade was to travel on the arms ship. Monteith wrongly said that 200,000 rifles were to be shipped.

Casement's immediate reaction was total opposition to the plan. He complained bitterly that the Germans had repeatedly refused his requests to send arms to Ireland. There is nothing in his diaries or letters to support his claim that he had asked them to do so. He realized that it would be unwise to reject this chance of getting a large shipment of arms for the Volunteers, but he was equally convinced that it would be folly to challenge the British occupation forces in an armed struggle. Nevertheless he made it clear to Monteith that, if a Rising was to take place, he was determined to be there with his comrades.

Monteith returned to Berlin and Casement followed him a day or two later. However, he was still a sick man and had to return to Munich and spend more time in bed before returning to Berlin on 16 March. Realizing that history was being made and that every move and statement was important, Casement began a diary on 17 March which he called 'The Last Page'.

His first move was to go to the German High Command and ask them about his request, made in a letter from Munich, to be sent to Ireland by submarine to enable him to co-ordinate the plans between the Irish and the Germans. Casement wanted badly to go to Ireland, but he made it plain in his diary that his real purpose was to persuade the Irish leaders not to go ahead with the Rising.

Captain Nadolmy of the German High Command told Casement that it would be too risky to send a submarine to the east coast of Ireland, and then have it come back to collect him two weeks later.

Casement decided to go to see the German Admiralty in the hope that he could convince them that it would be safe to send a submarine with himself and Monteith on board to the east coast of Ireland. They could then work out all plans with the Irish leaders to ensure that the discharge arrangements worked properly. The two of them could be collected a week or two later and brought back to Germany. When he failed to satisfy the Admiralty that the plan was safe and feasible, he made an alternative suggestion. He asked them if they would help him to get an Irishman (McGeoy) who had volunteered to serve in the brigade, and who was under his personal control, to go to Ireland. If they would arrange for this man to be escorted across the border into Denmark, there were regular passenger liner services between Denmark and Britain, and he could easily make his way from England to Ireland. In Dublin he could see the Volunteer leaders and ensure that, when the arms vessel arrived, suitable arrangements had been made for the quick discharge of the munitions.

The German Admiralty agreed to supply a private detective to escort McGeoy to the Danish border and to see him safely across it. Casement was confident that McGeoy would be able to use his American citizenship to get him through Denmark and on to Britain. It was agreed that Casement would have McGeoy at his hotel that evening and that the Admiralty would send the private detective to meet him. Early the following morning they would leave Berlin by train for the border.

McGeoy came to the hotel that evening and was introduced to the detective from the Admiralty. Beforehand, Casement had a private talk with the emissary he was sending to Dublin. He explained to McGeoy that the Germans had agreed to send him to Dublin to co-ordinate the plans for the reception and discharge of the gun-running vessel. Casement told McGeoy he doubted that the vessel would succeed in getting safely through the British blockade and explained to McGeoy that his real mission was to get to Dublin and to go to Tom Clarke's tobacconist shop in Parnell Street. Clarke would put him in touch with the Volunteer leaders and he was to tell him that the help the Germans were sending was derisory, and probably would never arrive. Casement's advice was that the Rising should be postponed or cancelled. If the vessel with the 20,000 rifles did reach Ireland, it should be possible to hide the weapons in some cave until such time as they could be distributed to the Volunteers.

McGeoy was also to tell the Volunteer leaders that Casement's request to be sent to Ireland by submarine had been refused, but that if the arms ship was sent to Ireland, he was determined to travel on it, and if the Irish did stage a Rising, despite his advice, he hoped to be there to take his part in it with them.

It was still dark and cold the following morning when McGeoy and the German detective left the hotel for the railway station. Casement had some money which he insisted on giving McGeoy, who did not want to take it. They shook hands on the steps of the hotel and exchanged farewell greetings in Irish. (The spy had either been selected for his knowledge of the Irish language or had acquired a smattering of it from some of the men in the brigade.)

McGeoy must often have wondered how he was going to extricate himself from his position as a member of the Irish Brigade to report back to British Intelligence. Even in his most optimistic dreams he can scarcely have imagined being escorted by a German private detective to a neutral country from which he could easily make his way to England. When he arrived at Scotland Yard some days later, he was able to give the British a full picture of the German plans to help the Irish Rising.

Casement and Spindler were both captured on Easter Saturday in separate operations by the British and were sent to Scotland Yard for questioning. They both put on record their surprise at the extent of the British knowledge of the plans for the Rising. When Casement was brought in to be questioned, one of the intelligence officers said to him, 'We were waiting for you, Sir Roger.' McGeoy had told them that Casement was determined to go on the arms ship when the Germans had refused to send him by submarine. Based on what McGeoy had told them, the British were now satisfied that everything was fitting into place just as they wanted.

When the Germans replied to the Irish request for arms for the

Rising by saying that the shipment would be in two or three steam trawlers, they could not then have had any intention of sending the brigade to Ireland, because it would have been impossible to conceal the men in such vessels. But once the decision had been made to send a tramp steamer of 1,400 tons, the Germans realized that it would be feasible to install secret living quarters in the bottom hold of such a vessel. This made sense as a strategy. The Germans would get rid of the brigade, now a severe embarrassment to them, and the men would provide a well-armed guard to protect the vessel during the discharge of the arms. If the plan had been discussed with Casement rather than presented to him, he might have agreed to it, although this is not likely. Casement was by no means a pacifist. He knew about the plans for the Howth gun-running, and the main purpose of his trip to the United States was to collect funds to buy arms for the Volunteers. If he was willing and anxious to arm the Volunteers, he may have believed that the possession of arms would make their use unnecessary. He believed that the fact that the Volunteers had arms was the reason the British had not imposed conscription in Ireland.

Casement's opposition to the Rising planned for Easter 1916 was largely based on his knowledge of the inadequate help the Germans were sending, and his firm conviction that, little as it was, it would never arrive. A major influence in his thinking, even though it may have been subconscious, was his horror at the thought of the inevitable bloodshed. He was appalled at the prospect of the Germans landing an expeditionary force in Ireland and turning the country into a battlefield like Belgium. Casement knew that any Rising in Ireland would benefit the Germans, and he was then as anti-German as he had been pro-German when he had arrived in Germany in the winter of 1914.

Casement did not have the information to enable him to appraise the wisdom of the Rising that the Irish Volunteers proposed to undertake that Easter. He had not been in Ireland since the early summer of 1914, and his only knowledge of the situation there was based on what Joe Plunkett had told him in early 1915, updated by Monteith at the end of that year. He had no knowledge of the fundamental danger to the Volunteers of the British deciding to impose conscription on Ireland, or deciding to arrest the leaders and make the possession of arms illegal. Finally, neither he nor any-one else could assess the boost to the national morale which might

The O'Rahilly, in his Volunteer uniform, c. 1915, photographed by his sister Anna in the garden of 54 Northumberland Road.

The O'Rahilly family home, 40 Herbert Park, where they lived from 1910; The O'Rahilly left it for the GPO on Easter Monday 1916.

Four pencilled notes (part-overwritten in ink) sent by The O'Rahilly to his three sons and wife from the GPO during Easter week.

result from a Rising, regardless of its failure as a military operation.

Casement considered the German proposal to send the brigade to Ireland to be unfair and unwise, and he was determined to do everything he could to prevent it. He felt personally responsible for the safety of these men. They had deserted from the British army at his behest, and the British were entitled to shoot them, out of hand, as deserters, if they caught them. But the Germans were equally determined to get rid of the brigade and this seemed an ideal opportunity. Casement had several sessions of heated argument with officers of the German High Command, in which he did his utmost to convince them that it would be disgraceful to risk the men on the ship, which he was convinced would never get through the British blockade.

Despite this belief that the ship would be captured, Casement made it clear that, while he was determined to do everything he could to prevent the Germans shipping the men, he himself would travel on the gun-running vessel, to be in Ireland for the Rising, since the Germans would not send him by submarine.

Casement had convinced himself that he had taken the initiative in the formation of the Volunteers. It was true that he had come to Dublin shortly after the inaugural meeting in the Rotunda, and had given all the help he could until he sailed for New York six months later; but the Volunteers would have been formed if Casement had never come to Dublin.

However, he was fully and solely responsible for the recruitment of the Irish prisoners of war into the brigade. He had personally urged them to desert and join the brigade; he believed it was irresponsible for the Germans to ship them to Ireland.

When these discussions began, Casement thought that, if the Germans insisted on shipping out the brigade, he and Monteith would have no power to prevent them doing so. They believed that their only hope of saving the brigade would be for Monteith and himself to accompany them on the gun-running ship and, when they were near the English coast, they would mutiny, seize the vessel and sail her into an English port and surrender. They hoped that if they surrendered the vessel with the arms and the German crew, it might save the POWs from summary execution.

The necessity for this did not arise. In the course of an acrimonious discussion, one of the German officers said, 'We shall ship the men whether you like it or not.' Casement replied, 'Try it.

Without my instructions, not a man will board the vessel.' Casement then knew that he had won this battle.

The Germans also knew they were beaten. If they were to put fifty-five heavily armed men on board at the point of the gun and against their will, what possible purpose could they serve when they arrived in Ireland? It was also obvious that, as soon as the vessel was at sea, the men could take her over and sail her wherever they wished.

The German High Command decided to make one final effort. They sent a senior officer to the Zossen camp to tell Monteith that if he would agree to embark the men, he would be given a substantial sum of money which he could use in Ireland for propaganda purposes. This was a thinly veiled bribe. Monteith spurned the bribe and remained loyal to Casement and to the men of the Irish Brigade.

It seems likely that the training of the men in the use of the German machine gun then ceased. It is also probable that no machine guns were sent to Ireland on the arms vessel, although in the first German reply to the request for help in the Irish Rising, they had agreed to include ten machine guns. This suggests that, from the very start, the Germans intended to send the brigade, armed with machine guns to cover the landing, on a small, disguised tramp steamer, and that mention of steam trawlers was intended to mislead the British.

Although Casement had saved the men of the brigade from being shipped on the gun-running vessel, he was still determined to travel on her himself. It would have been unthinkable for him to have remained safely in Germany while the men he had encouraged to enlist into the Irish Volunteers were dying in a hopeless Rising in Ireland. He was determined to participate in the Rising if it took place and, since the Germans would not send him by submarine to Ireland, he intended to travel on the arms ship.

Monteith and a powerfully built member of the brigade insisted they would accompany him. Casement suspected that when they were waiting in their hotel for the gun-runner to set out, these two men intended to overpower him and keep him tied up until the vessel had sailed in order to protect him from what they regarded as certain capture. This ultimate effort to save Casement, if this was what Monteith intended, was in the end not necessary.

In his efforts to enlist help for the Irish cause, Casement had become acquainted with a number of the top people in the German administration, and was held in considerable esteem by many of them. One such was a senior official in the German Foreign Office named Count Arthur von Zimmerman, who was made German Foreign Secretary about this time. Von Zimmerman wrote thus of Casement:

It was never my lot to know a man of loftier mind, of higher honour, or of more burning love of home. It was a matter of personal grief to me when I heard he had made up his mind to accompany the expedition, which I greatly feared was fantastic. So I urged him, as far as I could in propriety, to remain with us and do work among the prisoners. I felt sure Casement could not escape capture, and I knew what that meant. But he only shook his head saying: 'I must go — I must be with the boys!'

In Casement's anxiety to get to Ireland, he had approached several people whom he knew in the German Establishment. He asked them to use their influence with the Admiralty to send him to Ireland by submarine. If such representations were made, they were not successful.

However, when it became generally known that Casement was determined to go to Ireland on the arms ship, which they all feared had a slender chance of finding its way through the British blockade, sending him by submarine became an issue of greater importance. It was no longer just a matter of helping this remarkable man, who was held in such high public esteem, but of the harm it would do to the Germans, if he were captured, for having allowed him to travel in such a risky way when a submarine journey would have been so much safer. This consideration led to political pressure on the Admiralty and they gave way.

Casement was elated. He now hoped that he would reach Ireland in time to convince the leaders of the Volunteers to postpone their plans for a Rising. At the very least, the Dublin men would know the nature of the help the Germans were sending.

Casement was told that the submarine would not be leaving for about a week, and there was little else for him to do other than to arrange for his papers to be preserved and to make a trip to Zossen to bid farewell to the men of the Irish Brigade. He could not tell them where he was going or why or for how long he would be away.

Some days later, while Casement was waiting in Berlin for instructions to embark on the submarine, he got word that a letter had come to the German Foreign Office for him. It was delivered to his hotel that afternoon. It had come from Berne and was signed, 'A friend of James Malcolm'. It had the code word 'Ashling', which had been agreed between Casement and Joe Plunkett the year before.

The letter began by saying that the writer had been sent as a delegate by the president and the Supreme Council of the Irish Volunteers. The president was Eoin MacNeill, and this message proves conclusively that he was fully involved in the preparations for the Rising:

Berne 5th April 1916. 'Ashling'

Dear Roger Casement,

I am sent here as a delegate by the President and the Supreme Council of the Irish Volunteers, and through the courtesy of his Excellency, the German Ambassador, am enabled to give you this urgent message from Ireland.

(1) The Rising is fixed for next Easter Sunday.
(2) The large consignment of arms to be brought into Tralee Bay must arrive not later than dawn on Easter Monday.
(3) German Officers will be necessary for Volunteer forces. This is imperative.
(4) A German submarine will be required in Dublin Harbour. The time is very short but is necessarily so for we must act of our own choice and delays are dangerous.

Yours very sincerely
'A friend of James Malcolm'

Casement puzzled over this letter. The fact that it carried the code word 'Ashling' confirmed its authenticity. He thought the handwriting was familiar but could not place it.

It was clear that the Volunteer leaders needed and expected much more help from the Germans that they were going to get. Casement drafted a reply to the 'friend of James Malcolm', which he sent to the German Foreign Office to be wired to Berne. He assumed that it would be sent in code to the German Embassy in that city.

The delegate in Berne was Count Plunkett, the father of Joe Plunkett. Casement's telegram to Berne said that there would be 20,000 rifles and ten machine guns going to Ireland, but no German officers and no submarine. The ambassador in Berne was instructed by his Foreign Office to tell the delegate from Dublin the 'particulars' of Casement's telegram. Count Plunkett was not told anything that might cause the Volunteer leaders to cancel their plans for the Rising. He was certainly not told that Casement's message had said that there would be no German officers and no submarine.

It was the secretary of the embassy at Berne who gave this misleading message to Count Plunkett. The ambassador had developed a rapport with Count Plunkett and was unwilling to be a party to the deception.

There was subterfuge on both sides. Casement pretended that his anxiety was to get to Ireland to ensure that all arrangements were in order for the safe discharge of the arms ship. His real intention was to inform the leaders in Dublin of the inadequacy of the German help and his belief that it was unlikely to arrive, and to persuade them to cancel plans for the Rising. For their part, the Germans wanted the Irish to believe that all the requested help was on its way.

Count Plunkett then sent a second letter to Casement in Berlin, signed with his own name. This letter did not arrive until after Casement had left for Wilhelmshaven to board the submarine. It reads:

> Berne 11th April 1916. Ashling
>
> Dear Roger Casement,
>
> The Secretary of the Embassy has kindly given me the particulars of your reply to my letter. I am very sorry that time presses so much that I have to leave Berne to-day for Rome. If I could I would discuss with you many matters which are difficult for both of us.
>
> Of course the arrangement for the Rising was made known to the Irish in America, but I was directed to re-affirm it in my letter to you. The timing of the landing of the arms in Tralee Bay is such an essential part of the beginning of the work, that we in Ireland rely on your urgency to see it exactly carried out.
>
> I would ask you to bring your influence to bear on the German Government with regard to the two questions more directly touching Germany. I am sure you have raised the question of the advantages to Germany and to Ireland in having Germans take part in the actual Rising. The effect of the presence of German officers and of a German submarine (which otherwise might not seem so important) in Irish waters assisting us would be very great. I may add that the Supreme Council of the Irish Volunteers desire to associate Germany in this marked way with the liberation of Ireland.
>
> I do not suppose that any material change has occurred in Irish affairs

since I left Dublin on the 29th of March, though there seemed a likelihood of disturbances through further arrests and attempts to take the arms from the Volunteers. My son Joseph seems to have had news pretty regularly from America, and he was in touch with all events in Ireland, of course. I cannot say if he heard fully and often from Germany.

I will call at the Poste Restante in Paris on my way to Ireland, in about a week, and I hope to have word from you through the kindness of His Excellency the Ambassador, who has done so much for me. It will be 'A long pull, a strong pull, and a pull all together' to set the old country free.

With kind regards, yours very sincerely,

George Noble Plunkett

(A friend of James Malcolm)

There is no indication in this second letter that Count Plunkett had been told by the secretary of the German Embassy in Berne that no German officers were being sent to Ireland and that there would be no German submarine.

It is important to note that MacNeill considered it necessary to send Plunkett to Berne with this message for Casement, despite the fact that the Volunteers had been sending and receiving messages through the German ambassador in Washington. It is likely that MacNeill was not satisfied with the assurances of German help he was getting, which purported to be from the German ambassador in Washington via Clan na Gael.

MacNeill's message also makes clear another important point: until Count Plunkett's letter reached Berlin, there had been no request for German officers to act as advisers or for a German submarine to be in Dublin Bay. Plunkett was told to emphasize that such help was 'imperative'. This raises the possibility that MacNeill may have made his support for the Rising conditional on the Germans sending this help.

Count Plunkett's mission to Rome is also important. He had been brought up in Rome and was honoured with the title of a papal count in recognition of the knowledge he had acquired of early Christian art. He was on terms of personal intimacy with two Popes, and it would have been possible for him to have secured a tête-à-tête interview with the Pope, which few other lay members of Christendom could have done.

His mission to Rome was to get a papal blessing for the Irish Rising. Such an endorsement would have been a master stroke with the Irish people and would have ensured that the Rising got off to a flying start. Even if Plunkett had obtained some form of qualified approval, such as an assertion by the Pope of the right of the Irish to control their own country, it would have been a considerable achievement. Yet it was scarcely realistic to hope that, with Italy fighting on the Allied side in the war, the Pope could give an outright support to a country which was in alliance with Germany, the mortal enemy of Italy. Nevertheless it was decided that it was worth a try.

Count Plunkett is believed to have reported to MacNeill when he returned to Dublin that, while the Pope could not give an explicit blessing to the Irish Volunteers, or to give an endorsement of the right of the Irish people to rise in revolt, he would give his blessing to all men killed in doing what they believed to be their duty. This was the story current in Dublin at the time and was as much as the Volunteers could reasonably expect.

There has never been a credible official British account of the Rising and the events leading up to it. In the absence of such an account, it is only possible to make reasonable assumptions based on the moves the British made, both before and after the Rising had taken place.

When the British became aware, by reading and decoding the intercepted wireless messages and from what McGeoy was able to tell them of German plans and Casement's reaction to them, the War Office had to decide how to deal with the situation. The only two possible strategies were either to make a pre-emptive strike by arresting the leaders and making the possession of arms illegal, or to let the Rising take place and then crack down with all the force that could be mustered.

The political considerations involved making no move that might alienate the support Redmond and the Irish Party were giving to the war effort, or which might stir up trouble among the 200,000 Irish troops then serving in the British army, and the much larger number of Irishmen they were hoping to recruit when they were able to impose conscription. In addition, there was a vital political consideration of making no move that might antagonize the large Irish-American population and endanger the support the Allies were getting from the United States.

It was finally decided to do nothing that might alert the leaders of the Volunteers and lead to a cancellation of the Rising. This strategy of encouraging the Rising also required the assembly of a substantial army unit not far from the Welsh port of Holyhead, available for instant despatch to Ireland as soon as the Rebellion took place. There was no danger that the assembly of such a force would excite any suspicion in Ireland because such units were being assembled constantly, all over Britain, for despatch to France.

This part of the plan was carried out smoothly; the first British troops to suppress the Rising began arriving in Ireland early on Easter Wednesday, less than two days after the Declaration of the Republic. If the War Office had any misgivings as to how their troops to suppress the Rising would be received by the Irish population, these were allayed when reports came in that the troops had been given an enthusiastic welcome by the Irish people, who regaled them with refreshments of all kinds as they marched from Kingstown into Dublin.

The only snag in the developing situation, from the British viewpoint, was the news that the gun-running steamer, instead of pulling into an Irish port to discharge her cargo, had weighed anchor and was moving out of Tralee Bay. The arrival and discharge of the German munitions ship in Ireland was fundamental to the British strategy; it would justify the planned crack-down on the Volunteers and the arrest of their leaders.

The War Office then feared that the anticipated and hoped-for Rebellion would not take place. These fears were confirmed when it was reported that all was quiet on Easter Sunday, and that the Volunteers had cancelled all manoeuvres for that day. The British then assumed that all their plans for a crack-down on the Volunteers, following a Rising, had miscarried. These anxieties abated when the reports came in on Easter Monday afternoon that an Irish Republic had been declared at midday and that the rebels had occupied many important buildings in the centre of Dublin.

There must be a large element of speculation in any attempt to give a coherent account of the motives, hopes and fears among those who staged the 1916 Rising. The plans had to be made in the utmost secrecy. The leaders hoped that the British knew nothing of their plans, and would be taken by surprise when the Rising erupted.

Inevitably there were different views among the dozen or so people who made the decisions. There was general agreement that it was the duty of the Volunteers to strike a physical blow at the occupation forces at the appropriate moment; but there was no general agreement as to when this moment had arrived.

The opening move was the message that Philomena Plunkett brought to New York for wireless transmission to Berlin early in 1916. This message began 'Unanimous opinion here that action cannot be delayed much longer'. It is now known, beyond any doubt, that the conviction that the time to strike had arrived was not unanimous. The leaders were divided into groups.

James Connolly in effect had been co-opted as a member of the Volunteer executive and, if he was not accepted as the leader of the group of 'ultras' (those 'out and outers' who were itching to use their weapons against the British), he was one of the most determined of them. This group included Pearse and the cabal of senior Volunteer officers he had organized to obey his instructions; these included the five men besides Pearse and Connolly who signed the Proclamation of the Republic.

Pearse had sworn these men into this cabal on the understanding that they would support a Rising even against the orders of the official leadership of the Volunteers. In some accounts of the period, it is often assumed that this group of 'ultras' were the IRB. This is incorrect. Only two of the signatories of the Proclamation are known to have sworn the IRB oath. Despite the IRB's claim that it had played an important and indeed a fundamental part in the Rising, it would have been wholly out of character for Connolly, Pearse or Plunkett to ever have been members of the IRB.

Both Seán T. O'Kelly and Countess Markievicz have recorded how O'Rahilly had refused to join the IRB. I recall him coming home to lunch one day not long before the Rising and telling Mother how he had been asked to join a secret society. He said that he had refused to join on the grounds that, if he had done so, he would have to swear an oath of secrecy and could not then discuss with her matters that were of vital concern to both of them. The group he had been asked to join would have been Pearse's cabal. The reason he gave for his refusal was a compliment to his wife, but he would have realized that, to be effective, an organization needed the loyal support of its members and that the purpose of the cabal was to undermine this support.

Many years after 1916 I asked Eamon de Valera about his role in the Rising. He told me that one day at a meeting of the officers of

183

the 3rd Battalion, of which he was the commanding officer, he noticed that, when certain subjects were being discussed, there were nods and winks among some of the officers, which led him to believe that these men, who were junior to him, had information to which he was not privy. De Valera's senior officer was Thomas MacDonagh, and he went to him to complain about this. MacDonagh asked him, 'What would you do if you were told there was to be a Rising?' De Valera replied that as an officer in an army he would obey the commands of his senior officer. 'In that case', said MacDonagh, 'I will swear you in.' When de Valera told me this, he believed that he had been sworn into the IRB. He added that he supposed that he should not have sworn this oath, which he realized was a conspiracy to subvert the official leadership of the Irish Volunteers.

There is little in the way of written evidence to indicate which of the leaders were determined to rise and which were either opposed or doubtful. In a letter that was published in the *Workers' Republic* early in 1916 (see Appendix 3), O'Rahilly spelled out clearly his belief that the Volunteers should and would rise in revolt, and clearly implies that he and Connolly were in agreement about this. There is no doubt that when Pearse organized the senior officers who had sworn to take his instructions, he wanted to be in a position to stage a revolt, even against MacNeill's orders.

A document dealing with this issue was found among Bulmer Hobson's papers. It purports to have been issued by MacNeill and is largely concerned with making the case against the Volunteers rising in revolt against the British occupation. While it is alleged to have been written by MacNeill, it is supposed not to have been circulated by him to the senior Volunteer executive, but to have been given to one of them (presumably Hobson) who was to pass it to the others.

Any such assessment of the case for or against a Rising, to have any credibility, would have had to consider the possibility of German help being available. In this document there is no reference of any kind to such help. The absence of any mention of German help establishes beyond any doubt that the document is a fake. It was almost certainly concocted between Hobson and MacNeill when the Rising was over and MacNeill had decided to stand trial. Its purpose would have been to convince a British court martial that MacNeill had always opposed the Rising. Such a faked document could not have made any mention of German help, which, in British eyes, would have been the worst crime an Irishman could commit. The document was not used at MacNeill's trial.

As Easter approached, the Supreme Council of the Volunteers, with the exception of Hobson's group, were actively involved in implementing the plans for the Rising. MacNeill had misgivings about the nature and extent of the German help and he had sent Count Plunkett to have Casement impress on the Germans that their officers were 'imperative'. Count Plunkett's son was one of Pearse's 'ultra' group and would have known of Plunkett's mission.

The Germans were sending help, but it was minimal, and there were no officers coming. Indeed, the Germans seemed to have been more concerned with the possibility of getting their vessel and crew safely away than with helping the Rising. They had been asked to send the rifles and munitions to Limerick but they had substituted Fenit, Co. Kerry without consulting the Irish.

Casement was on his way to Ireland and hoped to arrive in time to convince the Volunteer leaders to cancel plans for the Rising. If, against all the odds, the arms ship did find its way through the British blockade, Casement hoped they could hide the rifles, and then distribute them throughout the country.

By early April the British were fully briefed by McGeoy on what the Germans were sending in the way of help, and that Casement was determined to travel on the arms ship. An essential part of their strategy was to allow the arms ship through the blockade. This meant the withdrawal of all their blockading vessels from the route of the arms ship. Furthermore, they must make no move in Ireland that might alarm the Volunteers and lead to a cancellation of the Rising. The British strategy was to wait until the German arms ship had berthed in an Irish port and was discharging its cargo; then they would need no further excuse to crack down on the Volunteers. Naval guns would bombard the vessel, and the British expeditionary force, assembled and waiting in Wales, would embark for Dublin. When the Volunteer leaders had been arrested or killed, it would then be possible to impose conscription on Ireland and obtain several hundred thousand additional soldiers who were badly needed for the British army.

Captain Spindler brought the *Aud* into Tralee Bay on the afternoon of Thursday, 20 April, in accordance with the earliest arrival time he had been given. His instructions were emphatic on the importance of arriving on time. The second message sent to Germany warned that the arms ship must not arrive before Easter Sunday, but by the time this message reached Germany, the *Aud* had already left.

Spindler expected to be met by a pilot vessel which was to show two green lights, close together, at short intervals. He looked in vain for these ' lights. No vessel of any kind approached him that afternoon in Tralee Bay. He circled slowly around the bay and then sailed over to the west side, dropped anchor and remained there that night.

The following morning a white vessel emerged from the Shannon estuary, turned towards Tralee Bay and then headed straight for the *Aud*, which was anchored under Mount Brandon. This white ship was a British Admiralty patrol vessel, and she tied up to the *Aud*. A party of armed British marines came on board the gun-running vessel and the officer in charge proceeded to question Spindler about the nationality of his vessel, the nature of his cargo, the details of his voyage and his reason for anchoring in Tralee Bay. They inspected his log, his ship's papers and the manifest of his cargo. Spindler was able to satisfy them, or so he thought, that he was a Norwegian tramp steamer on her lawful occasions bringing a cargo from Oslo to Spain. He said that his vessel had developed engine trouble the previous day and that he had availed of the shelter of Tralee Bay to enable his engineers to repair the engine. The British search party appeared satisfied that everything was in order. They reboarded their patrol vessel and returned to the Shannon.

Spindler says in his book that there were boxes of ammunition, clearly marked as such, lying on the deck, ready for a quick discharge when they tied up at Fenit pier. He could not understand how the British had not noticed them, although the markings would have been in German or Russian (the weapons were captured Russian rifles).

Spindler did not suspect that the purpose of this British search was to confirm their strong suspicion that the *Aud* was the German gun-runner. The boarding officer had been instructed not to alert the Germans to the fact that he knew about their mission, no matter what he found. If he saw the boxes, and realized what was in them, he was able to report back to the British Admiralty that this vessel was without doubt the German arms ship.

To complete the British plan, it was now essential for them to intercept the German ship in the act of discharging her cargo of arms for the Irish Volunteers in an Irish port. Capturing or sinking the arms ship on the high seas would not achieve this purpose.

All Friday the crew of the *Aud* watched anxiously for any sign of a pilot boat to bring them into Fenit, but no vessel appeared. It is difficult to believe that the Fenit pilot did not see this large merchant vessel anchored in Tralee Bay. His living depended on keeping a lookout for any vessels seeking a pilot to enter Fenit, and such vessels cannot have been frequent at any time, and still less during the war. The conclusion is inescapable: the pilot decided to have nothing whatever to do with this dangerous business of piloting a German gun-running vessel into Fenit. This is understandable and excusable. It is not so easy to understand or excuse why Austin Stack or the other officers of the local Volunteers made no effort to approach the vessel lying all day in Tralee Bay. If the professional pilot decided he was not going to get involved, it was surely possible for the Volunteers to have found a small boat to bring a party of Volunteers out to the *Aud*.

Casement's submarine had arrived in Tralee Bay at midnight on Friday, about ten hours after the *Aud*, and the three Irishmen had landed on Banna Strand in the early hours of Saturday morning. Casement had decided to hide in McKenna's fort until a car could be found to bring him to a safe house. Stack, the commanding officer of the local Volunteers, could legitimately plead that he had been busy all that morning trying to get a car for Casement. However, that effort was at an end by lunchtime when all the local Volunteers knew that Casement had been arrested and locked up in the RIC barracks in Tralee.

But by this time also, Monteith had informed the local Volunteers that Casement's mission to Ireland was to use all his influence to cancel the plans for the Rising became the German help was altogether inadequate, even in the unlikely event that it did arrive. The confusion caused by the knowledge of Casement's mission may have been the reason why the local Volunteers made no effort to make contact with the *Aud*.

If the local Volunteers made no effort to establish contact with the *Aud*, she was being closely watched by the British. During World War I there were coastguard stations at many points around the Irish coast and the British also had watchtowers at prominent headlands from which there was a good view of a large area of coastal waters. Any observation posts that could see the *Aud* were warned to keep a close watch on her and report immediately if she made any move.

Had Spindler waited until darkness made it impossible for the observation posts to see his vessel, she might have been able to reach the open sea during Friday night and been well out of reach of any British patrol vessels by dawn the next morning. But towards evening, while she was still visible, Spindler concluded that something had gone wrong with the plans for his reception. He considered that he had carried out his orders and that he was entitled to try to escape to the open sea.

The word that the *Aud* was moving out was immediately sent to the British Admiralty at Queenstown (now Cobh) and an armed patrol vessel, the *Bluebell*, which was waiting somewhere off the west coast, set off in pursuit. The chase went on all night and shortly after dawn on Saturday morning the *Bluebell* overtook the *Aud*. When an order to halt was ignored, a warning shot was fired across the *Aud*'s bows. Spindler then obeyed the order to halt.

The next order from the British vessel told the *Aud* to head for Queenstown. As the two vessels approached the entrance to this port, about 10 o'clock on Saturday morning, Spindler gave his last orders as the captain of the *Aud*. German naval uniforms were issued to the crew and, when all those on board had donned these, the German flag was hoisted. The lifeboats were lowered and, as the sailors were clambering into them, the fuse to the explosive charge was ignited. This gave them about five minutes to get the lifeboats clear of the ship before the explosion. The Germans were lucky that the *Bluebell* did not open fire on them as they rowed away from the sinking ship, but they hoisted white flags as soon as they were in the lifeboats and they were taken on board the *Bluebell* and treated as prisoners of war.

In Spindler's account of this last episode of his odyssey to Ireland, he says that they sank the *Aud* in the mouth of Queenstown harbour. When divers went down to see what they could find, the wreck was five miles from the harbour mouth. This detail, like almost any item of Spindler's account that can be verified, turns out to be false. Having said this, he must be given full marks for having brought the *Aud* through the British blockade and for arriving on schedule in Tralee Bay. He had no means of knowing that in making this voyage he had the full co-operation of the British Admiralty.

There was never any evidence of machine guns in the *Aud*'s cargo, which suggests that when the Germans did not succeed in getting the Irish Brigade to travel to Ireland on the *Aud*, they saw no purpose in sending weapons which the Irish had not been trained to use.

When the submarine (U19) in which Casement, Monteith and Bayley had travelled from Germany reached Tralee Bay, it approached the shore on the surface, using electric propulsion to avoid the noise of the diesel engine; the submarine spent some time cruising around the bay on the lookout for the pilot boat with the agreed signal — two green lights close together.

If the pilot had been in Tralee Bay to meet the submarine, Casement and his companions could have been brought ashore in comfort and safety to meet the local officers of the Volunteers. But the U19 had been misinformed about the pilot boat. The German reply to the initial Irish request for arms said that they would be delivered in two or three steam trawlers and the pilot was to be on the lookout for these vessels. In a later message (which may never have reached Ireland), the Germans added a small steamer to vessels bringing the arms.

The decision to send Casement to Ireland by submarine was made only a week before the U19 left, and there was no time to send word to Ireland. It is also significant that, before they left Germany, Monteith was practising how to handle the small dinghy carried by the submarine. This indicates that they intended to come ashore in Ireland by dinghy. When the submarine saw no sign of the pilot boat, the hatch of the compartment housing the dinghy was opened and it was put in the water. There was an outboard motor for the propulsion of the dinghy. This was the motor Monteith was practising to start, before the submarine left Wilhelmshaven, when it backfired and gave his wrist a bad strain. Monteith stated in his book that the Germans had refused to give the Irishmen this out-board motor, but Casement makes it quite clear that it was the Irishmen who refused to take it because they were nervous that the noise it made would attract attention. They should have realized that leaving the dinghy on the shore after they landed, where it would inevitably have been found, would result in a hue and cry, with searches of houses and watches on railway stations.

Instead of using the motor, Casement, Monteith and Bayley had elected to row ashore, a distance of about a mile. None of the trio had any experience of handling a small boat and when the German sailors saw the ineptitude of the three land-lubbers trying to manage the dinghy, one of them offered to land them. If they had accepted this offer and allowed the sailor to use the outboard motor, the chances of detection would have been remote.

The captain of the U19 was nervous that if his sailor failed to find the submarine when he returned, he would have been faced with the prospect of going away and leaving him alone in a small boat in the middle of Tralee Bay.

When the Irishmen were ready to board the dinghy, the Germans gave them three Mauser pistols. Monteith described these weapons as the 'supreme masterpiece of the gunsmith's art'. They could be held in one hand as a pistol, or the wooden holster could be clipped to the pistol grip to make a small semi-automatic rifle that would fire about eight shots. This pistol-cum-rifle was always known in Ireland as a 'Peter the Painter'. (A painter whose name was Peter used one in the Sydney Street siege in London.)

Monteith wanted to show Casement how to load his Mauser, but Casement had no interest and said to him, 'You load it for me.' Casement found this instrument for killing people repugnant, and did not want to know how to use it. The first thing these three men did after landing in Ireland was to bury their weapons in the sand not far from the dinghy. Even this was done so carelessly that when a local man, who had been commissioned by the police to keep a watch along the shore, returned from his own dawn patrol, he found his three children playing with the Mausers.

When the three Irishmen left in the dinghy, the U19 headed out into the Atlantic and proceeded with her normal work of sinking cargo vessels. She sank one that Friday off the coast of Ireland.

Casement was exhausted when the dinghy reached Banna Strand. The three rested there for some time and then set off on the ten-mile trek to Tralee. A mile or so along the road there was a Viking rath, known locally as McKenna's Fort. At this point Casement could go no further and decided to remain there and let the other two go into Tralee to find a car to bring him to a safe house. When Monteith and Bayley were leaving, Casement impressed on them that if he was found and arrested before they returned, they were to send an urgent message to the Dublin leaders that the German help was much less than they had requested and was unlikely to arrive. If the Rising was based on the arrival of substantial German assistance, it would be folly to go ahead with it.

Casement was tired, cold and miserable when he first sat in the fort that Good Friday morning, but the sun came out and warmed him up and he began to feel much better. Realizing that there was a serious risk of his being arrested, he buried some of his papers, but he did not empty his pockets carefully and he overlooked several incriminating items. One of these was the sleeper car ticket from Berlin to Wilhelmshaven, with a date on it only a week old. Another was a diary which stated, 'Left Wicklow in Willie's yacht.' This was to be interpreted as 'Left Wilhelmshaven in the Kaiser's submarine'.

Monteith and Bayley walked into Tralee, a town neither of them had ever been in before. Since they knew no one who could help them, they decided to look for a newsagent's shop that sold radical Irish papers. The proprietor would be able to put them in touch with the local Volunteer leader. When they found such a shop, they had to convince the shop owner that they were legitimate nationalists and not British spies. This took some time but eventually a message was sent to Austin Stack, the leader of the local Volunteers, asking him to come immediately to the shop. The word came back from Stack that he would be there in an hour and, despite messages urging him to hasten, it was mid-morning before he arrived. He was told that a motor car was required urgently to collect Casement. When the car arrived, it was sent with local Volunteers to McKenna's Fort. But they were delayed when the car got a puncture and then they lost their way! It was almost noon by the time they reached McKenna's Fort.

Meanwhile, the local man who had been commissioned by the RIC to keep a watch on the coast, and who had found his children playing with the loaded Mausers and had seen the dinghy on the shore, told the police in Ardfert what he had found. A search party went out to see if they could find anyone suspicious. When they saw Casement sitting in the fort, they covered him with their rifles and ordered him to put up his hands. He told them he was an English author named Morton, writing a book about St Brendan the navigator, and that he had come to the area to get local colour for his book. There was such an author with whom Casement was friendly, and Casement later said that he knew Morton would not mind him using his name.

When the police found the German railway ticket, they knew they had made an important catch. They stopped a passing pony and trap, put Casement into it and brought him to Ardfert barracks. As he was getting into the trap, Casement attempted to drop a piece of paper into the hedge at the side of the road. The boy driving the trap picked it up and said, 'Hey, mister, you have dropped this paper', handing it to him. When the police read it, they saw 'Left Wicklow in Willie's yacht', as well as some notes of a code that could be used in sending messages. Casement was not a competent conspirator, whatever other talents he may have had.

The RIC realized that they had made an important arrest and hired a car to send their prisoner into Tralee. In the barracks in Tralee, Casement still kept up the pretence that he was an English author called Morton. But when the district inspector of the RIC came in to see him, Casement decided that his best chance of getting his message to Dublin was to come clean and admit who he was. He knew he was in serious trouble himself, but he was entirely unconcerned about his own safety. His one thought was to get his message to the leaders of the Volunteers in Dublin.

When he told the inspector that he was Roger Casement, the officer said to him, 'We guessed who you were and I only hope it does not end like Wolfe Tone.' The police officer then asked him why he had not shot the policeman who had arrested him. Casement replied that he would not think of committing such a murder; he might have added that he and his companions had left their guns on Banna strand, so they could not have shot anyone.

When Casement realized that the police officer's sympathies were with the Volunteers, he asked him if he would send a message to the Dublin leaders to tell them that the help from Germany was inadequate and was unlikely to get through the British blockade. (It is surprising that Casement was so sure that the arms ship would be intercepted. The submarine on which he had just arrived had travelled almost the whole way on the surface and they had not seen a single British patrol vessel.)

It was scarcely realistic of Casement to expect a district inspector of the RIC to arrange for a message to be sent to the leaders of the Volunteers, urging them to cancel plans for the Rising. Even if the inspector had agreed to do this, a message from an RIC officer would not be accepted by the Dublin leaders, but in an effort to be helpful, the inspector sent in a doctor to see Casement.

The doctor did not want to get involved, even though his role would have been to try to cancel the Rising, and he in turn sent a priest, Father Ryan, to see Casement. It was not likely that the priest would get into trouble even if it became known that he had sent such a message to Dublin. It may seem surprising that the police allowed a private consultation between Casement and the priest, but everyone in the barracks was doing everything they reasonably could to help.

When the priest conveyed Casement's message to Austin Stack, it confirmed what Monteith had already told him. To avoid any mishap, Stack sent two messengers to Dublin. One took the train going via Killarney and Mallow, and the other the train going through Limerick.

It is not known when the messengers reached Dublin or when they reported to MacNeill. The reason so little is known about these messengers is that the Rising had no sooner been suppressed, and the executions carried out, than Irish nationalists considered it to have been the greatest achievement in the history of Ireland and no one was going to admit to having played a part in the efforts to cancel it. It has often been said that the messengers reported to Liberty Hall, but this can be positively refuted. Cathal O'Shannon put it on record that he was with James Connolly on the Saturday night until midnight when Connolly said to him, 'I had better go to bed now as I am not likely to get much sleep for the rest of the week.' Connolly then went into an inner room in which he had a bed. When he fell asleep that night, he was fully confident that the Rising was to start the following morning.

In anticipation of the Rising, to which he was fully committed, O'Rahilly had to make personal arrangements in case he became a casualty. Shortly after the outbreak of World War I, he had informed the Pembroke Urban District Council that their house was to be put in his wife's name. He was concerned that, if he was killed, an attempt might be made to evict his widow, and he wanted to ensure that this was legally impossible. The Council paid no attention to his request and continued to address the rates demand to him. O'Rahilly then informed them that no more rates would be paid on the house until the demand was sent to the correct tenant. This had the desired effect.

O'Rahilly also made arrangements with the companies in which he held shares to ensure that the dividends would continue to be paid to his wife if he died. Then some weeks before Easter he and

Nannie decided to go on a short holiday together to the Poula-phouca Hotel in Blessington, County Wicklow. Nannie was again pregnant and the baby was due some time in July.

When they returned some weeks before Easter, he decided to try to remedy a deficiency in the Volunteers' munitions. Many of them were equipped only with shot guns, normally used for fowling, but if cartridges for such weapons were loaded with buckshot, they could be quite effective in short-range fighting. There were plenty of shot-gun cartridges but very little buckshot.

O'Rahilly knew that casting lead shot for cartridges was as old an activity as making gunpowder, and he set about finding out how to do it. His first thought was to use plaster moulds; these would be used once and then discarded, and a new mould made for the next casting. A friend of his from Ballylongford, named Michael Creedon, was then a plastering contractor in Dublin, and O'Rahilly enlisted his help in making plaster moulds.

It did not prove feasible to cast buckshot in this way and O'Rahilly then made a wooden pattern and had brass castings made from it in the Brooks Thomas foundry in Abbey Street. These rough castings had to be filed to a close fit and put together in pairs to form a mould. This mould would have spherical holes, 9mm in diameter, into which the molten lead was poured. When the lead cooled, the mould was opened and the buckshot could be taken out.

This shot had still to be 'rumbled'. This meant putting about a hundred of them into a steel cylinder, made from perforated sheet metal, and rotating the cylinder to make them smooth and clean. The fins on the shot were rubbed off by the friction. O'Rahilly designed this rumbler and had it made in a Dublin engineering shop. The proprietor was told that it was to be used for roasting coffee, which indeed it could have been.

Michael was adept at metalwork of this kind, and he was working at this just before Easter. I was sent down to Brooks Thomas to collect the brass castings. The parcel in which they were wrapped did not seem heavy leaving the foundry, but by the time I had walked home it felt like a ton weight. I was warned not to mention the intended use of these castings, but someone in Brooks Thomas guessed the purpose for which they were to be used and, when the British held an enquiry into the Rising, Brooks Thomas volunteered to give evidence, and told the enquiry that the moulds had been cast in their foundry. The actual production of buckshot never got underway because the Rising took place before the equipment was ready for use.

This effort of armament production sounds pathetically primitive and amateurish, as indeed it was, but if a challenge to the might of the British empire was going to be made, it was important for every Volunteer to have a weapon of some kind.

The first overt move among the Volunteer leaders to express organized opposition to a Rising was made by Bulmer Hobson at a concert on Palm Sunday, a week before Easter. Sunday evening concerts for nationalists were common social events in those days. In the intermission, a leading political figure would speak on a topic of current interest.

Desmond FitzGerald was at this concert and, since he had recently been released from jail, after serving a six months' sentence for delivering an anti-recruiting speech, he was invited to make the interval speech. He declined, saying that his time in prison had put him out of touch with current events. Bulmer Hobson spoke instead.

The burden of Hobson's speech was a warning against any attempt at a violent uprising, which he argued would have disastrous consequences. Many of those in the audience, who were deeply involved in the preparations for the Rising, were unhappy, and indeed indignant, at the tone of Hobson's speech. In addition to making this public declaration against the Rising, he was known to be involved in private intrigues to prevent it taking place.

A group of the 'ultras' decided that Hobson was doing so much to wreck the plans for the Rising that he would have to be kidnapped to keep him quiet. This kidnapping took place about the middle of the week. Hobson was invited to a meeting at which he hoped he could continue his campaign of opposition to a Rising, but when he arrived he was confronted by a group of men armed with revolvers, who locked him up and kept him under guard until the Rising had begun.

One of his captors must have had some sympathy with Hobson because he was able to smuggle out a letter to Eoin MacNeill, telling him of his plight. When O'Rahilly heard of Hobson's kidnapping, he was furious; among his papers was found a letter which was never finished. It began: 'Commandant O'Rahilly to Commandant Pearse.'

The implications of a letter addressed in this way, between

comrades who had been on terms of personal intimacy for many years, was that they were both of equal rank in the organization. The letter then starts, 'A Chara', a most formal greeting, and then contains just three words, 'À pro pos'. Having written these words, O'Rahilly decided that this was not a matter for letter writing, and got into his car and drove out to Pearse's school at Rathfarnham.

Desmond Ryan, who had been at school there and was close to Pearse, said that O'Rahilly came into Pearse's study in a very bad humour. Sitting down in front of Pearse, he put a revolver on the table and said, 'Whoever kidnaps me will have to be a quicker shot.' Pearse said, 'Put away that gun; nobody wants to kidnap you.'

If O'Rahilly hoped to secure Hobson's release, he was not successful. Pearse convinced him that Hobson had to be kept out of the way in view of the efforts he was making to undermine plans for the Rising.

With Hobson locked up, the 'ultras' decided that it was essential to convince those Volunteer officers who might have fallen under his influence that they had no alternative to a Rising, because the British were determined to round up the leaders and suppress the Volunteers. The plot the ultras hatched was probably concocted by Seán Mac Diarmada. They invented a document, alleged to have been leaked from Dublin Castle, which spelled out the details of the steps to be taken to put an end to the activities of the Irish Volunteers.

This allegedly leaked document was circulated to the leading newspapers, but none of them would publish it. They probably checked with officials at Dublin Castle, who no doubt said that the 'leak' was a palpable forgery. The ultras then arranged to have the document read out at a meeting of Dublin Corporation, and the papers could not avoid publishing the proceedings of this public body.

I recall an episode that took place one morning during that week. My father was reading the paper at breakfast. Whatever he read had put him into a vile humour and for some trivial reason he snapped at one of us. Mother reproached him and said, 'It is not fair to take out your annoyance on the children; it is not their fault.' Some years later I wondered what had put him in such bad humour. I looked up that newspaper and decided that it was probably the 'leaked' document that was alleged to have come from Dublin Castle. This document listed a number of houses that were to be raided and our house, 40 Herbert Park, was one of them. O'Rahilly would not have been in any doubt that if there had been a general round-up of the houses of the Volunteer leaders, our house would have been included. Yet it was inconceivable that Dublin Castle would have decided to raid the house of the Catholic Archbishop of Dublin, and that they would have spelt the name of his house incorrectly.

O'Rahilly may have disapproved of the proposal to leak this faked document and assumed that it had been abandoned; then that morning he saw that they had gone ahead with the plan, despite his disapproval.

This faked document may have hardened the resolve of some of the Volunteer officers to take part in the Rising, although they all would have known that Dublin Castle had often considered the option of arresting the leaders and suppressing the Irish Volunteers.

By the middle of Holy Week, just a few days before Easter, everything was ready. With Hobson locked up, and any of those officers who might have been wavering now convinced by the faked document that there was no alternative to fighting or being interned, the die was cast. It can be assumed that MacNeill was satisfied with the message Count Plunkett had brought back from Germany and Rome. It would have been in line with the second letter Plunkett had sent to Casement before leaving for Rome. This letter implied that whatever 'particulars' of Casement's message Plunkett had been given by the secretary of the German embassy, he had not been told that there were no German officers coming to Ireland.

To be fair to the Germans, they could reasonably complain that the initial request from Ireland contained no suggestion of German officers being required or for a German submarine to be sent to Dublin Bay; and it was unreasonable to give them a message from Dublin asking for this additional help just as the *Aud* was getting ready to sail.

We must also question if MacNeill really understood what he was asking when he told Count Plunkett to insist that German officers were 'imperative'. This word suggests that without German officers there would be no Rising. Even if the Germans had been given advance notice of this requirement, could they have complied with it? Any German officers would have to volunteer for this duty, and the German High Command could not assure them of prisoner-of-war treatment if they were captured. They would have to be fluent

English speakers, and would be giving advice on a military campaign of which they had no knowledge or experience. The Germans were entitled to treat this last-minute demand as impracticable and could reasonably ignore it.

It is likely that the message Plunkett brought back to MacNeill in Dublin was that the Germans would do their utmost to comply with the Irish request. If this was not positively asserted, it was implied, and it was on this assumption that MacNeill gave his support for the Rising plans.

An essential step in the plans for the Rising was the wording of the Proclamation of the Republic. The men drawing it up would have been keenly aware that it was going to be read not only by millions of people of that generation, but by many generations of Irish people then unborn. If the cancellation had not been ordered by MacNeill, his signature would have been the leading one and the proclamation would have included O'Rahilly's name.

It was not possible for the Proclamation to be printed until the last possible moment, since it would have been unwise to let those involved in the printing know that a Rising was intended. This meant that the original plan was for the proclamation to have been printed on Sunday morning just an hour before the Rising commenced, and that the one issued was printed on Monday morning. There was a printing press in Liberty Hall and the proclamation was produced on this press.

On Saturday morning everything was back in the melting pot. MacNeill was given Casement's message from Tralee that the Volunteers had been deceived by the Germans and that the requested and promised help was not coming. The Dublin leaders had complete confidence in Casement. Everyone who knew the man was certain that his integrity and his commitment to the cause of Irish independence was unshakable. His shortcoming, and it was a serious one, was his overweening confidence in his own opinion, even in matters in which he did not have the necessary facts to enable him to form a valid judgment. In the present crisis Casement had information from Germany, not available to the Dublin Volunteers, but he had no knowledge of the situation in Ireland. Casement knew that a rising in Ireland would be a substantial advantage to the Germans because it would compel the British to withdraw troops from the Western Front.

Casement visualized the rebellion leading to the slaughter of thousands of Irishmen, and the devastation of Irish towns and cities, and ending as a disaster for Ireland and a great benefit to Germany. His opinion of the Germans at that time was such that the last thing he wanted to do was to help them, and certainly not at the expense of little Ireland.

MacNeill was alarmed and appalled at the news from Casement that the German help was derisory and probably would not arrive. He may not have been enthusiastic about a Rising, but had been persuaded that the present war, in which the British were strained to the limits of their war-making capacity, was an opportunity the Irish would be foolish to neglect, provided that substantial help was available from Germany.

The situation was now completely transformed. MacNeill called an urgent meeting, to be held on Saturday afternoon in Dr O'Kelly's house in Rathgar. All the prominent people in the 'Movement' who could be contacted were urged to come. The gathering may have been more a continuous discussion with delegates, as they arrived, rather than a formal meeting. It appears to have been generally agreed that, in the light of Casement's message, the Rising should be cancelled. Unfortunately O'Rahilly's views have not been recorded. He would have been conscious that it was his duty to obey the orders of Eoin MacNeill, the commander in chief, but it would have been out of character for him not to favour a Rising. He had made his views clear in his letter to the *Workers' Republic* some months earlier.

If Pearse opposed the cancellation, he agreed to accept it. He said that, no matter what orders came from the president of the Volunteers, 'his people' would not accept them without his endorsement and he agreed to send this endorsement to the officers who had committed themselves to accepting instructions from him. These officers would have been mostly, but not entirely, in Dublin.

When it had been agreed that the Rising was not going ahead in Dublin, it was imperative to get cancellation orders to the country officers that evening, or, at the latest, before any of them commenced action at noon the next day. Messengers would have to be sent to all centres of Volunteer support throughout Ireland. The Limerick area contained one of the most numerous and active Volunteer corps in Ireland outside Dublin. The courier who was either asked or offered to go to Limerick was O'Rahilly. The message that MacNeill wrote out for him to bring to Limerick reads: 'Volunteers completely deceived. All orders for special action are hereby cancelled and on no account will action be taken. Eoin MacNeill.' This order given to O'Rahilly was the only one of MacNeill's orders extant after the Rising.

When O'Rahilly set off on Saturday night to bring the cancellation order to Limerick, he decided not to take his own car because it was well-known to the police. Moreover, he might not have felt equal to such an arduous drive after being in bed with a heavy cold during the week. He went to the A. and B. taxi company in Portobello and selected a closed car in which he could sit unnoticed in the back seat.

This taxi ride cost £20, which Mother had to pay after the Rising, and it was this expense that Yeats referred to in his poem when he said that O'Rahilly had

> . . . Gone to great expense
> keeping all the Kerry men
> Out of that crazy fight;

He left Dublin at 10 pm and reached Limerick four hours later. He and his driver were given beds in Daly's, prominent Sinn Féiners. O'Rahilly went to an early morning Mass that Sunday and met the local Volunteer officers, all keyed up for the Rising, at noon. He showed them MacNeill's countermanding order, and no doubt explained why the Rising was being cancelled.

His route back to Dublin that day has not been recorded, but when he returned he sent word to MacNeill that he had visited Cork, Kerry, Limerick and Tipperary. I was in the front garden about 7 o'clock that evening when a taxi pulled up at the gate and my father stepped out of it. When I asked him where he had been, he said 'in the country'.

While he was having his meal, he told Mother about his journey and then wrote a note to MacNeill without mentioning the places he had visited. He thought it was not safe to refer to specific places because he had been served with a DORA order in 1915 prohibiting him from visiting the south-western counties. The purpose of this order was the British suspicion that in any of these counties it would be possible for him to have liaison with German submarines. (The deportation order to keep O'Rahilly out of these counties was brought to the bungalow in Kerry the morning after he had arrived there for a short holiday in the summer of 1915. He was uncertain if he should obey it or ignore it and let them arrest him, so he sent a telegram to the Volunteer headquarters in Dublin, asking for instructions. The answer was to obey the order, which was a considerable relief to Mother.)

I was given the note to deliver to MacNeill and my father impressed on me that it was of vital importance to memorize the names of the four counties. These were Cork, Kerry, Limerick and Tipperary. I kept repeating these four names on that bicycle ride up to Woodtown Park, beyond Rathfarnham; so much so that they are clearly in my mind to this day.

I had never been to Woodtown Park, so my father drew a small map to show me the road to take from Rathfarnham through Ballyboden and then out on the road to the Hell Fire Club. It was quite dark when I arrived at the house and delivered both the written note and the memorized verbal message of the four counties to MacNeill. I was sent back to Rathfarnham in a horse and trap and from there I got a tram to our house in Herbert Park, which I reached about 11 o'clock. My parents were not pleased that I had been sent home on my own so late. They thought the MacNeills should have given me a bed for the night.

It seems likely that MacNeill gave identical notes to all the couriers he sent around the country. O'Rahilly wanted his note kept as evidence that the Rising had been cancelled on MacNeill's orders, knowing full well that, although he had shown the officers MacNeill's order, the word that would go around and be remembered was that the Rising had been cancelled by 'O'Rahilly'.

On the morning of Easter Monday, as O'Rahilly was driving down to Liberty Hall with his sister Anna, he was particularly concerned that the Rising was now going to take place in Dublin, without any help from the country, and that he was responsible for calling it off in Munster. He gave MacNeill's note to his sister, telling her that he had carried it in his sock on his mission around Munster. He impressed on her that it was most important to keep it carefully. When Anna was settling her affairs in the 1940s she decided that such a historical document would be safest in the National Museum. She donated it to that institution, along with the last Order of the Day, dictated by Connolly in the burning GPO (see Appendix 4).

'O words are lightly spoken,'
Said Pearse to Connolly,
'Maybe a breath of politic words
Has withered our Rose Tree;
Or maybe but a wind that blows
Across the bitter sea.'

'It needs to be but watered',
James Connolly replied,
'To make the green come out again
And spread on every side,
And shake the blossom from the bud
To be the garden's pride.'

'But where can we draw water,'
Said Pearse to Connolly,
'When all the wells are parched away?
O plain as plain can be
There's nothing but our own red blood
Can make a right Rose Tree.'

(W.B. Yeats, 'The Rose Tree')

The decision to cancel the Rising was sent all over Ireland on Saturday night, but no one thought of conveying it to James Connolly and his Citizen Army right in the centre of Dublin. Connolly was awakened early on Easter Sunday by one of his Citizen Army men who had just read in the *Sunday Independent* that all Volunteer manoeuvres for that day had been cancelled. He woke Connolly and showed him the notice. Connolly probably sent a man on a bicycle to Pearse's school in Rathfarnham with a note, 'Come here urgently. We strike at noon to-day, with or without the Volunteers.' He had some breakfast while waiting for Pearse, who arrived about 10 o'clock. They are likely to have spoken as follows.

Connolly: What the hell has gone wrong? Many of us doubted if the bourgeois Volunteers would ever have the guts to take the fatal plunge and now we know we were right! Why was the Rising called off?

Pearse: MacNeill got word from Casement, who landed from a submarine in Kerry and was captured by the police, that the Volunteers had been completely deceived by the Germans and that the help that was coming from Germany was derisory and probably would never arrive.

Connolly: We always knew that the German arms ship had a poor chance of getting through the British naval blockade. We have enough arms of our own to stage a Rising if we have the guts to use them. But you assured me many times that you had enough of the top Volunteer officers sworn to obey your orders to rise, whether MacNeill agreed to it or not.

Pearse: When all the others agreed on a postponement, I decided to accept it.

Connolly: What about O'Rahilly? I hoped that whatever about the others, he was determined to have a go.

Pearse: O'Rahilly decided that it was a military organization and it was essential to obey the orders of the commander-in-chief.

Connolly: So where does that leave us? You don't suppose the British are going to allow us any more time. So do we sit here like petrified rabbits while they come and arrest the leaders and disarm the rank and file? We shall have missed the best chance that Ireland has had for more than a hundred years, due to our own pusillanimity. As far as the Citizen Army is concerned, we are going to strike at noon today. We will occupy the GPO or Dublin Castle and declare a Workers' Republic.

Pearse: If you do, the Volunteers will inevitably be disarmed and all the leaders arrested.

Connolly: That is your funeral. We, at least, will die with our boots on.

Pearse: Put it off until tomorrow and I will undertake to bring out the Dublin Volunteers, where almost all the top officers have sworn to obey my orders, and we can then have a joint declaration of an Irish Republic.

Connolly: Is that a firm commitment? Can I be sure there will be no more backsliding?

Pearse: Yes, that is a promise. I will send out the new mobilization orders immediately.

Michael was still in bed at 10 o'clock the next morning, recovering from his exhausting drive, when Desmond FitzGerald arrived at the house. Mother said to him 'Don't tell me there is more bad news.' FitzGerald said, 'I must speak to Michael' and Mother told him he was sleeping.

FitzGerald went upstairs and woke my father to tell him that the Dublin men, despite MacNeill's cancellation, had decided to go ahead with the Rising that day at noon. In his memoirs Desmond said that Michael's comment was, 'If men are determined to have a Rising, nothing will stop them.'

It did not occur to Michael that he would do other than join the Dublin men in the Rising, even though their action was contrary to MacNeill's cancellation order. As he was putting on his Volunteer uniform, my brother Mac and I, dressed in our Fianna uniforms, were getting ready to leave on a march to the country. This organization of Irish boy scouts normally went on such marches on public holidays. Our parents held a whispered consultation to decide whether they should allow us to go or not and decided that we were safer in the country than in the city.

Desmond FitzGerald was then asked to take Michael's bicycle from the garage, and to go up to MacNeill's house to tell him that the Rising was taking place. Michael assumed, correctly, that MacNeill also would want to take part.

The last view I had of my father was as he sat on the side of the bed winding on his puttees. These were long strips of cloth, about three inches wide, made of the same material as a soldier's uniform, which were wound spirally around the leg from the ankle to under the knee, and which kept it warm and gave it support.

When he had finished his breakfast, he collected all the weapons in the house and loaded them into his car. He was the director of arms for the Volunteers and there were always weapons of one kind or another in the house, ready for distribution. One of the last things he said to Mother when he was kissing her goodbye was, 'Don't forget about those papers I sent up to Mrs Hogan; the boys will be interested in them.' He then got into the car and backed it the short distance down to the road and, as he put it into forward gear, he waved her a last farewell. Mother felt that she was not likely ever to see him again and she closed the door with a heavy heart.

The papers to which Michael referred were some he wanted preserved. Some weeks before Easter we had all been at 9 o'clock Sunday Mass, and a group of friends and acquaintances were chatting outside Donnybrook Church before going home. The Hogan family, who lived at the top of Herbert Park, were among the group and, before we parted, Michael turned to Mrs Hogan and said 'I have some important papers which I am anxious to have preserved. Would you mind keeping them for me?' Mrs Hogan said this would be no trouble. Later that morning when we had finished our breakfast, my father told Mac, his eldest son, that he wanted him to take an envelope up to the Hogans' house. Mac recalled that the envelope had come from Mexico and, because he was collecting stamps, he was unhappy that he could not keep the ones on the envelope.

Some weeks after the Rising, Mother remembered about these papers and she called to get them. Mrs Hogan became confused and embarrassed and said, 'I was afraid we might get into trouble over them and the parish priest advised me to burn them.'

The family often speculated about the documents in this envelope which Michael considered so important. I used to think that, in anticipation of the Rising and the likelihood that he would be a casualty, he had written an account of how he had become involved in the movement. Such a document might have explained how he had come to the conclusion that, if Ireland was ever to raise her head again, the British occupation forces had to be expelled, and that he had become convinced that the only way they would leave was when we were strong enough and determined enough to drive them out. But there was nothing new in this. He had said the same many times, both verbally and in writing.

I now believe that, in anticipation of the Rising and the serious risk that he might not survive it, he had decided to summarize the work he had done on the family's genealogy. He would have assumed that, following the defeat of the rebels, which he knew was likely, his papers would be taken from Herbert Park for scrutiny by the Secret Service. If this were to happen, all the work he had done to trace the O'Rahilly background would be lost. This view is strengthened by his remark to Nannie that 'the boys will be interested in them'.

When the Rising was over and she had lost her husband, Nannie often wondered whether she should have attempted to dissuade him from joining the fight. Several of his most intimate companions in the movement, including Eoin MacNeill, Arthur Griffith and Bulmer Hobson, had not taken part in the Rising and had survived. When the prisoners were released about a year after the Rising, Arthur Griffith called to our house to condole with Mother on Michael's death. In her eyes, Griffith was the man whose ideas had inspired her husband and she found it difficult to understand how

O'Rahilly's mentor had escaped unscathed. Mother asked Griffith bluntly why he had not taken part in the Rising. He explained that his wife had been ill or away. He did not call again.

Mother came to the conclusion that if she had tried to keep Michael from taking part, he would have gone anyway and the parting would have been acrimonious. It was a subject frequently discussed in the weeks following the Rising. In the course of one such discussion, Mother said: 'Wouldn't you boys prefer if he had not gone "out" and you still had your father?' One of us replied, 'Not if he was called a traitor.'

When the car containing O'Rahilly and his sister Anna, laden with rifles, arrived at Liberty Hall on Easter Monday about 11 o'clock, many Volunteers and members of the Citizen Army were assembled outside. O'Rahilly, as usual, was meticulously dressed in his Volunteer uniform, and he was given a loud cheer of welcome.

Anna went with him into the building and joined the group of senior officers who were assembled in the hall. She told me later that she went up to Pearse, whom she knew very well (his school had benefited substantially from her financial support), and gave him a good pinch on the arm to attract his attention. Then she said, 'This is all your fault.' In this she was reflecting Michael's views, which he had conveyed to her in the car coming down. It was Pearse's action in organizing this cabal of senior officers to take their instructions from him, rather than the legitimate leadership, which made possible this partial Rising in Dublin. The British, in Michael's view, would have no trouble suppressing it, whereas if there had been a simultaneous series of uprisings throughout the country, the British might not have been able to do so.

The rifles were taken out of the car and Anna was about to drive it home when O'Rahilly was asked to leave it because the rebels had no other means of transport. He agreed to leave it, if his sister was willing, and she also assented and walked home.

Barricade at end of Moore Street which The O'Rahilly was trying to storm when shot. It is identified by the butcher's shop, 'Simpson and Wallace'.

The burnt-out shell of The O'Rahilly's De Dion Bouton in Prince's Street after the Rising, now buried under 'Hill 16' in Croke Park.

Dear Dada

26 of April 1916

I got your new letter I heard from Nell and Anno that the volunteers are winning. I dont suppose they will ever get the G. P. O. fo as long as you are in command. Father O'Mahony told us that up in Portello bridge there were two soldiers killed and twenty four wounded. We had Father O'mahony down here last night with anno and had a grand talk about the whole thing.

With Best Love

from
Egan

Written after I was shot —

Darling Nancy
I was shot leading a rush up Moore Street took refuge in a doorway while I was there I heard the men pointing out where I was & I made a bolt for the lane I am in now. I got more one bullet I think Tons & tons of love dearie to you & to the boys & to hell & Anna It was a good fight anyhow Please deliver this to Nannie O Rahilly 40 Herbert Park Dublin Good bye darling

A letter from the author to his father written during Easter week and sent to the GPO. On its reverse The O'Rahilly pencilled a farewell to his wife, after being hit by a bullet, which passed through his tunic, puncturing the paper.

16

Five Days That Transformed Ireland

All the leaders who took part in the Rising were in Liberty Hall that Easter Monday morning getting ready to take their units to the buildings that they were assigned to occupy. Countess Markievicz was one of the senior officers in the Citizen Army and she met O'Rahilly in Liberty Hall as final preparations were being made.

'Well, Michael', she asked, 'What do you think of it?' He replied, 'It is madness, but it is glorious madness.'

As noon approached, the different groups of Volunteers left on their various assignments. None of the buildings to be occupied was more than 30 minutes' walk from Liberty Hall. The General Post Office was to be the headquarters and, since it was only a few minutes' walk from Liberty Hall, the top officers were the last to leave.

The Volunteers knew that there was a guard of armed soldiers in the GPO, possibly protecting the switchroom for the telegraphic communication system. Connolly's union members, who worked in the GPO, would have known where the guard room was stationed.

O'Rahilly's mobilization order for the Easter Sunday Rising assigned him as aide de camp to Patrick Pearse. This order was signed by Willie Pearse. In this role, he may have been ordered by Pearse to lead the men into the Post Office, or he himself may have realized how easily the whole Rising could end as a tragic fiasco, if the guard of British soldiers succeeded in preventing the occupation of the building that was to serve as the headquarters.

Michael marched with the leaders along O'Connell Street. When they reached the GPO, he gave the order to charge and led the Volunteers into the building, with his drawn Mauser in his hand and the safety catch off. He dashed upstairs, guided by a man who knew where the guard room was situated. It was essential to disarm the guard before they became aware that the building was being occupied.

When O'Rahilly burst into the guard room, the soldiers were sitting around with their rifles stacked out of reach. He shouted to them to put up their hands. The sergeant tried to reach for his rifle and this resulted in a shot over his head from the Mauser. He made no further attempt at resistance.

Following the Rising, a question was asked in the House of Commons about why the guard had not resisted. The Minister for the Army said that they had forgotten to bring any ammunition with them. It was an utterly implausible excuse. He might as well have said they had never been shown how to load their rifles. The simple truth was that if there had been any attempt at resistance, the guards would have been shot. O'Rahilly's role is established beyond any doubt by a note he wrote to his son Niall the next day, when he said: 'I disarmed six Saxons and took their rifles.' All correspondence leaving the GPO was examined and passed by 'I.R.Censor', so it is not likely that he would have made any claims which those in the GPO knew to be false.

> Dst Niall,
> You are a good
> little boy to be so
> lonely after me yesterday.
> We are doing grand
> and are giving the
> English a run for their
> money.
>   I disarmed 6 Saxons
> and took their rifles.
>   Be good. Lots of love &
> kisses.   Ua Rathghaille

When the buildings had been occupied and the guard disarmed, O'Rahilly's next concern was that some of the Volunteers might decide to help themselves to the money in the cash boxes at the wickets. A British officer had been in the GPO when it was occupied and he was taken prisoner. To ensure that there was no pilfering of cash, O'Rahilly appointed him to take charge of the safe. A Volunteer officer was then sent around to all the desks containing cash. These were emptied and the money was given to the British officer, who put all the cash, stamps and postal orders in the safe. The safe was fireproof and, when the Rising was over and the GPO had been burned out, it was opened and all the cash was intact.

O'Rahilly was then ordered by Pearse or Connolly to take charge of the men on the top floor and the roof of the GPO. It is usually assumed that, although Pearse was the President of the Republic which had just been proclaimed, Connolly was the officer in charge of the GPO. It is unlikely that there was any formal command structure. After O'Rahilly was killed, an order was found in his pocket. It read: 'Go with bearer in car to get rifles', and is signed by James Connolly. It has not been reported that O'Rahilly ever left the GPO, in his car or otherwise. His nephew, Dick Humphreys, is reported to have taken out the car, but this was to get foodstuffs.

When Desmond and Mabel FitzGerald came into the GPO early on Monday afternoon, Pearse sent him to O'Rahilly to serve as his adjutant. Desmond writes in his memoirs:

When I reached the top floor O'Rahilly came forward, still smiling, 'They were determined to have a Rising', he said, 'so here we are.'

'How long do you think we can hold out?' I asked.

'By a miracle we might last for 24 hours', he replied, 'but I don't think that we'll go for that long.' I thought his estimate extremely optimistic.

Dick Humphreys joined them in the GPO on Monday afternoon. He had not received the mobilization order for the Rising, but when he heard that it had started he immediately went down to the GPO to take his part.

O'Rahilly wrote his first note to his wife on Monday evening:

> GPO 6.15 pm
> Darling Nancy,
>   All safe here
> so far.
>   Things going
> well I believe
> in most places.
>   Love & kisses to you
> & the boys. Ua Rathghaille

One of O'Rahilly's first concerns on Tuesday morning was to visit the prisoners he had taken the previous day. He was annoyed to find that they had not been given any breakfast, and went off to the catering department, set up by the Volunteers, to arrange for food to be brought to them.

Desmond FitzGerald writes that on Tuesday he again asked O'Rahilly how long he thought the Volunteers could sustain their resistance and that Michael had replied that they would be lucky to last 36 hours. It was quite clear to FitzGerald that his colleague had no faith whatever in the strategy adopted by those who had declared the Republic. This plan was to occupy important buildings all over Dublin, in the belief that the British army would not demolish them with artillery. This was based on Connolly's belief that capitalists would not destroy their own property.

O'Rahilly understood that, in the context of subduing a revolution right in the heart of the British empire, as a matter of urgent priority, a few million pounds' worth of property was of no significance.

On Tuesday Michael wrote notes to his four children. He began one of the notes (it has since been lost) with the words, 'Dear Boys' but then decided that each of us would want an individual note, and so wrote four of them. He also wrote a note to his wife every day. He could not, for obvious reasons, give details of any problems that had arisen, or any information about the fighting. In any case there was nothing of this kind to report other than the charge of the Lancers down O'Connell Street on Monday, and he knew that Nannie would not want to hear any news of that kind.

It was on Tuesday that Nell Humphreys, O'Rahilly's eldest sister, came down to the GPO. She was five or six years older than her brother, and believed that she might be able to influence him, as she had done when they were children. She argued that they had now made their protest and there was no point in waiting there like rats in a trap for the British to come and kill them. Nell realized that there was little possibility that Michael would come away on his own and leave the others to their fate. She knew that he was largely responsible for these men being in the GPO, so she hoped to persuade them all to call off the Rising.

Michael's wife and his two sisters were in a frenzy of anxiety about Michael and Dick, and Nell decided to go to the GPO to see if she could influence her brother to persuade the leaders to end the revolt. Nell argued convincingly that there could be only one end to this crazy fight, the slaughter of many Volunteers. She told Michael that whatever sacrifice he was willing to make of his own life, he was not entitled to inflict such a hardship on his wife, their four children, as well as the one yet unborn.

Michael had no answer to this. It was inconsiderate and irresponsible of him to inflict on his wife the worry and hardship his death would entail for her. Michael was convinced, and had been for many years, that the armed struggle was the only way Ireland could hope to end the British occupation which had improverished his country, destroyed its culture, almost ended the knowledge and use of the Irish language, and was sending millions of its young people away on the emigrant ship, never to see Ireland again. He believed, as he made clear to Desmond FitzGerald, that the strategy of occupying important buildings was bound to end in the slaughter, or surrender, of many Volunteers; but it was the armed struggle he had advocated, however foolishly or incompetently planned.

If he had 'chickened out' now, no matter how cruel a hardship he was inflicting on the wife he loved so dearly, he could never have looked himself in the face again.

In reporting Nell's visit to his wife, he said: 'I had a talk with Nell and dont agree a bit with that point of view. I am sure I have done right & would have been worse than a coward to do otherwise. Besides we never died a winter yet. I am sorry dearie for all the trouble I am giving you just now but [you will agree that] we must see it through.'

He crossed out the words in brackets, because he knew Nannie would not agree.

It is of interest to note that a month or two after the Rising when Nell was reporting it all to her sister-in-law in Australia, she made no mention of her visit to Michael in the GPO (see Appendix 5).

When Nell failed to move Michael, she turned her attention to her son Dick, who had just turned twenty years of age. It is said that in her efforts to influence him, she enlisted Pearse's help. He is supposed to have agreed that if Michael was killed, then Dick would be the only grown-up male member in the two families, and that they were entitled to one grown-up male.

Whatever arguments or authority were used, she persuaded Dick to come home with her. Dick told us later that they were in greater danger on the way home, with bullets whistling over their heads, than he ever experienced in the GPO.

When Nell was leaving, Michael gave her a message for his

children. 'Tell the boys', he said, 'never to join a secret society.' He regarded the split in the Volunteers, which had resulted in what he then believed to be an abortive Rising, was directly due to the cabal of senior leaders who had been organized by Pearse to subvert the authority of the accepted command structure of the Volunteers. He was fully convinced that if there had been a united rebellion of the 10,000 men of the Volunteers, with an entirely different strategy, it could have succeeded in driving the British forces out of Ireland.

Michael knew that the secret society of the IRB, which had been in existence for more than fifty years, had not even attempted any activity in all that time; and now he believed that it was Pearse's cabal, also a kind of secret society, that had destroyed the prospects of a successful Rising.

Michael wrote another letter on Tuesday after Nell had been down to the GPO.

> Darling Nancy,
>   We are still to the
> good and I dont think
> anyone will bother us till
> tomorrow. I had a talk
> with Nell and dont agree
> a bit with that point
> of view. I am sure I have
> done right & would have
> been worse than a coward
> to do otherwise. Besides
> we never died a winter
> yet. I am sorry dearie
> for all the trouble I am
> giving you just now
> but ~~you will agree that~~
> we must see it through.
>   Probably it will be only
> in ten years time that
> the value of our little
> fight will become known.
> Thousands of kisses
> dearie and lots of love
> from your own.
>   Ua R.

It was on Tuesday that O'Rahilly persuaded those holding

212

Hobson prisoner to release him. Seán T. O'Kelly recalled how he saw O'Rahilly in earnest conversation with Seán Mac Diarmada, and when O'Rahilly went away, the Leitrim man called O'Kelly and told him to go to a house in Dorset Street to instruct the Volunteers holding Hobson that they were to release him. When Hobson was released, he went up to Woodtown Park where he spent the rest of the week with MacNeill.

Dick Humphreys had a good night's sleep in his own bed on that Tuesday night. The following morning he got up with the others and they all went to 8 o'clock Mass in Haddington Road Church, only a few minutes' walk from their home. After breakfast Dick stood up from the table and said: 'Well I'll be off.'

'Where are you going?' he was asked.

'Back to the GPO. I told Michael I would be back.'

Nobody tried to stop him. They knew it would have been of no use. He went back to the General Post Office and joined his comrades, remaining with them until the end; he was captured with most of the garrison and was sent off to an internment camp in England.

On Wednesday one of the Volunteers saw a British officer in full uniform at one of the top windows on the opposite side of O'Connell Street; he had a pair of field glasses with which he was scanning the Volunteer positions. The Volunteer pointed him out to O'Rahilly and asked, 'Will I shoot him?' This was the moment of truth for Michael. Here was one of the enemy trying to find out about the defence of the GPO, and they had a good chance of killing him and wiping out any information that he might have gathered.

But this British officer was also a human being, possibly with a wife and family. To kill him for no better reason than that the colour of the cloth he was wearing was different from that worn by the Volunteers was something that does not come naturally to any civilized person. O'Rahilly had not yet arrived at that stage of dehumanisation, at which a soldier thinks no more of killing a man than he does of shooting a rabbit. He said to the Volunteer, 'Don't shoot; you would only give away our position. In any case, you would probably miss.'

During those five days in the GPO, the Volunteers were meticulous in their solicitude for the welfare of their prisoners, who numbered about a dozen. When the Rising was over, several of them paid particular tribute to O'Rahilly and said how well he had treated them. The Dublin Metropolitan Police prisoners were especially grateful.

In May 1916 the *Freeman's Journal* published an interview with one of the men who was held prisoner in the GPO. This is relevant in the light of a recent statement by a journalist that a number of the DMP who were held prisoner in the GPO were shot when the Post Office was being evacuated:

Next morning O'Rahilly called to them to see about their food. 'Hello' said he, 'Good morning to you all. How are you doing for food men?' 'We had nothing to eat' we said.

'Oh, damn' said he, 'you should have been attended to long ago. I'll see to it all right', and away he went.

In about a quarter of an hour two ladies in Volunteer uniform came along with two trays filled with food and tea, and O'Rahilly himself helped to distribute the stuff to us. They saw we were quite comfortable and in fact no one could be a finer gentlemen than The O'Rahilly who told us as long as there was food in the place we would get it.

In describing later events this man reported:

Then The O'Rahilly came to us and said, 'men this place is now in the zone of danger. I'll have to bring you back to your old room, but you'll be quite safe there.' We thanked him again and he said 'That's all right. I'll give you my word that you'll escape with your lives.' Again we thanked him and many of us said a prayer for him.

On Wednesday morning the British Expeditionary Force landed at Kingstown from Holyhead and marched into Dublin. From the windows of our house, it was possible to see the endless stream of British soldiers with their field guns moving into the city. After watching this for some hours, Mother could stand it no longer, and she decided to leave Herbert Park. The house was well known as a 'rebel house', and it seemed certain that it would be raided. She moved with the younger children to Dundrum, and Mac and I were sent to MacNeills, Woodtown Park.

Michael's note to Nannie on Wednesday reads:

> Darling Nancy,
> Just now at 12.15
> Nancy Power came in and
> will take this. We are

doing finely. Have been
more than 48 hours free
from English control.

   Thanks awfully for your
sweet letter and all the boys'
letters. Dont worry dearie.

   There is no doubt at
all that I did the right
thing. Everyone agrees about
it. Probably everything will
turn out well. For instance
we will stand as well as
Montenegro for instance.

   Don't worry, Darling,

   No matter what tragedy
may come it will be
really a glorious end.

   No one can ever again
say the Volunteers were
bluffing.

   They got a gunboat to
bombard Liberty Hall
& occupy it and they
are now lying about
Liberty Hall being 'our
'Head-Quarters'. Tons of love
& kisses to self & the boys.

   Ua Rathghaille

Desmond FitzGerald records in his memoirs that on Thursday he remarked to O'Rahilly: 'You said that the most we could last would be 36 hours and now we are into our third day.' Michael replied: 'We should have lasted only 36 hours. It is against all the rules of warfare that we are still here. But don't worry, it will not be long now.'

   The British had now got their artillery into Dublin, but they were not able to get a direct hit on the GPO. They could pump shells into the buildings on the opposite side of the street and they proceeded to do this and to burn and flatten them. The Volunteers in the Post Office could see the shells knocking holes in these buildings and then setting fire to them. There were no Volunteers in them and it seemed to be just wanton destruction.

O'Rahilly is reported to have asked one of the Volunteers: 'Do you know why they are blasting away those buildings?' 'I don't' was the reply. 'They just want to show us how little they think of us and our city', O'Rahilly said.

It was now clear that Connolly's hope that capitalists would not destroy their own property was not a valid assumption. He himself had now been badly wounded and was lying on a stretcher in the main hall. He was still in command, to the extent that there was any commanding to be done. However, as the net tightened around the Post Office, there is no evidence of any effort by the leaders to devise an alternative strategy to staying locked up in the GPO. Nor does there seem to have been any attempt at scouting to see which routes from the building were still open and which had been sealed off by the British military. Once the belief that capitalists would not destroy their own property had been exploded, the leaders do not appear to have had any hope of further resistance.

As evening closed in on Thursday, the days of the Irish Republic were coming to an end. Michael's note to Nannie reads:

> Dublin. Thursday Apl. 27
> 1916
> 4 pm
> Darling Nancy,
>   We are still going strong with hardly a regrettable incident.
>   The Sinn-Feiners & soreheads are putting up some fight.
>   God bless you little darling & the boys. Lots of love to you & them & Nell & Anna & everybody.
>   Buaid agus beannact
>   Ua Rathghaille

It seems clear that Michael thought that this was his farewell note to his family and friends. The British were now able to direct rifle fire through the tops of the windows into the GPO. These were not fully barricaded and the British used incendiary bullets. When these hit a wall, they disintegrated and left a blob of phosphorus on the wall which burst into flames within a few minutes and would ignite anything flammable. A continuous stream of these incendiary bullets were coming into the building, making it impossible to quench the flames which were arising everywhere. The Volunteers had a fire-fighting hose which O'Rahilly was using, trying to keep the flames from spreading. The British had not attempted to cut off the water supply from the building, but the pressure was weak and the flames were getting out of control. By Friday afternoon the two top floors were on fire and the Volunteers were driven down to the Central Hall, which the flames had not yet reached.

Connolly was lying on a stretcher, having been wounded twice the previous day, and O'Rahilly had taken charge of the fire-fighting. There has never been any report of a formal 'Council of War' having taken place among the leaders, but it is likely that some such discussion, no matter how informal, must have been held when the leaders knew that the flames were spreading out of control and it was only a matter of time before the building would have to be evacuated.

Five of those who signed the Proclamation were in the GPO and were the *de facto* leaders of the government of the Republic. If O'Rahilly had not been formally co-opted into the command structure, he seems to have been tacitly accepted as having taken over the role of commander of the garrison when Connolly was wounded.

Before Easter, Joseph Plunkett had been dying of tuberculosis in a Dublin hospital and was barely able to drag himself out of bed to come into the GPO for the Rising. FitzGerald reported that by the second or third day in the Post Office Plunkett was completely exhausted, and would not have been in any condition to contribute to that Council of War. Connolly had been badly wounded twice and could not move, so the Council had to be held around his stretcher. The leaders who gathered around it would have been Pearse, Clarke, Mac Diarmada and O'Rahilly.

What follows is speculation based on the assumption that Pearse, Clarke and Mac Diarmada then advocated the policy that they carried out on Saturday morning. These three would have argued that it was only a matter of a few hours before the fire would force them out of the GPO. There was no other large building available and further resistance was now impossible. It was clearly their duty to save the lives of as many Volunteers as possible. The only way to do this was to seek terms of surrender.

We know that Connolly and O'Rahilly did not agree. Connolly

called his secretary, Miss Carney, and dictated his last 'Order of the Day' which spelled out that any suggestion of surrendering was far from his thoughts at that time (see Appendix 4).

We know also that O'Rahilly had no such intention because he proceeded to organize a squad of twelve men, whom he intended to lead in a charge against the British barricade at the end of Moore Street. This appeared to be the only obstacle preventing them from moving from the GPO into the Williams and Woods jam factory, which was just around the corner from where Moore Street joins Parnell Street.

It seems reasonable to assume that if Pearse, Clarke and Mac Diarmada had favoured an assault on this barricade, they would have offered to take part in it. It is not recorded that any of the three offered to join O'Rahilly in the charge.

The options available to the rebels on the Friday evening were limited. When they decided on the strategy of occupying a number of large buildings in Dublin, and barricading themselves into them, they must have realized that the British were likely to demolish these buildings by artillery fire. Those occupying them would then have no alternative but to surrender or be killed. Even as the strategy was being devised, they must have intended to do so, as soon as the British were able and willing to demolish the buildings. Unless, of course, Connolly's theory was valid that capitalists would not destroy their own property. But the British had shown their scant regard for buildings when they had levelled all the buildings on one side of O'Connell Street, even though these were not occupied by Volunteers. It must have seemed to the leaders that by midday on Friday the time had come to save as many as possible of the rank and file by negotiating terms of surrender.

Despite the logic of this argument, Connolly proceeded to dictate his 'Order of the Day'. When this had been typed out by Miss Carney, Connolly read it to ensure that it expressed what he intended. He then wanted it read to the garrison to raise their morale and inspire their determination to continue the fight. It was clearly Pearse's role to do this. He was the leader, the President of the Republic which he had proclaimed at noon on Monday. Was Pearse so shellshocked by that time that he was incapable of doing so? Desmond FitzGerald said that Pearse, unlike O'Rahilly, was unable to sleep at night. Or did Pearse disapprove so strongly of what Connolly had said in this exhortation to the garrison that he refused to read it. It will never be known why Pearse did not read it, but it was O'Rahilly who called the members of the garrison together. They consisted of about 120 men and a dozen women, if most of the nurses were still in the GPO. O'Rahilly stood on one of the counters to read out what Connolly had written. The garrison listened and wondered. The 'Order' was so irrelevant to the realities of their predicament, they may well have pinched themselves to see if they were awake.

They had to resolve another problem in this last hour or two of crisis. If the policy of seeking terms of surrender was to be attempted, it was essential to have good light so that a nurse, carrying a large white flag, would be clearly visible to the British soldiers manning the barricade at the end of Moore Street. The soldiers could then be certain that she was an unarmed female nurse.

But if the alternative policy of attempting to storm the barricade was to have any chance of success, then the storming party had to be able to advance along Moore Street in darkness or at least semi-darkness, so the soldiers on the barricade would not be able to see them until the last possible moment.

When he had read out Connolly's 'Order', O'Rahilly folded it and put it in his pocket. He knew that if he survived, it would be an interesting historical document. There was still too much light to have any realistic hope of storming the barricade. The upper floors of the GPO were on fire and there was a serious risk that the ceiling would come crashing down, but this was a risk they had to take. To gain time and to instil courage into the garrison, O'Rahilly asked them all to join with him in singing John Kells Ingram's popular ballad, 'Who fears to speak of Ninety-eight?' Every Irish nationalist who could carry a tune would be able to sing it. By the time he had finished the song, with the men joining in the chorus, it was nearly dark and the twelve men who were to accompany him were ready.

Desmond FitzGerald's memoirs contains an account of those last minutes before O'Rahilly left the GPO to lead the charge up Moore Street. He knew that the chances of any of them surviving the charge were slender and he was concerned about the twelve men who had offered to accompany him. A number of them were *Gaeilgeoirí* and three or four of them came from Kerry. It seems likely that, during the five days in the GPO, O'Rahilly had sought out native Irish speakers on whom to practise his Irish, and when it came to looking for volunteers for the charge, a number of these men offered to go with him. In his eyes these native Gaelic speakers were precious assets. He showed his concern for them by saying, jokingly, to FitzGerald: 'When I give the order to charge, I will say, "English speakers to the fore: Irish speakers to the rear. Charge!"'

Desmond FitzGerald tells how O'Rahilly came to him as he was getting ready to lead the twelve out of the GPO. 'Good-bye, Desmond' he said. 'This is the end now for certain. I never dreamed it would last so long.' Then, as he turned to go, he said with a smile, 'But fancy missing this and then catching cold running for a tram.'

I suspect that FitzGerald's memory was not quite accurate and that what O'Rahilly said to him was: 'But fancy missing this and then getting killed running for a tram or catching cold.'

If my surmise is correct, the reference to getting killed running for a tram relates to when we lived in Leeson Street. The tram-stops were some distance from our house and Michael, instead of going to one of them, would wait until the tram was passing our door and then would take a flying leap to board it. Mother warned him that if his foot slipped, he might get killed and begged him not to do it. In his reference to catching cold, Michael was thinking of his own father. He had caught a cold riding his bicycle home from Listowel on a wet night. The cold developed into pneumonia and he was dead within a week.

Jack Plunkett, the youngest of the three Plunkett boys, in his memoirs recalled that, as the twelve were preparing to go, he asked O'Rahilly if he would like another twelve, but O'Rahilly declined the offer and said that 'any more would only draw their fire.' If any more were needed, Jack would have been the first to join them.

As they were about to emerge by the side door opening onto Henry Street, O'Rahilly saw a priest near it. He walked over to him, took off his hat and, kneeling down, said: 'I don't suppose, Father, that we will ever meet in this world again. Please give me your blessing.'

The barricade at the end of Moore Street was the only obstacle preventing the Volunteers getting to the Williams and Woods factory in Parnell Street. If it could be overrun, the garrison could move into this factory.

This barricade was also, and this was probably a fundamental consideration in O'Rahilly's eyes, the only possibility of a direct confrontation with the British army of occupation, which was what he wanted before he died.

When the thirteen emerged from the GPO into Henry Street, they were not visible to the British. The Volunteers had erected their own barricade across Henry Street at the junction of Moore Street and some of this had to be removed to allow them into Moore Street. O'Rahilly told six of the men to follow him to the opposite side of Moore Street. The other six were to remain on the near side and, keeping close to the buildings, they were all to advance at a slow run towards the barricade at the end of the street. There was to be no firing until they reached the barricade. It is not known how many of the men obeyed these instructions and followed O'Rahilly along Moore Street. I spoke to a number of the survivors, but it was fifty years later and their memories were dim. What I can testify is that even to have volunteered for the charge proves that they were all heroes.

We know that Paddy Shortis and Cremmins followed O'Rahilly. Shortis was killed and his body was found not far from O'Rahilly's, and Cremmins was wounded in the leg, but was able to crawl to an unoccupied tenement building and remained there until Sunday, when he was found by the British and brought to the hospital in Dublin Castle.

O'Rahilly knew the basic rule for an officer leading a charge: never stop and never look back. If the officer gives any indication of a lack of confidence, it is certain that the men behind him will also lose their confidence and their resolution to continue the charge.

The distance O'Rahilly covered from the corner of Henry Street to where he was shot was about 180 yards, and he was then only 30 yards from the barricade. It is possible, but unlikely, that the British saw the Volunteers as soon as they had left the shelter of Henry Street and held their fire until they were close to the barricade. The reason for thinking this unlikely is that, after he was shot, when O'Rahilly took shelter in a doorway, just before Riddal's Row, he was near the barricade and yet not clearly visible to all the soldiers at it. In his note to Nannie he said, 'I heard the men pointing out where I was', which indicates that some of them could see him and were shouting to the Lewis gunner so that he could get another burst of machine-gun fire to finish him off. That note also read, 'I got more than one bullet I think'. If he was correct in this, it would most likely have been bullets from a machine gun which hit him.

Even after being hit by two bullets, he was still able to make 'a bolt' across Moore Street to the shelter of what was then Moore Lane and is now called O'Rahilly Parade. The fact that he was able to get, unaided, across Moore Street, which is quite a wide street, proves that he was not very badly wounded and, if any medical help had been available, he could have survived.

When he got into the shelter of Moore Lane, where he could no longer be seen by the British soldiers manning the barricade, he knew that he was dying and wrote his last note to his wife.

The British officer in charge of the barricade was a Captain G.J. Edmunds. He told Max Caulfield, author of *The Easter Rebellion*, that he had sent a sergeant to search O'Rahilly's body, presumably after the surrender on Saturday. Among the papers he found was this last note. Edmunds was kind enough to take the trouble, and possibly the risk, of either delivering it himself or having it delivered to 40 Herbert Park.

> Written after I was shot —
>
> Darling Nancy
>
> I was shot leading a rush up Moore St & took refuge in a doorway.
>
> While I was there I heard the men pointing out where I was & made a bolt for the laneway I am in now.
>
> I got more than one bullet I think. Tons and tons of love dearie to you & the boys & to Nell and Anna. It was a good fight anyhow. Please deliver this to Nannie O Rahilly, 40 Herbert Park, Dublin. Goodbye Darling.

Michael's last note to Nannie was written on the back of a note I had sent in to him on Tuesday. He had it folded in his pocket and one of the bullets had gone through the folded note.

> 26 of April 1916
>
> Dear Dada
>
> I got your ne— letter. I
> heart from Nell and Anna that
> the volunteers are winning. I don't
> suppose they will ever get the G.P.O
> for as long as you are in command.
> Father O'Mahony told us that up
> in portello bridge there were two
> soldiers killed and twenty four
> wounded. We had Father O'Mahony
> down here last night with Anna
> and had a grand talk about the
> whole thing.
>
> > With Best Love
> > From
> > Egan

On Saturday morning Pearse surrendered. One of the nurses offered to go to the British barricade at the end of Moore Street under the protection of a white flag, to speak to the British officer in charge. She hoped the Volunteers might be given prisoner of war status. The message the nurse brought back was that the British would accept nothing but unconditional surrender. Pearse and the other leaders decided to accept these terms.

It was stated at the time that the decision to surrender was influenced by the sight of two dead women on Moore Street. Miss Kelly, who lived on Moore Street, told me there had been no such tragedy: she and her sister could see the whole of Moore Street from their house and no women had been killed on this street.

When Pearse walked along Moore Street to surrender, he saw O'Rahilly's hat and Mauser pistol in the roadway, and then, looking down Moore Lane, saw his dead body. As Pearse was awaiting execution, he remarked to a comrade, 'I envy O'Rahilly: that is the way I wanted to die.'

The sergeant who searched O'Rahilly's body removed all his papers and gave them to Captain Edmunds, the British officer in command of the barricade. The note he sent to his headquarters with these papers reads:

The above interesting Orders which were typewritten, were found on the body of the O'Rahilly [*sic*], one of the rebel commandants who was shot by the 2/4 Sherwood Foresters as he was leading a charge on one of their barricades in Moor [*sic*] Street near the Post Office. Upon him also was a letter written to his wife after he was wounded in which he said he was shot leading a charge. He got into an entry on the side of the street and later endeavoured to crawl to an opening on the other side. He was wounded again and before he died he wrote in a firm hand a pencilled note to his wife and children.

By a lucky chance, the 'above interesting Orders' were recovered. Captain Edmunds sent them to his commanding officer in the barracks which was the headquarters of the British military. The officer to whom they were sent left them on his desk when he was leaving his office that night. Early the following morning an Irish girl who was employed to clean the offices saw the papers and read them. She decided that if the British were entitled to take these papers from the body of a dead Volunteer, she was entitled to take them back, which she did, stuffing them in her blouse. She asked her boyfriend what she should do with them and he found out where O'Rahilly's sister lived and gave them to Anna O'Rahilly.

The shop outside which O'Rahilly died was owned by two Miss Kellys. One of them told me all she knew about his death. When she saw his body the next morning she first thought that he had vomited a pool of black porter on to the street, but then she realized it was blood. O'Rahilly's last act as he lay dying was to dip his finger in this blood and use it to write on the doorway beside his head:

'Here died The O'Rahilly R.I.P.'

It was a typically extrovert gesture. A similar urge, but in very different circumstances, had led him as a student to carve his name on the wooden rail in the 'Gods' of the Gaiety Theatre. The carving was quite professional, and when the theatre was being rebuilt fifty years later, the builder preserved this piece of timber, which is now in the Kilmainham Museum.

In 1916 O'Rahilly had made, consciously and deliberately, a sacrifice of his life to redeem Ireland's honour, and wanted the Irish people to know it. In this last gesture, he used the title 'The'. His name when he came back to Ireland in 1909 was the name he was christened, Michael Joseph Rahilly. The first change was to restore the 'O' and he became O'Rahilly. Later, about 1911, he began signing himself in letters to the paper and articles, as 'The O'Rahilly'. He may have initially intended it as a non de plume, but it soon took on and it was how he was generally known by 1914. In connection with the Volunteers in 1914, Redmond always referred to him with this prefix. However, there were Irish people with a knowledge of heraldry and an interest in titles who pointed out that this plebeian from Kerry had no right to any such title.

When W.B. Yeats heard that O'Rahilly was being criticized for having assumed this title, he wrote his poem 'The O'Rahilly' in which he made the plea 'Do not deny his right' and said that he had 'christened himself with blood.'

It was probably Desmond FitzGerald who inspired Yeats to write this poem, and gave him the information it contained about O'Rahilly. I have consulted a number of Yeatsian scholars about the refrain 'How goes the weather?' after each verse, but none of them can explain it. It was possibly a password used by O'Rahilly which he gave to Desmond FitzGerald who, in turn, passed it to Yeats.

It has been suggested that O'Rahilly was still alive on Saturday
afternoon, four or five hours after Pearse had agreed to surrender
on b⸏⸏⸏ ⸏⸏ all th⸏⸏⸏⸏ ⸏⸏⸏ers who had taken part in the Rising. It
h⸏⸏⸏⸏ ⸏⸏⸏ been s⸏⸏⸏d th⸏⸏ ⸏⸏en an ambulance was collecting the
⸏⸏⸏⸏ and b⸏⸏⸏⸏⸏ ⸏⸏⸏⸏ ⸏⸏ hospital, on Saturday afternoon, a
⸏⸏⸏⸏ ⸏⸏⸏⸏⸏⸏⸏ ⸏⸏⸏ ⸏⸏ ambulance man, in reference to
O⸏⸏⸏⸏⸏⸏ ⸏⸏⸏⸏ ⸏⸏⸏⸏⸏ ⸏⸏⸏⸏ing him. Let him die where he is. It
⸏⸏⸏⸏⸏⸏ ⸏⸏⸏⸏⸏⸏⸏⸏⸏⸏⸏ ⸏⸏ ⸏⸏⸏⸏ting him.' This is complete fantasy.
⸏⸏⸏⸏⸏⸏ ⸏⸏⸏⸏ ⸏⸏⸏⸏ ⸏⸏⸏⸏ ⸏⸏ believe that O'Rahilly's comrades,
⸏⸏⸏⸏⸏⸏ ⸏⸏⸏⸏⸏ ⸏⸏⸏⸏ ⸏⸏⸏⸏ had surrendered, saw that he was
⸏⸏⸏⸏ ⸏⸏⸏ ⸏⸏⸏ ⸏⸏⸏⸏⸏⸏ ⸏⸏ ⸏⸏⸏⸏ him.
⸏⸏⸏⸏⸏⸏⸏ ⸏⸏⸏⸏ ⸏⸏⸏⸏ ⸏⸏ ⸏⸏⸏ in the middle of that night, either
⸏⸏⸏⸏⸏⸏ ⸏⸏⸏ ⸏⸏⸏ ⸏⸏⸏ ⸏⸏⸏⸏urs of Saturday. She had been in a
⸏⸏⸏⸏⸏ ⸏⸏ ⸏⸏⸏ ⸏⸏⸏⸏⸏⸏⸏ ⸏⸏ at week. She went to bed as it was
⸏⸏⸏⸏⸏ ⸏⸏⸏⸏ ⸏⸏⸏⸏⸏⸏⸏ ⸏⸏⸏⸏ and then, for no apparent reason,
⸏⸏⸏⸏ ⸏⸏⸏⸏⸏ ⸏⸏⸏ ⸏⸏ ⸏⸏⸏⸏⸏⸏ ⸏⸏ the night, and was overcome, at
⸏⸏⸏⸏ ⸏⸏⸏⸏⸏⸏ ⸏⸏⸏⸏ ⸏⸏⸏ ⸏⸏ a sense of overwhelming loss and
⸏⸏⸏⸏⸏⸏ ⸏⸏⸏⸏⸏⸏⸏⸏ ⸏⸏⸏ ⸏⸏⸏⸏⸏⸏⸏ uesday she heard the news of his
⸏⸏⸏⸏ ⸏⸏⸏ ⸏⸏⸏⸏ ⸏⸏⸏ ⸏⸏⸏⸏ ⸏⸏ at the moment of his death was
⸏⸏⸏⸏ ⸏⸏ ⸏⸏⸏⸏ ⸏⸏⸏⸏⸏⸏⸏⸏

⸏⸏⸏⸏ ⸏⸏⸏ ⸏⸏⸏⸏⸏⸏ ⸏⸏ o die, and the news of his death
⸏⸏⸏ ⸏⸏⸏⸏⸏⸏ ⸏⸏⸏⸏⸏⸏ ⸏⸏ ⸏⸏⸏⸏ ⸏⸏ the British news agencies. His
sister-⸏⸏⸏⸏ ⸏⸏⸏⸏ of it in Australia, before his wife did in Dublin.

His sister, Nell Humphreys, heard that he had been killed and
found his body in the morgue. She found it difficult to get an
undertaker to bury him. They did not want to be associated in any
way with the rebels. Corrigans agreed to do it and my Aunt told us
that she herself was to be buried by Corrigans because they were the
only undertakers in Dublin who would bury her brother.

The funeral cortège consisted of one horse-drawn cab, which
contained his two sisters and a priest who was a relation of the
family. The coffin was given a temporary grave in a remote corner of
Glasnevin cemetery, and in 1917 was removed to what is now known
as 'The Republican plot'. Forty-four years later, in 1961, Nannie
joined him in the same grave.

APPENDIX 1

Manifesto on Behalf of
The Gaelic League (Ireland), 1911
(Written by Michael O'Rahilly)

The Gaelic League preaches the doctrine that Ireland's language is one of her most priceless National Treasures, that that language must not be permitted to die, and that it is the imperative duty of this generation to revive and re-establish it.

The League first propounded this doctrine to an apathetic public, nearly all of whom were indifferent to Irish, many of whom despised it, and not a few of whom were, until then, ignorant that the Language of their country was a highly developed tongue, possessing a literature as ancient and as valuable as that of any vernacular in Europe.

In 1891, the Irish Language was regarded as an archaic survival, to be heard only in fishermen's cottages, and to be read only in musty manuscripts, and at that period the number of Irish speakers in Ireland was decreasing at the appalling rate of 27,000 a year. Largely as a result of the League's activity in championing the language, the industries, the art, the literature, and the music of Ireland, Irish is today not a picturesque antique, but a real and living issue in modern Ireland.

Education, industries and temperance have also benefited enormously by this movement, which fact alone should suffice to show that the League is worthy of the support of everyone who desires either industrial development or educational progress, or who has at heart the moral welfare of our people.

Irish is now taught in thousands of schools, its study is part of a University training, a modern Gaelic literature has been created, newspapers, banks, and public institutions have recognised the Language, and proficiency in it has come to be a qualification for a business career.

But, notwithstanding this progress, the recent census returns disclose a condition that not only all Irishmen, but all men of sensibility must view with the gravest concern. For although Irish shows a uniform advance

227

throughout the more prosperous parts of Ireland, although Ulster and Leinster have converted a former loss of 2,000 Irish speakers per annum into a now continuous gain of 1,400 every year, these gains are not sufficient to compensate for the drain which, though diminished, still continues to flow from the more Irish-speaking districts of Ireland.

Immediately upon the publication of these census figures the Gaelic League unanimously voted that an extra £1,000 per year be spent on propaganda and teaching in the Irish-speaking districts, and it now contemplates the adoption of further measures involving additional expense, with the same object. These expenditures are not provided for in the League's estimates. The League has not the money to meet them. It has realised that these and many similar measures are essential and urgent. It has adopted those measures, and for the financing of them it relies on the patriotism of the Irish race, and on the practical sympathy of those who are interested in their efforts to preserve their national characteristics.

To save it the efforts of the League – and of those outside the League – must be redoubled, probably quadrupled. Sacrifices, personal and pecuniary, will be necessary. Money, men and enthusiasm, and unflinching determination, are wanted. And they are wanted now.

The Irish-speaking districts are the last stronghold of the Gael. If they fall Irish is dead, and with it will die, beyond doubt and beyond redemption, Ireland's nationhood. But that stage must never be reached; and while the League can command either cash, credit, or a single volunteer worker, it will leave nothing undone to avert that catastrophe.

Will you, the reader of this manifesto, do your part?

Will you, by your Subscription and by your personal efforts, help save this generation from the eternal infamy of being the one which permitted Ireland's Language to perish?

(Signed)

Douglas Hyde,
  President
Lorgan J. Sherlock,
  Lord Mayor of Dublin
Henry O'Shea,
  Lord Mayor of Cork
Philip O'Donovan,
  Mayor of Limerick
Richard Power,
  Mayor of Waterford

Daniel O'Donnell,
  Mayor of Sligo
Joseph Purcell,
  Mayor of Kilkenny
Thomas Fitzgibbon,
  Mayor of Clonmel
Stiophan Bairead,
  Treasurer, Gaelic League,
    25 Parnell Square, Dublin, Ireland

APPENDIX 2

Redmond's Ultimatum

Dear Sir,

I regret to observe the controversy which is now taking place in the Press on the Irish National Volunteer movement. Many of the writers convey the impression that the Volunteer movement is to some extent, at all events, hostile to the objects and policy of the Irish Party. I desire to say emphatically that there is no foundation for this idea, and any attempt to create discord between the Volunteer movement and the Irish Party are calculated, in my opinion, to ruin the Volunteer movement, which, properly directed, may be of incalculable service to the national cause.

Up to two months ago I felt that the Volunteer movement was somewhat premature, but the effect of Sir Edward Carson's threats upon the public opinion in England, the House of Commons and the Government; the occurrences in the Curragh Camp, and the successful gun-running in Ulster, virtually altered the position, and the Irish Party took steps about six weeks ago to inform their friends and supporters in the country that, in their opinion, it was desirable to support the Volunteer movement, with the result that within the last six weeks the movement has spread like prairie fire, and all the Nationalists of Ireland will shortly be enrolled.

Within the last fortnight, I have had communications from representative men in all parts of the country inquiring as to the organisation and control of the Volunteer movement and it has been strongly recommended to me that the Governing Body should be reconstructed and placed on a thoroughly representative basis so as to give confidence to all shades of national opinion.

So far as my information goes, the present Provisional Committee is self-elected. It consists of some 25 members, all of whom are resident in Dublin, and there appears to be no representation on it from any other part of the country. It only claims to be a strictly provisional and temporary body, and holds office only pending the constitution of a permanent governing body. In deference to the representations which have been made to me, and in the best interest of the Home Rule cause, which the Volunteer movement has been called into existence to vindicate and safeguard, I suggest that the present Provisional Committee should be immediately strengthened by the addition of 25 representative men from different parts of the country, nominated at the instance of the Irish Party, and in sympathy with its objects and aims. The Committee so constituted would enjoy the confidence of all Nationalists, and would proceed with the work of completing the organisation of the movement in the country, so that at the earliest possible moment a conference of Volunteer representatives might be held by which the permanent Government Body could be elected. If this suggestion is accepted, the National Party, and I myself, will be in a position to give our fullest support to the Volunteer movement, but failing the acceptance of some such arrangement as that above suggested, I fear it will be necessary to fall back on County Control and government, until the organisation is sufficiently complete to make possible the election of a fully representative Executive by the Volunteers themselves.

     Yours very truly,
     J. E. REDMOND.

(Freeman's Journal, 10 June 1914)

APPENDIX 3

Letter to the *Workers' Republic*

22 January 1916

Dear Sir,

In recent issues of your paper correspondents have, with timely foresight, dealt with the analogy which exists, more or less, between Grattan's Volunteers and the Irish Volunteers of the present day. One in the issue of the 8th inst. sums up the comparison in two well-known verses.

What I would like to say on this, and what I have proved by experience, I am prevented from saying publicly, by the fact that your paper, as well as all others of a national tendency, are permitted to exist solely as a barometer, by which the trend of public affairs can be gauged by Dublin Castle.

However I hope I am perfectly clear when I say that up to the present we have 'mustered and paraded' a good deal. And with 'patient endeavour' as the goal there is no doubt but we will be able to complete the analogy.

Whether in the end we shall have a repetition of history I am not going to express an opinion for reasons already given. I am confident of the sincerity and determination of the rank and file, and am in complete accord with the Editor that they cannot nor will not be deflected from their obvious duty at the present moment.

Their immediate concern should be watchfulness and preparation to be on the alert against those who may desire to postpone action, and to provide as much arms and ammunition as they can.

The present day leaders do undoubtedly hold allegiance to Ireland as their most sacred duty, but what that really means has not been defined with absolute precision, and having close connection with many of them, both prior to and since the formation of the Volunteers, a private exchange of views would I believe lead to good results. If the Editor would arrange for a short conference with his two correspondents 'B.F', 'J.J.B' and myself the outlook may be more clearly defined.

Our opportunity has arrived, if we have but the will and the courage to use it. We are strong enough to rid ourselves for ever of English domination, if we strike at the proper moment. If we wait till the war is over, the task of crushing a hostile armed force will be an easy one for the English. Any resistance we then make will be of no avail and we will have no redress.

With apologies, I remain, Sir, respectfully yours, M.O'R

APPENDIX 4

Connolly's 'Order of the Day'

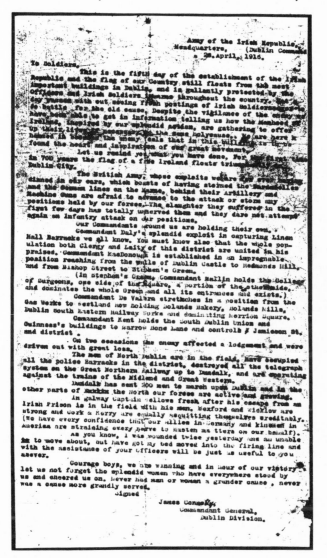

APPENDIX 5

From Nell Humphreys's
Letter to Nora*

Dear Nora,

It is too long to give you the reasons why it [the Rising] was put off on Sunday. MacNeill was a scholar NOT a soldier. He got the country stopped though there was to be the best organised universal Rising that was ever in Ireland. On Monday morning the first shot was fired at 12 o'clock. Dick had gone out sometime after breakfast, just to see was there anything going on and remained wandering around town till he went into the Post Office at 2 o'clock, knowing Michael would be there.

It is said Michael was the greatest martyr and it is true. . . .

On Saturday when it was put off, messengers were sent to every part of the country with orders from MacNeill to disband and go quietly home. Michael was sent to Limerick and only got back in time for Monday's Rising.

This all seems very confusing and it was, and by that change MacNeill broke the back of the Rising. As they said in a paper, only half or less of each battalion went out. There were two sets of plans, one to be carried out if every one rose [every Volunteer], the 2nd if they had not enough men, which they had not. Oh, it was pitiable, Nora, the few men they had and the fight that was made by these few. Here in our own road two men held a house and there were over ninety soldiers killed or wounded. Anna and Sighle saw nearly all who fell.

I find I cannot write this, there is too much to tell. I will get Dick to describe the Post Office events and I will keep to our own family.

We had to think of Nannie before anything, as you know the state she was in at the time, so I went over to her house, not seven minutes walk and remained with her. She bore up wonderfully, but the nights were terrible, rifle firing and machine guns and the sound of burning houses. (I cannot describe, so you must imagine what occurred and know that everything was far worse than your wildest imagining.) Anyhow Nannie was not able to

---

*Nora Humphreys, Nell's sister-in-law, a nun in Australia.

endure it longer and she sent me looking for a house in the country. On Friday morning I cycled out to Dundrum and found an empty house and she and I and the maid and the youngest boy went out there in the afternoon. That saved her; we were not continually looking at millions of soldiers, as we thought, and wagon loads of ammunition passing into the town against our HANDFUL of men.

Anna and Sighle were left alone here with our maid (who was a regular Ann Devlin). When she (Anna) could get a pass (under pretence of going to buy milk) she used to cycle out to see us, but she had no news, only wild rumours, till Tuesday morning, a week and a day after the Rising began. She came out to tell us Michael had fallen. In the afternoon I came in to town (I will never forget the way I left poor Nannie, sitting in a strange bare bedroom, her head bowed down on a shabby dressing table, such a forlorn little figure).

Well, I cycled into town with my cousin, the Carmelite Rector in Clarendon Street, and after passing numerous sentries and riding over heaps of broken glass we got to the Morgue. There was Michael, stretched out on a stand. He was even honoured there, all the others were lying on the ground and he did look fine Nora. His head thrown back, he had a very high forehead and he looked as brave and peaceful as ever a warrior sculptured in marble on a tomb. Nobody but myself saw him and tis a pity. If Nannie could only have had that impression for her life, it would have made up for much.

By the great kindness of an undertaker, whose own two sons 'were out' as we now say, we were able to get a plain coffin, and even buried him in Glasnevin, temporarily on Thursday.

We were only home an hour, just had time to have lunch, when an officer and three soldiers came to the house, while ten more guarded the front of the house, searched every nook and corner for four hours and took me prisoner. I never could tell you of the cross examination I had to go through, first at one barracks and then another; how I was marched through our own street between seven soldiers, how they threatened ten years penal servitude for Dick unless I told everything. I had nothing to tell, but anyway I wasn't going to say anything.

All this time our worst trouble was that we had no idea of where Dick was. On Wednesday morning I heard he was killed and had a very bad hour or two looking for him at all the hospitals etc. My cousin was still with me; a placid priest who gave me a good laugh all to myself, EVEN THEN, fancy, as he would insist on ordering a hearse and everything to take TWO coffins, and seemed a bit put out when Dick's body could not be found.

When I had been in prison a few days Anna came to see me, indeed she came every day, in fact spent her time going around looking for me, as I always was moved with only a few minutes warning from one place to another. I was in a horse box in Ballsbridge (R.D.S. grounds) to begin with, then I was sent to Richmond Barracks, then to Kilmainham (you know of it) then to Mountjoy where I spent ten days (and before I forget it, there I was on the 13th May, and one of my most bitter thoughts was 'would David be ashamed of me, making such a muddle of my life that I was in one prison & Dick in another?') Your letter the other day comforted me so.

As I was saying I was only a few days in Mountjoy when Anna came to say that Dick had been sent to England with a batch of prisoners. It was a relief to be sure he was alive. I did not mind things a bit after that.

One day Anna asked the governor of the Prison if she might have a solicitor for my case. She was only gone home when I was released without any more ado, and I arrived home quite unexpectedly.

After a week I went to London and saw Mr Dillon M.P. and asked him to get Dick liberated on account of delicate health. Then I went to Wakefield and spent five really enjoyable days seeing the men all day: the rules there not nearly as strict there as they have since become. I will never forget the joy I felt at seeing Dick the first day, we were SO sure he was dead.

Now Nora, I will say no more about that, only of the good the Rising has done. We have been shunned by almost all our society acquaintances, so I cannot vouch for the truth of the saying that it was not worth losing all those valuable lives, that the conversions to our side are not sufficient, but I can speak for the working classes. We have met so many of every sort and they are all proud of being Irish, of having lived and suffered for this, so anxious to do anything for the men who were out, for the wives and families of those who have fallen. It is again an exquisite charitable world as it must have been at the time of the early Christians, it is great to be alive now and to feel your heart warm as mine does over the goodness of man. You will say that I am heroic and absurd, but it is what I feel Nora. Trouble has drawn us all together as we were originally meant to be.

Did you hear at all of the part women took in the Rising? I used to feel ashamed of Sighle, as being unwomanly, when Anna told me that at times it was difficult to keep her from taking a shot herself, that the way she gloried when the enemy fell was actually inhuman, and her nerve during the whole time was wonderful. But it is only the spirit of the age; every girl in every centre, the G.P.O., Jacobs, the College of Surgeons, was just as cool and brave. They gave the men INVALUABLE help and kept things normal. The only place where they were not present, Boland Mills (as de Valera, the Commandant, would have none of them) they became so highly strung that a young Volunteer lost his head and shot one of their best men.

I have not said half what I should say especially of the good it did in rousing up the people and making them think.

Dick has put in a little sketch of the worst areas and a short account of his time in the G.P.O. I wish I could send you a few post cards of streets but they are now allowed, and I don't want this parcel to be too large. A priest has kindly offered to take it out for me. I know you will pray hard for our men who got penal servitude, some boys younger than Dick & pray for the Frongoch men that they may get home before winter and for a man who has a bullet in his lung. Dick and Anna join me in best love and thanks for all your nice presents, dearest Nora,

Yours affectionately, Nell.

APPENDIX 6

Eoin MacNeill and the Rising

It is generally accepted that the Rising of 1916, which led directly to the withdrawal of the British occupation forces from twenty-six of the Irish counties, was the most important political event in Ireland since the Act of Union of 1800. If this is true, it follows that Eoin MacNeill's attempt to call off this Rising was the most important decision of his political career. Yet in 1973 a book about MacNeill, *The Scholar Revolutionary*, was published, dealing with almost every aspect of his life, in which there is no reference to this most fundamental quasi-political decision, even though on the dust cover of this publication there is a facsimile reproduction of the order cancelling the Rising which MacNeill sent to de Valera, one of the Dublin commandants. Anyone interested in this aspect of MacNeill's activities must be curious about this omission.

It is now commonly stated that MacNeill was not told about the arrangements being made for the Rising, and that when he heard of them, some weeks before Easter, he reluctantly agreed not to oppose them. His cancellation decision on Easter Saturday is often supposed to have been due to word reaching Dublin of the capture of the arms ship. If these assumptions were valid, it would mean that not one of the senior officers, who would have had to be told about the Rising at least a month before Easter, had sufficient loyalty to MacNeill to inform him what was afoot.

This disloyalty would have had to include O'Rahilly, who was extremely close to MacNeill. I can recall my feeling of shame when it was stated at MacNeill's trial that he had not been aware of the plans of the Rising. We knew my father was aware of the Rising plans, and if MacNeill was ignorant of them it could only mean that my father had deceived his closest comrade in the Volunteer organization. There is no evidence to support any deception of this kind.

MacNeill's knowledge of the Rising is established beyond any doubt by the message he gave to Count Plunkett to convey to Casement at least a month before Easter. It was also spelled out by Seán T. O'Kelly when he was giving a talk on RTE in 1966 about the events of Easter Week. He said that during that week in the GPO, Tom Clarke said he would like to have a talk with him. Clarke told him there was little possibility of the leaders surviving the Rising and he thought it was important that someone like Seán T., who was likely to survive, should be given as many details as possible. One fact which remained clearly in O'Kelly's memory was of Clarke telling him that MacNeill had known all about the plans for the Rising.

If it is suggested that the message brought by Count Plunkett to Berne to deliver to Casement was false, and had never been given by MacNeill, it is relevant that this message was first published in the Irish papers in 1922, and would inevitably have been read by both MacNeill and Plunkett, both of whom were then alive and politically active. However, they were on opposite sides in the Treaty conflict, so that there would not have been any question of personal loyalty having prevented MacNeill stating that he never gave this message to Plunkett to deliver to Casement.

MacNeill's decision to call off the Rising was similar to his decision not to send the motor boat to tell Childers to land the arms at Howth, not to issue any ammunition to the Volunteers who were given the Howth rifles so they could defend themselves, and, some weeks later, not to allow O'Rahilly to carry out a coup d'état by seizing Dublin Castle. MacNeill was incapable of making any decision which might result in violence or in people being killed or wounded. This may be a commendable aspect of his character, but it rules him out as in any way competent to lead a revolutionary organization.

APPENDIX 7

Documents Relative to the
Sinn Féin Movement

This pamphlet, 'Presented to Parliament by command of His Majesty' in 1921, is one of the most important sources of information about the events that led to the Rising of 1916, and the liaison between the leaders of the Irish Volunteers and the Germans.

While it does not explicitly say so, the fact that all the wireless messages between von Bernstorff, the German ambassador in Washington, and the German Foreign Office are given in precise detail, with dates and code numbers, indicates beyond any doubt that the British had broken the German wireless code and were intercepting these messages and decoding them in room 40 of the Admiralty.

It might be suggested that the British received these messages from the German archives after Germany had been defeated in the war, but there is no evidence that any German archives were given to the British following World War I, although the Americans obtained similar papers after World War II.

One important piece of evidence proves that the British were intercepting and reading these German messages as they were transmitted. This was the message from the German ambassador in which he stated that the Germans in the United States had purchased a large consignment of arms for India, adding that 'Devoy says they cannot be shipped to Ireland'. The clear implication of this message is that these arms had been offered to John Devoy for Ireland and that he had refused them. The following morning the ban on the importation of arms to Ireland, which had been lifted following the Bachelor's Walk atrocity, was reimposed. The British were not taking any chances that Devoy might change his mind.

It is in this *Documents Relative . . . .* pamphlet that the British sent the first Irish message to Germany to say that they had decided to start the Rising at Easter 1916, and wanted the German arms on Easter Saturday.

The ability of the British to read these German messages, including those between their warships and their naval headquarters in Berlin, may well have played a decisive part in the defeat of the Germans in World War I.

Appendix 7

As a result of intercepting and being able to decode the German wireless messages, and getting the report from McGeoy, the British were well-informed on almost all the plans for the Rising. The one mistake they made is of some interest.

It emerged at the enquiry into the Rising, and the events leading up to it, that the Admiralty in London had sent a message to the commander of their base in Queenstown that the arms vessel was accompanied by two submarines. When von Bernstorff read this report, he was a happy man. He resented Devoy's accusation that the British had obtained their information from papers that had been left carelessly on von Igel's desk and which were found by the FBI, who gave them to the British.

Von Bernstorff sent a message to his Foreign Office in Berlin, pointing out to them that if the British obtained information that the gun-running vessel was accompanied by two submarines, they could not possibly have been given this information from any leak in New York or Washington. He said that the only information the Germans on the ambassador's staff had on this subject was that the arms were to arrive on two or three steam trawlers. The Germans in the US could not have leaked information which they did not have.

We can only speculate why the British believed that the arms ship was accompanied by two submarines. What seems most likely is that when the U19 was leaving German waters with the three Irishmen on board, they sent a wireless message to the German Admiralty in Berlin, 'U.19 Leaving German waters for Ireland'. When this vessel returned a day later for what they hoped would be minor repairs, this was reported by telephone to Berlin, and when it was found that the repairs would take several days, a second submarine, the U20, was sent with the three Irishmen. If this submarine also sent a message by wireless to the German Admiralty, 'U.20 leaving German waters for Ireland', and if the British picked up both messages, they would have concluded that both submarines were escorting the gun-running vessel to Ireland.

Sources

PRIMARY SOURCES

The O'Rahilly Papers
The O'Rahilly was an inveterate, almost compulsive, collector of personal and other memorabilia. Fortunately, most of these have survived and are the main source of information on his life and work.

The O'Rahilly collection is housed at University College, Dublin and the National Museum, Dublin.

National Library of Ireland
Redmond Papers, Plunkett Papers, Alice Stopford Green Papers, William Bulfin Papers, Eoin MacNeill Papers, Constance Markievicz Papers, Bulmer Hobson Papers and Roger Casement Papers.

New York Central Library, 42nd Street
Maloney Papers.

University College, Dublin
Eóin MacNeill Papers.

Other
State Paper Office, Dublin. O'Connell School (Christian Brothers), Dublin. Foreign Office Archives, Bonn and Military History Archives, Koblenz, Germany.

Contemporary Printed Sources
Secret History of the Irish Volunteers by The O'Rahilly, 1915. Pamphlet in NLI.
Reports of Royal Commissions: Landing of Arms at Howth (1914) and the Rebellion in Ireland (1916).
Sinn Féin Rebellion Handbook, Easter 1916 – compiled by the *Weekly Irish Times*, Dublin 1917.
Documents relative to the Sinn Féin Movement, London n.d.
Hansard.

243

Sources

SECONDARY SOURCES

Asquith, Margot, *Autobiography*, Vol. III (London 1922)

Bourke, Marcus, *The O'Rahilly* (Tralee 1967)

Birrell, Augustine, *Things Past Redress* (London 1937)

Caulfield, Max, *The Easter Rebellion* (London 1963)

Childers, Erskine, *The Riddle of the Sands* (London 1934)

Connolly O'Brien, Nora, *James Connolly: Portrait of a Rebel Father* (Dublin 1935)

Curry, Charles, (ed.) *Sir Roger Casement's Diaries, His mission to Germany and Findlay Affair* (Munich 1922)

Davis, Richard P., *Arthur Griffith and Non-Violent Sinn Féin* (Tralee 1974)

De C. Permiter, Geoffrey, *Roger Casement* (London 1936)

Dineen P. and O'Donoghue T., (eds) *The Poems of Egan O'Rahilly, Irish Texts Society*, Vol. III (London 1911)

Edwards, Ruth, Dudley, *James Connolly* (Dublin 1981)

———, *Patrick Pearse, The Triumph of Failure* (London 1971)

Figgis, Darrell, *Recollections of the Irish War* (London 1927)

FitzGerald, Desmond, Pierce, Fergus and Garret, (eds) *The Memoirs of Desmond FitzGerald* (London 1968)

Gwynn, Denis, *The Life of John Redmond* (London 1932)

Gwynn, Stephen, *John Redmond's Last Years* (London 1919)

Hobson, Bulmer, *Ireland Yesterday and Tomorrow* (Tralee 1968)

Inglis, Brian, *Roger Casement* (London 1973)

Kee, Robert, *The Green Flag* (Suffolk 1972)

Lavelle, Patricia, *James O'Mara* (Dublin 1961)

Lynam, E.W., *The Irish Character in Print, 1571-1923* (Shannon 1969)

Lynch, Florence Monteith, *The Mystery Man of Banna Strand* (New York 1959)

Lyons, F.S.L., *Ireland Since the Famine* (London 1971)

———, *John Dillon: A Biography* (London 1968)

Mac Coll, Renee, *Roger Casement* (London 1960)

Mac Entee, Sean, *Episode at Easter* (Dublin 1966)

MacGiolla Choille, Breandan, *Intelligence Notes, 1913-1916* (Dublin 1966)

MacLochlainn, Piaras F., (ed.) *Last Words* (Dublin 1971)

McHugh, Roger, *Dublin 1916* (Dublin 1966)

Macardle, Dorothy, *The Irish Republic* (London 1937)

Martin, F.X., (ed.) *The Howth Gun-Running, 1914* (Dublin 1964)

———, (ed.) *The Irish Volunteers, 1913-1915* (Dublin 1963)

———, (ed.) *Leaders and Men of the Easter Rising, Dublin, 1916* (Dublin 1967)

——— and Byrne, F.J., (eds) *The Scholar Revolutionary* (Shannon 1973)

Moore, Maurice, *History of the Irish Volunteers* (*Irish Press*, January and February 1938; See Ó Mordha, Muirís, below)

Sources

Monteith, Robert, *Casement's Last Adventure* (2nd edn., Dublin 1953)

Norman, Diana, *Terrible Beauty, a Life of Constance Markievicz* (London 1987)

O'Brien, W. and Ryan D., (eds) *Devoy's Post Bag 1871-1928 Vol. II 1880-1928* (Dublin 1953)

O'Broin, Leon, *The Chief Secretary, Augustine Birrell in Ireland* (Edinburgh 1969)

———, *Dublin Castle and the 1916 Rising* (Dublin 1966)

———, *Revolutionary Underground* (Dublin 1976)

O'Mackey, Herbert, *The Life and Times of Roger Casement* (Dublin 1954)

Ó Mordha, Muirís, *Tús and Fás Oglach na hEireann* (B.A.C. 1936)

Pearse, Patrick H., *Collected Works, Political Writings and Speeches* (Dublin 1922)

Spindler, Karl, *The Mystery of the Casement Ship* (Tralee 1965)

Stephens, James, *The Insurrection in Dublin* (Dublin 1916)

Tierney, Michael, *Eoin MacNeill, Scholar and Men of Action, 1867-1945* (New York 1980)

Woodham-Smith, Cecil, *The Great Hunger* (London 1962)

Yeats, W.B., *Collected Poems* (London 1963)

NEWSPAPERS AND PERIODICALS

Claidheamh Soluis

Evening Telegraph

Freeman's Journal

Gaelic American

Irish Citizen

Irish Freedom

Irish Independent

Irish Press

Irish Times

Irish Volunteer

Irish Worker

Irish World

Leader

Scissors and Paste

Sinn Féin

Sinn Féin Weekly

Spark

Times (London)

United Irishman

Workers Republic

Index